Oaklawn School for Girls

OAKLAWN SCHOOL FOR GIRLS

JUVENILE REFORM IN RHODE ISLAND

KELLY SULLIVAN PEZZA

For Abby, Delia, Minnie, Mattie, Loraine, Maggie, and Mary—the lost girls. May you rest in peace.

America Through Time is an imprint of Fonthill Media LLC
www.through-time.com
office@through-time.com

Published by Arcadia Publishing by arrangement with Fonthill Media LLC
For all general information, please contact Arcadia Publishing:
Telephone: 843-853-2070
Fax: 843-853-0044
E-mail: sales@arcadiapublishing.com
For customer service and orders:
Toll-Free 1-888-313-2665

www.arcadiapublishing.com

First published 2019

Copyright © Kelly Sullivan Pezza 2019

ISBN 978-1-63499-183-4

All rights reserved. No part of this publication may be reproduced, stored in a retrieval system or transmitted in any form or by any means, electronic, mechanical, photocopying, recording or otherwise, without prior permission in writing from Fonthill Media LLC

Typeset in Sabon 10pt on 13.5pt
Printed and bound in England

Acknowledgments

Many thanks go to:

Jay Slater of Fonthill Media for recognizing the importance of this project and making it possible for me to share it with a wider audience.

Ken Carlson of the Rhode Island State Archives and Michelle Chiles of the Rhode Island Historical Society for all of their help with research.

Kathan Lambert, Linda Pearson, Crystal Trementozzi, and Jennifer (Van Ostrand) Wilcoxson for helping me to put faces to these words.

Matthew Ryan for his professional help with photography questions.

Rene Tougas for bundling up and walking through those woods with me for hours.

Karen Bruscini for her insight and total willingness to share her gift, as well as for the grilled cheese lunches that turned her from source to friend.

Angela Harvey for making it possible for me to get this book better than it ever would have been otherwise.

Lastly, Andy Hall for his unending generosity in sharing not only his research materials with me but for celebrating along with me the crazy obsessions that only "our kind" understand.

CONTENTS

Acknowledgments		5
Introduction		9
1	I Am Going to Be A Good Girl	11
2	The Quiet Home-Like Life They Lead	64
3	The Staff	115
4	Oaklawn Girls	130
5	The Cemetery	172
6	The Only Happiness They Ever Had	184
Bibliography		191

Introduction

While a great deal of effort has gone into making certain all information is as accurate as possible, historical records are often at odds with each other, difficult to read, or erroneously documented. Some names are spelled differently depending on what document they are recorded on, just as birthdates often differ depending on which source of information one looks at. When this has happened, I have gone with the spellings, dates, and information that appear most often. Undoubtedly, there will be some errors in this work as the original records themselves contain many errors. I have sought to collect, correct, and corroborate the facts as much as the decades will allow.

1

I Am Going to Be
A Good Girl

Prior to the early nineteenth century, children who committed crimes were not known as "juvenile delinquents." They were merely young criminals who would face the same consequences as adults for the laws they had broken. Teenage girls who were caught fornicating would be thrown into cells with dangerous criminals twice their age. Young boys walking the streets past curfew would be incarcerated with thieves and rapists. They were decidedly damaged young people, lost causes whose only lot in life was to be shut away from the community.

In 1824, in New York, the first of America's institutions for the reform of juvenile offenders opened. Unfortunately, such schools of the mid-nineteenth century were merely centers of punishment. The children would be secured with a goal of merely punishing them for the wrongs they had done.

There was little investigation completed, at that time, into the mindset of the child being admitted to a reform school. Many such children, who did not readily conform to rules or laws, had mental handicaps or disabilities that prevented them from making the same rational or logical decisions of others. Many more were emotionally scarred by abuse, abandonment by one or both parents, or the death of a mother, father, or sibling. It was not until 1899, in Illinois, that the nation's first Juvenile Court came into existence, allowing for the outcome of a case to take the individual's age and circumstances into account. As interested parties and organizations began looking into the inner workings of the country's reform schools, great changes were about to be made. It was suggested that instead of using the incarceration as merely a time of punishment, the children should be given every opportunity to better their lives once they were released, so that they did not become inmates again, later in life, in adult prisons. Soon, most reform schools were following a curriculum that included schooling, industrial training, outdoor exercise, entertainments, religious education, and teaching on the importance of etiquette, rule-following, and law-abiding.

In Rhode Island, the Providence Reform School opened in 1850. Both males and females were taken into the school as inmates until 1882 when the school was abolished, and the inmates were relocated to two different institutions that had been erected in Cranston. One building would house the female inmates and be known as the Oaklawn School for Girls. The other would hold the male inmates and be known as the Sockanosset School for Boys. Each school would be under the care and control of a superintendent appointed by the board of State Charities and Corrections. For Oaklawn School, that superintendent would be Mrs. R. S. Butterworth.

In 1880, 8.78 acres of land had been purchased from Job Wilbur, at a cost of $1,200, along New London Turnpike (now called Brayton Avenue) for the construction of the school. On May 28 of that year, the Rhode Island General Assembly passed an act directing the Rhode Island Board of State Charities and Corrections to proceed with plans for Oaklawn School. Additional land was purchased from the state to bring the total acreage of the school grounds to 27.21. The main building, to be called "Oaklawn Cottage," was a beautiful structure completed in 1881. Water was supplied by a well which had been sunk that year, about 36 feet deep, by digging and drilling a 3-inch hole into an underlying ledge. The water was pumped to the school by the use of a windmill constructed over the well, carrying it to a tank inside the school's attic. Until autumn, this proved to be effective. The cost of the well, windmill and tower was $582.11. The total cost of the school's construction was $20,880.81.

The school had been built using a "cottage plan," meaning that it would be more home-like than institutional, without bars or fences. The completed three-story building appeared more like an elegant Victorian home than a place of incarceration. A sewing room within the school was warmly decorated with framed portraits on walls, ornate hanging lamps, and elegant furniture. The schoolroom, located on the second floor, had rows of large desks all facing the chalkboard and the desk of the instructor. Maps and other learning materials were affixed to the walls around a beautiful clock, and lush potted plants made the room exquisitely comfortable.

Located on a hillside about a quarter of a mile from Oaklawn train station, the school contained six single bedrooms and one large dormitory. The inmates would share a single washroom and each would be given a locker and key in which to keep her personal belongings. As the superintendent would be living at the school, private quarters were set apart on the second floor for this purpose. The layout, however, was not the most logical. The superintendent's living room, kitchen, and bedroom were located on the east side of the building, while her bedroom and bathroom were located on the west side, requiring that the superintendent cross one of the halls used by the inmates to get from the living room or kitchen to the bedroom or bathroom. Oaklawn School for Girls officially opened on July 13, 1882, and twenty girls from the reform school in Providence were transferred there as Oaklawn's first inmates.

The Oaklawn School for Girls in 1885. (*Rhode Island Department of State*)

Some of the girls were determined, with or without intervention, to live life on the wrong side of the law. Yet, for others, the care they received at Oaklawn School, along with the family atmosphere, would be the first opportunity they had ever had to feel safe and wanted. Some of the girls had come from homes where they had been physically abused. Others had lived with parents who struggled with the effects of addiction or who engaged in their own criminal behavior.

Girls who were more attracted to the opposite sex than what was deemed acceptable were decidedly "lewd and wanton" and a young girl of that time could have been hauled into court for simply kissing a boy. Some of the "vagrant" girls committed by the courts to Oaklawn School may have been simply youngsters who stayed away from their homes because those homes were too emotionally or physically violent. Others had been deposited at orphanages as babies because their families had far too many children to care for already. Many of these girls had begun their lives knowing they were unwanted.

It is interesting to notice how many of the inmates at Oaklawn School were committed immediately following the death of a parent. We will never know if some of these young girls went down the wrong path due to the sudden loss of a motherly influence, or if they had long been engaging in delinquent behavior and the parent remaining could not handle such behavior on their own. We will never know if, back when many families regularly boarded numbers of grown itinerant men in their homes, some of these girls found themselves living within nightmarish situations; we will also never know the personal stories of most of these girls. Yet what seems evident is that Oaklawn School was not only a safety net, but an institution devoted whole-heartedly to clearing the slate and giving these girls another chance at life. Many former inmates went on to become teachers, private governesses, nurses, and some even went on to graduate from Ivy League schools. Most became the wives of respectable men and, later, the mothers of well-loved children. Over the decades, Oaklawn School, as a whole, seems to have succeeded in its goal of reforming a large number of girls deemed to be "juvenile delinquents" in Rhode Island. In addition, it provided care and concern to those girls who had never experienced such things.

1882

Thirty bedsteads and bureaus—made of ash and white-wood, and ornamented with black walnut scrolls—were constructed at Rhode Island Prison for use in the school. Twenty-five desks, which had formerly been used at the Rhode Island State House, were re-varnished and placed in the schoolroom.

The sum of $1,774.98 was added to the cost of construction, bringing the total to $22,655.79. The most expensive undertaking was the well, which ended up costing $1,066.44. By December, it was necessary to drill into the 3-inch hole again. Reaching a depth of 90 feet below the platform of the windmill's tower, it became possible to pump about 5.25 gallons of water per minute, for a straight

The schoolroom within Oaklawn School for Girls. (*Rhode Island Department of State*)

twenty-four hours. By February 7, the depth reached 141 feet. For years, this well never failed to provide adequate amounts of water.

Another additional expense resulted from the need to lay a new concrete floor in the basement as the first one laid was too soft.

Later that year, a report was made by the Rhode Island Board of State Charities and Corrections:

> Mrs. R. S. Butterworth was, in May, appointed Superintendent of the Oaklawn School and, in June, entered upon her duties by assisting in the final preparation of the building. On the thirteenth of July, the removal took place. Since the opening of the school, four girls have been received and none discharged. There have been no escapes and no deaths. Twenty-four remain in the school at the close of the year. Three of those committed were sentenced by the Justice Court of Providence and one by the Justice Court of Pawtucket. All were sentenced to remain during minority.

The expenses for the school that first year were reported to be as follows: provisions and groceries, $373.67; meat, vegetables, milk, etc. from the Rhode Island State Farm, $285.56; salaries, $779.37; books, stationary, etc., $125.08; fuel, $205.20; clothing and bedding, $240.54; medicines, etc., $18.91; lights and kerosene oil, $13.44; and miscellaneous, $112.20. This resulted in a total of $2,153.97. It was estimated that the expenses for each girl, per week, was $4. The Board's report went on to state:

> There are as many matrons for twenty girls as for fifty, and the cost for heating, lighting and cleansing is nearly the same whatever the number. When the Board took charge of the school, the number was thirty and it was thought that there would be an increase with better provisions for their care. The Board has been pleased to note a marked improvement in the girls since their removal to the new building, where they have enjoyed a degree of freedom and received an amount of personal instruction in useful occupations and right living from their Superintendent and teachers that could not be given them at the old school. Their surroundings are pleasant and elevating and they are with those who are earnestly endeavoring to prepare them to go forth into the world, moral and useful women. It will be their own fault, resulting from a perverse nature, if they fail to reap due benefit from the generous provision made for them by the State. The Superintendent reports that the girls have made 994 garments and other articles, have repaired 2,424, and have washed and ironed 8,177.

The salaries of the staff consisted of $50 per month paid to R. Butterworth and $25 per month paid to H. Buffington, E. Bacon, Ella Armes, Alithea Hutchins, and Ermina Eiler.

1883

In January, the Women's Board of Visitors to the Penal and Correctional Institutions of the State visited Oaklawn School; they subsequently submitted the following report:

> Each year confirms the necessity of a Board of Visitors for Institutions Where Females are Imprisoned. Great benefit has accrued, and many happy results have been realized from this organization. When necessities are acknowledged and decided progress follows, we can but feel that our efforts have been recognized favorably. It is a pleasant duty to speak of the great improvement in the moral element of the girls at the reform school for the past few years. Mr. and Mrs. Eldridge, in their relations with the school, were earnestly interested in sowing seeds of virtue and correct principles, and by their firmness and kindness trained them to habits of self-reliance and self-government. We would also commend the services of Mr. and Mrs. Howe. They have been most faithful and efficient and by their experience elsewhere have acquired a degree of ability both as regards instruction and discipline, which has brought about valuable results. The curative experiment with dispensing with bolts and bars and the abolishment of bodily chastisement are among the prominent methods. Their systems of wise gentleness are working out a great reform. With these changes, the inmates perform their various tasks with more cheerfulness than formerly. They are taught the moral value of industry and their hands, hearts and heads are in harmonious activity which will help to make good citizens. We believe the influence of Mr. and Mrs. Howe will be an uplifting power, acting upon all who may come under their guidance. It is cheering to know that a number of the girls have gone out from the institution in the last two or three years and are now in families, doing well. We feel confident that with more appliances and greater facilities, the new State Schools at Cranston will, by their spirits and methods, effect great practical advancement. The appropriations made by the Legislature to establish and furnish suitable buildings, and all needful appointments for a new home for the unfortunate boys and girls who have been deprived of the resistless power of a mother's love, will make an effective change in their character and encourage them to self-respect and self-control in the future. In this home, they will be guided by watchful care through the slippery paths of youth and protected from the seductive allurements which beset the young on every side. With such results the expenditure will be worth far more to the State than it has cost. 'Time's buildings are not all of stone' and in the removal of the girls to the Oaklawn School, we feel sure that a foundation is laid for character and uprightness which shall always endure.

The Women's Board report continued:

> The school for girls is really a retreat, not only from the world, but from its cares and temptations. It has the charm of solitude with pleasant surroundings, with the

advantages of an industrial as well as a moral education. Mrs. Butterworth, the new Matron, seems to be eminently qualified for her position and her management thus far is very satisfactory. The benefit rising from the system of discipline which she has established, is already manifest.

The Women's Board report went on:

> It is a pleasant feature that the girls have had a change in the hours of study, having the morning for labor and the afternoon for school studies. By the faithful labors of competent teachers, they are making proficience in their studies and their attainments will compare favorably with some of our public schools. In one of our visits, after their recitations, they repeated Longfellow's Psalm of Life and the sentiments uttered in concert, day after day, by them, cannot fail to leave a lasting and salutary impression upon their minds. Habits of order are being formed by the girls. The neat and tasteful little bureaus and beds, manufactured at the prison, which furnish their rooms, are a source of pleasure to them and they feel grateful to the Board of State Charities for their new privileges.

Twenty-four inmates remained at the school as of January 1, 1883. Within the next year, fourteen more were committed, one who had been discharged on probation on February 25, 1882, and voluntarily returned, and one was there as

The Oaklawn School for Girls. (*Rhode Island Department of State*)

a boarder. Three inmates were discharged during the year. Ten of those committed were from Providence, one was from Newport, one was from Pawtucket, one was from Bristol, and one was from East Providence. Eight of the girls committed were sentenced for being idle persons, one for being an idle person with a doubtful reputation, four for theft, and one for being lewd and wanton.

Oaklawn School's yearly report to the State's Board of Charities and Corrections stated:

> The girls attended a concert in the Baptist Church on the evening of January 4th. The girls are well-contented, loving their home and school. We have taken many walks, enjoying the trees, grass and flowers. I have taken six of the girls to visit their parents in the city. (May) The girls are doing well enjoying their delightful home. (June) The girls are ambitious and happy. (July) Through the kindness and generosity of Charles H. George, the girls partook of and enjoyed a very nice shore dinner at Nausauket Farm near Apponaug on Tuesday, August 28th. On their return they were surprised in receiving an invitation to lunch at Superintendent Hunt's house, which was exceedingly pleasant for them. The day from early morning till evening was filled with comfort and enjoyment for the Oaklawn School girls. We passed a very pleasant Christmas. The girls enjoyed the evening very much, knowing they had been improving their minds by preparing themselves for such an entertainment (dialogues, recitations, etc.). The appropriation of twenty-five dollars, for singing birds and cages for the school, has been expended in the purchase of four canaries and the same number of brass cages with the necessary cage furniture, hooks, etc.

The salary of the staff consisted of $50 per month being paid to R. Butterworth and $25 per month paid to Ella Armes, E. Gibson, Kittie Eiler, Alithea Hutchins, and Ermina Eiler.

The only construction done on the grounds that year was the setting of a line of posts for the purpose of enclosing the property against stragglers by a barbed-wire fence. The wire had been purchased but not yet attached to the posts. Plans were being made to place granite posts and ornamental gates, perhaps of iron, at the two entrances to the school. The cost for the posts, wire, and surveying was $274.61.

An unnamed inmate wrote a letter on behalf of herself and the other girls, explaining to the Women's Board of Visitors how much they liked the school and how they had spent Christmas. Included in the Board's report to the State, it read:

> As we were short of officers, Mrs. Butterworth, our dear matron, was in the kitchen most of the day. Miss Eiler and Miss Hutchins were in the sewing room preparing our tree and we were trusted all alone most of the day. You do not know how nice it is to be trusted. Mrs. Butterworth is not afraid to trust us anywhere. We have got so much to say to you, and all of the Board, and we hope to repay by being good

and upright girls. Mrs. Butterworth is so kind to us. She is like a mother and works from morning until we retire at night. She gave us at Christmas some tea spoons for our table, and it seems so nice to think we are living like other people and are learning to be polite and ladylike. Mrs. Butterworth works with us and she takes so much pleasure in teaching us to do all kinds of work. We go to school at half-past two and learn to read and write and spell. We study arithmetic and geography and many other things. We could not have a better teacher than Miss Hutchins. She is so patient with us, as some of us are hard to learn. We have half an hour for singing. Miss Eiler is very kind to us. She is an excellent music teacher.

1884

A Rhode Island General Assembly report that year stated that of the inmates committed over the course of the year, one was ten years old, one was twelve years old, two were thirteen years old, one was fourteen years old, three were fifteen years old, two were sixteen years old, and four were seventeen years old. It also stated that no inmate had escaped that year or even attempted to. The report went on to say:

> The Superintendent reports that the girls have made 1,140 garments and other articles, repaired 5,963 and have washed and ironed 25,132. They received four premiums for needle work at the fair of the Rhode Island Society in September. As the material had been mostly furnished by the officers of the school and friends of the girls, and the work had been done in recreation hours, the money, four dollars, was handed to the Superintendent for the benefit of the girls.

Ten ash bedsteads, five ash bureaus, a large table, and a pine bookcase were constructed for the school in the carpentry shop at the men's prison. A shed was being constructed on the grounds in which to house the horses of visitors to the school. Gate posts, which had been purchased the previous year, were set and gates were hung upon them at the two entrances to the property to prevent unnecessary driving on the rods of the school grounds. A picket fence was built at each entrance to connect the gateways. Barbed wire, which had also been purchased the previous year, was attached to posts by mechanics of the Rhode Island State Workhouse to enclose the property—not to keep the girls in, but to keep bad influences out. Workhouse inmates also painted the exterior of the school and the shed.

The expenses of operating the school that year were salaries, $1,510.17; provisions and groceries, $702.99; meat, vegetables, milk, etc. from State Workhouse and farm, $742.37; clothing and bedding, $427.04; fuel, $360.63; repairs, $198.77; books and stationary, $102.68; furniture, $91.65; lights and kerosene oil, $6.69; postage, $19.50; medical supplies, $3.87; and miscellaneous, $68.75. This brought the total cost to $4,235.12.

The sum of $64 had been collected for the board of one girl admitted in June. The school continued under the management of Mrs. R. S. Butterworth, who took charge of it at the time the girls, twenty in number, were removed from the city a year and a half ago.

Twenty girls had been committed to the school by the courts between January 1, 1884, and January 1, 1885. Three girls were returned to school after escaping, and one was returned from a home in which she had been placed. Ten girls were discharged from the school on probation, two were discharged upon the expiration of their sentences, one boarder was discharged, one inmate was discharged upon bail, and three were removed to the State Workhouse and House of Correction. Eleven of the girls had been committed from Providence, three from Bristol, two from Newport, two from Westerly, one from Pawtucket, and one from East Providence. Thirteen were sentenced for being idle persons or for vagrancy, three for theft, two for lewdness, one for destroying property, and one for lying, stealing, and trying to poison herself. Of those committed, one girl was seven years old, two were eleven years old, two were thirteen years old, four were fourteen years old, two were fifteen years old, five were sixteen years old, three were seventeen years old, and one's age was unknown.

The General Assembly report went on:

> The circumstances attending the escapes and the subsequent conduct of the girls made it evident that they were utterly incorrigible, and the Board caused them to be removed, after they had been returned to the school, to the Workhouse and House of Correction.

The report continued:

> Mrs. Butterworth reports that the girls have made during the year 1,455 garments and other articles, have repaired 8,528 and have washed and ironed 29,741. Several of the girls who have been discharged on probation are now in families and are known to be doing well. Mrs. Butterworth occasionally hears from them by letter and receives information regarding them from the persons in whose care they have been placed. A shed for sheltering the horses and vehicles of persons visiting the school is being constructed. It is thirty-three feet long and twelve and a half feet wide. The front roof projects four feet so that the area covered is sixteen and a half feet in width. Some friends of the school are endeavoring to obtain for it a piano, and two hundred and thirty-five dollars for the purpose have been subscribed. (Post scriptum February 9, 1885) The piano was purchased and delivered at the school on February 7th. By the terms of the subscription, the instrument becomes the property of the State.

The school's farm had a partial failure of its potato crop that year. In 1883, the farm had produced 6,000 bushels of potatoes. In 1884, it produced only 3,791 bushels. Twice as much corn was raised than the previous year, and there was an increase of 781 bushels of onions, 20.5 tons of hay, 130 barrels of cabbages, and 96 bushels of tomatoes. Other of the numerous types of vegetables raised there saw a decrease in the harvest that year. A disease of an unknown nature attacked the small pigs, causing many of them to die. This lessened the sales of pigs to a considerable extent. The superintendent of State Institutions, in cooperation with Rhode Island Society for the Encouragement of Domestic Industry, experimented that year with different fertilizers upon the school's farm. The different plots were fertilized with no manure, old rotted manure, green manure, ground bone, bone and ashes, commercial fertilizers, and phosphate.

The salary of the staff consisted of $600 per year being paid to R. Butterworth; $50 per month being paid to Ermina Eiler; and $25 per month being paid to Mary Merrill, A. Barber, A. Gaskill, Alithea Hutchins, Maud Clossen, Mary Pendleton, and H. Bullard.

A girl named Jenny Stowe was committed to the school on September 15, 1884, after being charged with being a wanton and lascivious person in speech and behavior. She pleaded guilty to both charges and was sentenced to remain at the school for her minority.

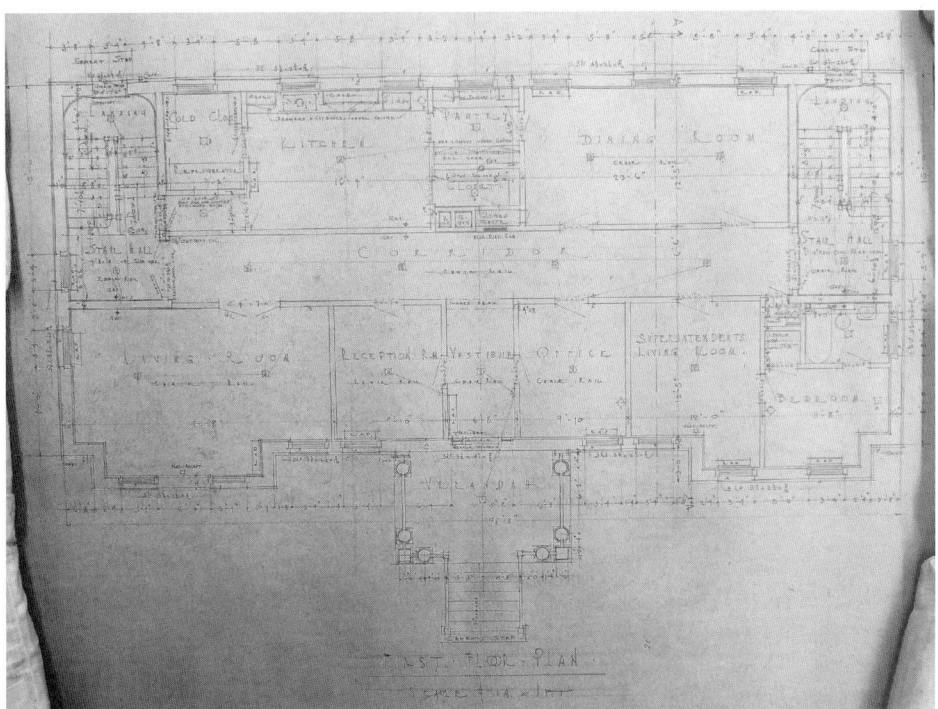

Building plans for Oaklawn School's first floor. (*Rhode Island State Archives*)

1885

Ten girls were committed to the school; one was ten years old, one was eleven years old, two were fifteen years old, five were sixteen years old, and one was seventeen years old. Five of them were determined to be idle persons, two were night-walkers, two were accused of theft, and one was said to be an idle person of doubtful reputation. The cost of sheltering one girl for a year was estimated to be $2.14.

Two girls escaped and were returned. One girl was discharged in order to accompany her parents to England. One girl was discharged due to illness and subsequently died.

The physician was called to attend to one case of eczema (skin rash) and one case of phthisis (lung infection).

The construction of the shed was completed at a cost of $257.03.

The salary of the staff consisted of $600 for the year being paid to R. Butterworth; $50 per month being paid to H. Bullard; and $25 per month being paid to Mary Merrill, Eliza Goodman, A. Baker, Alithea Hutchins, and Lizzie Conley.

1886

In early 1886, construction of two strongrooms in the basement of Oaklawn School (similar to those in the basement at Sockanosset School for Boys) began. These rooms would be used for discipline.

A report of RI Board of State Charities and Corrections that year outlined the arrival of one inmate, Fanny Nesbit, who had severely frostbitten feet:

> The girl who was sent to the Rhode Island Hospital was subsequently removed to the Rhode Island Almshouse. She came to the school with feet so badly injured by frostbite that a surgical operation was necessary. Naturally feeble, both physically and mentally, the effect of the operation was such that it was deemed best to cause removal.

She later returned to school and was reportedly "greatly benefited" from the amputation of some of her toes.

The Board's report continued:

> Most of the girls discharged on probation have been placed in families, there being a demand for all the school can supply. Many have given satisfaction while some have failed to do so, having returned or been sent back to the school. It is not, however, always wholly through fault of the girls that they return from places. At times, too much seems to have been expected from girls and not sufficient allowance made for

hereditary defects and lack of early home training. And discipline in a family cannot, of course, be so strictly maintained as in an institution. Two, having fallen into evil ways after their discharge, were removed, upon their return, to the Workhouse and House of Correction. A third was kept there a few days and returned to the school, since which time she has conducted herself properly. The two strongrooms in course of construction in the basement of the school building, which is dry and warmed, will be an efficient aid in maintaining good order, seclusion in a place removed from the other inmates, where the making of noise fails to disturb the rest of the household being, perhaps, the best form of discipline. There is no special need of these rooms at present, nor any anticipated greater than in the past, but it has been thought wise to have them for their preventive effect, if for nothing more.

Of the girls committed that year, one was ten years old, one was twelve years old, one was thirteen years old, two were fourteen years old, five were fifteen years old, and one was sixteen years old. Eight were there for being vagrants, one as an idle person, two for theft, one for making false pretenses, one as a lewd person, and one for truancy. Inmate Abby Shepard died on March 25 of consumption.

The salary of the staff consisted of $800 being paid for the year to R. Butterworth; $50 per month being paid to Alithea Hutchins and Lizzie Conley; and $25 per month being paid to M. Baker, Eva Downs, Rebecca Bliss, A. Wright, and Mary Lamb.

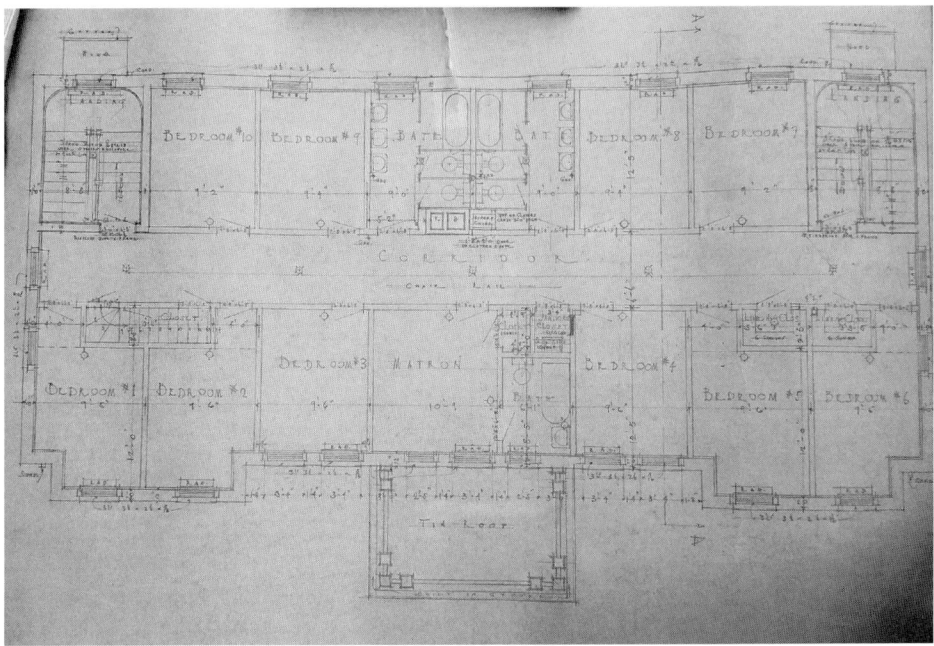

Building plans for Oaklawn School's second floor. (*Rhode Island State Archives*)

1887

A Rhode Island General Assembly report that year read:

> The Oaklawn School for girls was first opened in July 1882. Before this date, the reform school in the city of Providence had received boys and girls who were proper objects of its care. When the institution at Oaklawn was initiated for the girls, it was put under the care of Mrs. R. S. Butterworth and in the years that have passed since then, it has been proved to our board beyond any doubt that she is eminently qualified to fill the position that she assumed. We see in her appointment a striking illustration of the poet Cowper's statement that everyone falls "just in the niche he was ordained to fill." In reviewing our experience in the old reformatory, we call to mind many interesting cases, but the memory of some obstinate and wicked inmates who refused to yield to necessary order cannot but awaken painful thoughts. One instance is well remembered of a girl who set fire in the drying room which was fortunately discovered before any damage was done. It can readily be seen that natures like these cannot be controlled by moral suasion alone and that discipline of a sterner sort must be used to guard against such dangerous acts of insubordination. Before the girls were removed to their new quarters at Oaklawn, all of their number that were eligible for situations in families were sent out to service. Those that remained in the school when Mrs. Butterworth assumed her duties were for the most part depraved in nature and seemed very discouraging material for her work. Recognizing the responsibility of her trust, she has with untiring zeal and patience pursued the even tenor of her way and given these girls that were neglected in their earliest years such training as would enable them to go out into the world prepared for honorable self-support. It has been highly gratifying to witness the satisfactory progress that has been made by the girls under her charge. By the aide of efficient teachers, they obtain a fair share of book knowledge. Moral and religious instruction free from the bias of sectarianism has also been a feature in their education. Another lesson that has been taught them is prompt and respectful obedience, and loyal submission to the authority of law in all its forms. Unhappily, from their want of early training and guidance, these girls had a very inadequate idea of yielding to any rule of duty beyond their own wills, a germ of rebellion fruitful of much evil. As discipline is one of the greatest advantages gained by the martial training of boys, so in like manner some definite system should be carried out in the training of girls in reformatories like the Oaklawn School. We consider that this school is in good working order.

At the time that this report was completed, there were thirty-three inmates at Oaklawn School.

Twenty-four girls were committed that year. Two were twelve years old, three were thirteen years old, two were fourteen years old, six were fifteen years old, seven were sixteen years old, and four were seventeen years old. Sixteen-year-old inmate Delia Flaherty died on March 10 of pulmonary consumption (lung infection) and was buried in the school's cemetery.

The two strongrooms were completed at a cost of $120.41.

The salary of the staff consisted of $800 being paid for the year to R. Butterworth; $50 per month being paid to H. Bullard and Mary Lamb; and $25 per month being paid to Rebecca Bliss, I. Van Riper, Nellie Dean, Nellie White, Alithea Hutchins, Jennie Sherman, and A. Mason.

1888

A Rhode Island Senate Committee gathered in February to address charges of cruelty committed upon the inmates at Oaklawn School. The Committee reported to the state:

> Written complaints were received by the Committee from one or more ex-officers of the Oaklawn School for Girls as to harsh and cruel treatment towards several of its inmates, giving names and details of the alleged ill treatment. The Committee placed a copy of these complaints in the hands of Mrs. Butterworth, the principal of the school, as soon as received, deeming it due to her that she should be at once acquainted with the charges as well as the names of those making them. The Committee subsequently visited this school and made a personal and careful inspection of the methods of government and the daily routine observed by its inmates, the sleeping, dining, cooking, and in fact every department of the institution. We also questioned the girls upon whom alleged cruelty had been practiced, both apart and in the presence of the principal, thus gaining as thorough a knowledge as possible of the facts.

The Committee's report continued:

> We afterwards gave a public hearing in regard to this particular matter and invited those who had made the complaints to appear and make oaths to the truthfulness of their written statements. None appeared however and the Committee were left with the statements of the girls themselves and the sworn testimony of the principal. The little ones, while complaining of harsh treatment in the past, agreed that they were well cared for and do not now complain. We are firmly of the opinion that this institution is economically and humanely managed and have no hesitancy in commending the conduct of this school. It is a credit to the State.

One of the complainants, a former teacher who had removed to Boston, had accused R. S. Butterworth of forcing eleven-year-old inmate Fanny Nesbit to be confined in a cold room, causing both of her feet to become frozen. The teacher had promised to come and testify but did not appear at the hearing. Fanny Nesbit reported to the Committee herself that her feet had been frozen while she was living at home in Newport, not while at the school.

There were twenty-two girls committed to the school that year. Two were ten years old, one was twelve years old, one was thirteen years old, five were fourteen years old, eight were fifteen years old, one was sixteen years old, and four were seventeen years old. One inmate died that year of hereditary phthisis, a condition of the lungs that one is born with, making that person susceptible to tuberculosis (a lung infection). This may have been Minnie Pherson, who was buried in the school's cemetery.

The doctor was called to attend to one case of bronchial catarrh (inflammation of the mucus membranes of the sinuses and throat), two cases of general debility (weakness), one case of eczema, one femur fracture (broken thigh bone), one fracture of the lower extremities, one case of hysteria, two cases of malaria (mosquito-borne illness), one case of paronychia (fungal infection of the fingernails), three cases of scabies (mites under the skin), and two cases of acute rheumatism (pain in the joints and muscles).

The salary of the staff consisted of $800 being paid for the year to R. Butterworth; $52.50 per month being paid to Alithea Hubbard; and $25 per month being paid to Nellie White, C. Cheney, S. Main, H. Bullard, M. Goodman, and A. Mason.

In December, a nineteen-year-old boy named Frank Lawrenz arrived up at the school, looking for his seventeen-year-old sister, May. He had been living with May, their three-year-old brother, Joseph, and their parents, James and Margaret Lawrenz, in Brockton, Massachusetts, until 1876. James, a native of Germany, found himself unable to support his family that year. All three kids were handed into the custody of the Home for Destitute Children in Brockton. Frank was eventually placed with a family named Smith, where he stayed for about a year before being sent to Kansas. He continued moving around until he found himself in Missouri in the winter of 1888. Having never forgotten about his family, he set out to find them. He journeyed to the institution they had been taken to in Brockton and asked if they knew where May was. They informed him that she had been adopted by a Mrs. Burton of Providence, Rhode Island, but was currently an inmate at Oaklawn School and Mrs. Burton had since relocated.

Frank continued on to Cranston and arrived at Oaklawn School, where he was greeted by R. S. Butterworth. He asked her if he could see May; soon, the girl was brought to him. The look on her face, upon seeing her brother, was one of astonishment. He asked her if she remembered that she had a brother once. She replied that she did, but she thought he was dead. He told her that he was her brother and that he had come from Kansas City to find her.

She continued to stare at him in shock and then finally ran to his outstretched arms. They conversed for a while before contacting the chairman of the Rhode Island Board of Charities and asking what they could do to secure May's release from the school.

As May was a minor and the legal child of Mrs. Burton, she could only ever be released into her care. She was informed that Mrs. Burton had been trying to secure her release already. May explained that life with her adopted mother had not been a happy one, that she was happier at the school, and that she would never return to the Burton home for any reason.

Frank planned to continue attempting to have his sister released into his care and to locate their little brother, Joseph. No one had seen their father since 1876 and it was assumed he had either moved or died. Their mother was said to have relocated to Wyoming.

1889

A Rhode Island Board of State Charities and Corrections report to the state noted that, within the year, six girls had been committed for theft, four for vagrancy, two for truancy, two for being wayward, one for being lewd and wanton, one for being a disorderly person, one for running away from home, and one for "maliciously injuring certain plants."

Of those committed, one was ten years old, one was eleven years old, five were twelve years old, three were thirteen years old, three were fourteen years old, two were fifteen years old, one was sixteen years old, and two were seventeen years old. The Board's report went on to read:

> At seventeen years, and even at sixteen, girls are believed to be in most cases too old for a reform school. They early mature in evil ways and in such cases the Workhouse and House of Correction is the more appropriate institution for them, rather than a school where they become the companions of little girls, some of whom may be but slightly more than eight years old and are innocent through their very youthfulness. The law now permits any person under eighteen years of age to be sentenced to the reform school.

A girl named Alice Foster, who was believed to be about twelve or thirteen years old, was committed to Oaklawn School on December 9, 1889, after being charged with being a vagrant and disorderly person. She was sentenced to remain at the school for five years.

The salary of the staff consisted of $800 being paid for the year to R. Butterworth and $25 per month being paid to A. Main, E. Sheldon, Mary Lamb, A. Mason, and A. Holmes.

The physician was called to attend to one abscess (pus-filled sore), one case of diarrhea, one case of incontinence of urine, one case of necrosis (interrupted blood supply), one case of phthisis, and one case of acute rheumatism.

1890

Inmate Mattie Malvose died of pneumonia on May 12 and was buried in the school's cemetery.

1891

The salary of the staff consisted of $800 being paid for the year to R. Butterworth and $25 per month being paid to Rosa Eames, W. Bennett, A. Atwood, E. Sheldon, Emily Cope, Annie Hackett, Lillie Hollister, M. George, Ella Foote, and S. McDonald.

An inmate paroled to thirty-six-year-old Arthur Gilbert Billings received permission from him to invite her school friends over to enjoy his home and farm for the day. Billings lived on Prospect Hill in Warwick with his wife, Etta, and children, Herbert (aged eight), Hattie (aged seven), and Arthur (aged four). Approximately twenty-eight girls arrived and spent a wonderful Saturday there.

1893

Eighteen girls were received at the school that year. A report by Mrs. R. S. Butterworth to the Rhode Island State Board of Education stated:

> The Oaklawn School, located in the town of Cranston, is a reform school for girls only. Girls are received between the ages of eight and eighteen years, being sentenced by the various courts of the state for terms varying from two years to the years of their minority. It would be for their interest if all sentences were made to expire with their reaching twenty-one years of age. Few would remain in the school so long a time, yet they would continue members of the school, subject to its authority and liable at any time to be returned for cause to its precincts. The policy is to send each girl, so soon as this can be done with safety and profit to her, into a family where she will be surrounded by good influences and receive such religious, moral and mental training as is calculated to make of her a good and useful woman. A girl is not legally bound to the person who shall receive her into his family but may be recalled at once when her interest requires this, or she may be returned to the school without delay if she proves in anywise unsatisfactory. She does not go into the family as a mere servant, this would in a majority of cases secure her ruin, but it is

in every case expected that she will be received into the family, treated as a member of the family, and by the woman at its head guarded and guided as a child of the family. Such conditions being imposed, the applicants for girls are doubtless fewer than they would be if less were required on behalf of the girls, those whose only care is to get the most service possible out of the least possible outlay are not likely to accede to our terms. And yet there is never any lack of approved persons who seek our girls to give them homes and home training, indeed the applications are always more numerous than are the girls whom we have ready to leave us. Circumstances sometimes require that a girl who has done well in the school shall go to her parents, or to relatives with whom she formerly lived. In such cases, the result is usually disastrous for the girl. Of those, however, who are sent into the country and among strangers, nearly all grow up to a reputable womanhood, the exceptions being in almost every case those whose term of sentence is short, who at the most critical age are released from the school's control, and who then very naturally gravitate back to the vicious associations of their childhood.

Butterworth's report went on:

During the year 1893, twenty-three girls were sent to homes, making, with those who were absent and yet members of the school at the beginning of the year, fifty-four girls for who's well-being the school was responsible, and over whom a constant supervision was exercised. Of this number, only three were returned as unsatisfactory to those who had them in charge. In the school, the certainty that if she try faithfully to improve herself, she may at an early date go to a better home than she ever knew is presented to every girl, and the number is very small upon whom this does not act as a powerful stimulus to doing well. All the teaching and the discipline of the school has in view the same end. It is regarded as of the first importance to know how to do general housework. There is a kitchen, a laundry, and a sewing room, each of which, with the halls and dormitories, is under the charge of a different teacher, the girls being changed from one department to another at the beginning of each fourth month. They are taught that it is the part of a woman to make her home as attractive as possible, and that no employment is more honorable than the worthy discharge of household duties. They accept this teaching, many of them being apt to learn, ambitious to excel, going about their work cheerfully, doing it with a neatness and a promptness that are full of promise. Three hours of each day are spent in the exercises of the schoolroom under the care of an experienced and successful teacher. They are nearly all backward for their years and the instruction is largely in the elementary branches. The following text books are used: Monroe's fourth and fifth readers, Normal third and fourth readers, Normal spelling course, Normal copy books, Harper's geography, Higginson's history of United States, Franklin arithmetics, and an approved text book in physiology, etc.

Her report continued:

> The girls are more studious than one might expect in view of their antecedents, some of them making good progress. There is a well-supplied library for their use. Much attention is given to vocal music, in which a considerable proficiency is acquired, excellent voices are common. At the regular Sunday service, they furnish singing of a quality which excites the surprise of those who may be present as visitors. In the morning, when the weather is suitable, the younger girls go out of doors without a teacher, staying as may be convenient from one to two hours, roaming anywhere upon the broad grounds connected with the school, often out of sight and hearing, being often permitted to go upon the street to the store, to the railroad station, and about the neighborhood, on errands, and it may be said that not one of these smaller girls ever betrayed such a trust reposed in her. When the older girls are out of doors, they are always accompanied by a teacher. It is hardly necessary, after what has been said, to add that Oaklawn School is in no sense a juvenile prison, and those committed to its care are neither regarded nor made to feel like they came to be punished for crimes committed. Their wrongdoing is less the expression of innate viciousness than it is the result of vicious surroundings in which they have been compelled to live, and for those whose existence they are in no wise responsible, and they have come to the school that under more favorable circumstances than they ever yet knew, they may be helped on to a virtuous and honorable womanhood. The school is invested as much as possible with the atmosphere of a home, in which the Superintendent stands as a mother, and the teachers as her assistants, toiling in all ways for the good of their charge.

Ten girls were sent to homes on parole that year and three of them were returned and sent to different homes. Butterworth's report noted:

> Incompatibility of temperament is an element of failure in the placing of girls in families as it is in other relations of life … It not infrequently happens that a girl fails to give satisfaction or is herself dissatisfied in one family, who will be both satisfactory and contented in another.

Five inmates had been removed to the Workhouse and House of Correction, one of whom was removed from the school due to her incorrigibility while there. She was later returned to the school and paroled to a family where she was said to be doing well. Another, an eighteen-year-old girl, was determined to be unfit for residency at the school due to her maturity and the poor physical condition she was in, resulting from the life she had been leading. The other three had been inmates at the school previously and had been discharged from custody several years earlier. Their misconduct had caused them to be committed again. Due to their return at an older age, with morals that made them inappropriate associates for the other girls, they were not accepted at the school a second time.

A group of twelve men worked for a total of five weeks removing stumps of trees, brush, and dead wood to improve the appearance of the groves that surrounded the school.

On July 25, an African-American girl named Florence, residing in Arctic Center, was committed to the school for five years on charges of "being disobedient and annoying her parents in many ways."

The physician was called to attend to one case of scrofulous glands (swollen glands in the neck), one case of hysteria, two cases of phthisis, and one case of pneumonia, in which the girl had been sent to the Almshouse several months earlier in critical condition, and had died there.

The salary of the staff that year consisted of $800 being paid for the year to R. Butterworth and $25 dollars per month paid to L. Phillips, Emma Dutton, S. Wardwell, Annie Crowell, N. Leighton, A. Holmes, A. Hubbard, L. Foster, E. Hinman, M. Pierce, E. Sheldon, Lena Horne, Mac Young, Lena Welton, A. Mason, Alice Wilder, and Ethel Kenney.

1894

Thirty-four girls were received at the school that year. The Rhode Island State Board of Education report noted that one inmate had died, which may have been Loraine Kerwin, who was buried in the school's cemetery. Seventeen girls had been committed for being idle and disorderly, five for theft, three for truancy, two for vagrancy, and six for being lewd and wanton persons. Of those entering the school that year, one girl was eight years old, one was eleven years old, five were twelve years old, one was thirteen years old, four were fourteen years old, eight were fifteen years old, five were sixteen years old, six were seventeen years old, one was eighteen years old, one was nineteen years old, and one's age was unknown. The report stated:

> As the girl was released on bail within a few hours after commitment, her age was not ascertained. The girls whose ages are given respectively as eighteen and nineteen years must have stated their ages differently to the court, for the courts are not authorized by the law to sentence minors to the reform school who are over eighteen years of age. It is believed that these girls gave their ages correctly as given above. The two girls who were removed to the Workhouse and House of Correction had been inmates of the school several years before. They had then been removed to the Workhouse and subsequently returned to the school, to be from there discharged on probation to live in families, two cases in which the results of the efforts made in their behalf were very disappointing. Of the five girls discharged to go to the Almshouse, four went there for treatment which they could not properly receive at the school, and the fifth is a simple-minded girl who had been an inmate of both the school and the almshouse before.

The physician was called to attend to one abscess, one case of hysteria, one case of malaria, two cases of pulmonalis phthisis (lung infection), one case of tuberculosis, and one case of pulmonary consumption (lung infection), of which the girl died. Again, this may have been Loraine Kerwin.

The salary of the staff consisted of $800 being paid for the year to R. Butterworth and $25 per month paid to M. Tilotson, Jennie Parker, J. Durant, H. Hutchinson, A. Helfin, A. Wilder, Emma Dutton, E. Hinman, M. Young, A. Mason, and Jennie Jones.

1895

Eighteen girls were received at the school that year. One was eight years old, two were nine years old, one was thirteen years old, five were fourteen years old, one was fifteen years old, six were sixteen years old, one was seventeen years old, and one was nineteen years old.

Superintendent Butterworth notified the board in July that she had meditated for some time on retiring from the reform school life and work and had decided to resign her position. The resignation was to take effect whenever her successor was chosen. In August, Mrs. M. F. Hopkins was hired to fill the position temporarily and in October, James Eastman was installed.

It was decided to lay a new water pipe leading to the school from the pump at the Workhouse and House of Correction. Previously, the school had been provided with water pumped from an artesian well by the power of the windmill on the property. The windmill had been causing many problems (as it failed to furnish enough water during calm weather) and needed frequent repairs, including the necessity of replacing the wheel after it was blown off in a gale. In addition, gravity did not allow water to reach the tank in the school's attic, creating a dangerous situation should fire break out. Now, the school would receive its water from the same main as the other nearby institutions.

The salary of the staff included $800 being paid to R. Butterworth for the year and $25 per month paid to M. Hopkins, A. Wilder, E. Smith, Bessie McNab, E. Hinman, A. Mason, Mary Kinnicutt, M. Tyler, Jennie Jones, Lillian Walker, M. Young, and A. Hubbard. Income for the school included $13.14 for the sale of old rugs.

1896

That year, several girls had been reported missing from their homes in Providence. Officials from the Society for Prevention of Cruelty to Children began an investigation and, that February, located many of them in Burrillville roadhouses.

One of the girls was committed to Oaklawn School while the others were taken to a mission home in Providence.

A sixteen-year-old girl named Katie Shea was committed to the school on March 3, charged with being an idle person. She was sentenced to remain there until she turned eighteen.

Inmate Edith Bailey escaped on the afternoon of July 15. Mr. Eastman and several others immediately set out looking for her. In less than an hour, she was located at the home of George Shields in the West Warwick village of Lippitt and brought back to the school. During the search, the horse that one of the men was riding became exhausted and died. Edith had left the school and walked along back roads towards the west end of Cranston, headed for Fiskeville. She later reported that as she passed through the woods, she was criminally assaulted by a man there. She was then found by Shields and another man, who brought her to Shields's house in their carriage. Once she was returned to the school, she made out a statement detailing the assault and gave a description of the man who attacked her. Police believed they knew who the man was—a resident of Warwick—and set out to find him. In total, fourteen inmates escaped that year; twelve of them were located and returned.

An eighteen-year-old girl named Elizabeth Bullock was committed on August 8 after being arrested for and pleading guilty to being an idle person of dissolute habits. She was sentenced to the school for her minority.

In November, inmate Agatha Northup wrote to Superintendent Eastman:

> I now take the time to write you a few lines. Since you have been our superintendent, I have made up my mind to do just what is right, to do my work just as good as it can be done, to be good to the girls, to be kind to all that are around me and not let my temper get the best of me. I will try to help the teachers all I can and to help you. I will try to have good lessons in school. I wish I had come here long before I did. I am going to try all the harder now. I am one of the girls that told Mrs. Eastman I couldn't write to you because I didn't know what to. I must close my letter with best wishes to you and Mrs. Eastman.

The girls, wishing to show their appreciation to the superintendent and his family, gave an entertainment in their honor on the evening of Thanksgiving. The girls performed recitations and songs.

The school grounds were improved by removing boulders and unsightly trees, evening the ground surface, and draining the wet portion of the opening in the woods in front of the school. A new clothes yard and playground were constructed on the grounds. It was planned for a picket fence to be built around the playground. A stone foundation was laid by the inmates of the State Asylum, upon which a new henhouse would be built. Additionally, a portion of the driveway, leading from the road to the school, a distance of about twenty-eight rods, was rebuilt and underlaid with stone. The school generated some income that year by selling wearing apparel made by the inmates, earning $26.09.

The physician was called to attend to one abscess, two cases of acne, two cases of anemia, one nasopharyngeal catarrh (inflammation of airways), two cases of cephalalgia (headache), one case of chancroids (bacterial infection of the genitals), one case of herpes (sexually transmitted disease causing genital pain and sores), one case of hysteria, three cases of leucorrhoea (vaginal yeast infection), one case of menorrhagia (heavy menstruation), one case of poison ivy, three cases of syphilis (sexually transmitted disease causing sores on genitals), three cases of vaginitis(infection of vagina), one case of constipation, four cases of coryza (inflammation of the lining of the nose), two cases of diarrhea, one case of dyspepsia (pain in the abdomen), one case of erysipelas (acute bacterial infection), six cases of enlarged glands, one case of indigestion, nineteen cases of influenza, two cases of malaria, two cases of pharyngitis (sore throat), one case of scrofula (infection of lymph nodes in the neck), and nine cases of tonsillitis (infection of the tonsils). Inmate Maggie McCoy died on February 12 and was buried in the school's cemetery.

The State Institution religious instructor, in his yearly report to the Board of State Charities and Corrections, stated:

> I have had ample opportunity to note the good results which follow from placing girls of the Oaklawn School in carefully selected homes, nearly all such girls growing up into a good and useful womanhood. This is true of some whose antecedents have been of the worst. The evil results which often follow when girls are dismissed to their old homes are equally manifest, a very large majority of these turning out badly, even when their natural proclivities seemed the very opposite of vicious.

The salary of the staff consisted of $800 for the year being paid to M. Hopkins; $50 per month paid to Emma Silver, M. Boomhower, and Ida Smith; $40 per month paid to Clara Forbush; and $25 per month paid to M. Mills, E. Hinman, Rosa Marwood, M. Tyler, Cora Ray, Ida Smith, Jennie Jones, Mrs. Welch, Alice Wilder, Miss Spears, Hannah Rowand, Miss Searle, K. Buckelew, Olive Richardson, H. Brayton, Lillian Walker, Dora Williams, E. Hopkins, and M. Kinnicutt.

1897

On January 13, an inmate named Edith M. wrote to the superintendent from the home she had been paroled to in North Sterling, Connecticut:

I want to thank you for the home you got me and I think there couldn't be a better home than I have. I will show you how I appreciate my home by just doing the best I can. I am trying hard not to get homesick but sometimes I think of you all. I have made my mind not to come back but I want to grow up a good woman so that the State can be proud of me. We have thirteen cows, three horses, five cats, one dog and over one hundred hens and there are over 140 acres of land. We have a great many apple trees. I am going to commence school the week after next. I have got acquainted with my teacher and I think she is very nice. Last night she invited me to go with her to the bean supper and we had a very pleasant evening. I have all the apples I want to eat and also all the milk I want to drink. Clara Carter was over to see me this week and I hardly knew her, she has grown so tall. She said she was glad that I had come to this home. Please give my love to Mrs. Eastman, also to Miss Grace and tell her I hope the girls are trying hard in their marching. There isn't a day goes by that I don't think how I used to drill them. Please give my love to Mrs. Forbush and all the girls. I close, hoping to hear from you soon. I remain one of your girls.

Inmate Sadie Trainor, who was paroled to a Mr. and Mrs. Gardner who resided in Voluntown, Connecticut, wrote to Mr. Eastman on January 14, 1898:

Have been intending to write but have not any reason why I did not. Hope all the girls are well and doing right because it is right. I enjoyed their entertainment very much. Each girl did her part well and there certainly is an improvement in their singing. I am well. Have never been sick since I left the school. I like my home very much. Mr. and Mrs. Gardner are very kind to me. I belong to the Epworth League. Will close now, with love to Mrs. Eastman.

Sadie wrote to Eastman again on April 17:

I have been doing housework during the quarter. Have been regular in attendance at church and Sabbath school. Have been careful regarding my habits and associates. I am satisfied and contended with my home and present occupation. I am getting along all right. Have not got angry since coming here.

Mrs. Gardner then wrote to Mr. Eastman the following report:

Sadie has been invaluable to me during the past weeks. She has improved in many ways and is to be especially commended for the willing, cheerful manner in which she relieved me of every household care in our recent time of sorrow.

That same month, a man named W. H. Allen went to inspect the Howard complex and the reform schools. He later wrote a letter to the superintendent:

Inmates engaging in the required physical culture. (*Rhode Island Department of State*)

My visit to Howard has made a deep impression upon my mind. Since my return I have talked much about the institutions at Cranston. The reformatory work in which you are engaged is hopeful in a large degree. I believe that the average boy in that school would compare favorable with the average boy on the streets of Woonsocket. I admire your method of treating the girls. You are introducing them into a new world, both of thought and manners. The majority of them are there because they have not had the love and care of discreet parents and I think it is well to tell them so. I wish that it were possible to keep the "fallen girls" apart from the orphans. The little ones learn too much from the big ones. Time and a deeper public interest may make such a separation possible. You may count me among the friends of the school and, when possible, I will put you in a way to find a home for some girl.

Also in January, Clara Myles was admitted from Woonsocket, and Carrie Bingham was admitted from Providence. *The Howard Times*, the newspaper of the Sockanosset School for Boys, reported that they were "two very bright girls" who had "stepped aside from the true path." The article went on to say:

The hope is that they may appreciate their opportunities while in the school, that they may not persist in ways that culminated in their being sent there, or in other words, that they may turn their backs upon their past history and, looking to the future, may show themselves willing to do whatever is required of them in the daily routine of the place. And most important of all, that they may take counsel of their matrons, to heed it to the uprooting of old habits of thought and action and the substitution of such will conduce to womanhood.

On February 6, an inmate named Viola was returned from her placement in the home of the Turner family of Oaklawn Village, as they stated they had no further need of her services. Another inmate, Mattie, was returned from the State Almshouse by order of the Board. Inmates Nellie Fry and Katie Shea returned from a voluntary exile from the school.

The physician was called to attend to two abscesses, one case of anemia (lack of red blood cells), one case of acute bronchitis (inflammation of the airways), one case of cephalalgia (headache), one case of conjunctivitis (eye inflammation), one contusion (bruise), one case of coryza, fourteen cases of diarrhea, seven cases of dysentery (intestinal infection), one case of dyspepsia (indigestion), two cases of hypertrophied tonsils (enlarged tonsils), five cases of tonsillitis (swelling of the tonsils), two cases of vaginitis (vaginal infection), one incised wound (sharp-edged cut), two lacerated wounds (tear-like wounds), two cases of eczema, three episodes of epilepsy, two cases of rheumatism, two cases of enlarged glands, two cases of granular lids (drying of the eye), one case of herpes (sexually transmitted disease), one case of hysteria, six cases of indigestion, twenty-seven cases of influenza, one case of leucorrhoea, one case of malaria, one case of otorrhoea (discharge from the ear), five cases of pharyngitis, one case of pityriasis (skin rash), and three sprains.

That winter, the Grippe (influenza) had been very prevalent at the school, affecting the matrons and the girls. Emma Silver, the kitchen matron, was confined to her room for several days. Many of the girls were confined to their rooms for days at a time as well, and even those who had not come down quite as sick were coughing incessantly and suffering with bad colds.

On March 7, inmate Isabel "Bella or Belle" Mont, who had previously been paroled to the Burdick family, penned the following letter to school authorities:

> I have a good home and I like my home. Mrs. Burdick is good to me and I am good to her too. I like to take care of the baby. She is a good little girl for me. I am a good girl, Mr. Eastman. I don't have much work to do. I sit down every afternoon and sometimes mornings and I do my work good. Please tell Mrs. Eastman I would like to see her if I could. Please give my love to Mrs. Forbush and all the girls.

An agent from the school visited the Burdick home twenty-two days later and reported the following to the school, via letter:

She has made a very favorable impression. Mrs. Burdick had many complimentary things to say; Isabel was the best humored girl she ever knew. Under all circumstances, she is good humored. She can do good work, makes a good loaf of bread, likes the little girl. They are much pleased with the girl and the girl is much pleased with her home.

On March 23, a paroled inmate, E. B. G., wrote the superintendent:

I received your letter dated February 4 and was very glad to hear from you. I read your letter several times. I would like to have a letter from the girls. I think about the girls every day and wish I could see them; also, the teachers. I do not know any of them, but I wish to see them just the same. I had a nice little letter from Bella Mont. I did not know who she was, but I thought a little while then I knew who she was. She said she liked her home, especially the baby, and she was trying to do right. I was sorry when I heard Katie had gone back to the school.

On March 26, an inmate named Jennie penned a letter to fellow inmate Agatha Northup, whose behavior had recently become unacceptable:

I promised to write you a little letter this afternoon, and now I find the time. Agatha, what makes you act so disagreeable lately? You were getting along so nicely a little while ago. Now won't you commence again and try hard to do better? You promised to behave while Mrs. Forbush was away this afternoon. I hope you have kept that promise. Now, Agatha, when you are about to do anything, you should not when I am around. I shall remind you of your promise. Then don't take it in a cross manner, but remember I am only trying to help you a little. You would not say the Lord's Prayer this morning. Perhaps you have been neglecting your prayers for some time. If you have, I shouldn't wonder if that's what is making you go wrong. I am sure if you ask our Lord every morning when you rise to help you overcome your temper through each day, you will get on better. But you must make some effort yourself, you know. You must try hard. It lies with you. Our Lord can't make you good even if you pray to Him to do so, if you don't try yourself. I am much pleased to write a letter to you now or any time if it will help you along. Just now as I am writing, the sun shines on my desk and all around me, so lovely and bright. Then all of a sudden it hides behind a cloud and the room looks so dark. I thought it would not come out again but, by and by, it came out far brighter than before then went and hid again and the last time it came out, it stayed out and all was sunshine. And as I noticed this, I thought how much that sun was like us girls. We shine for a while and all is bright and happy, then a cloud of wrongdoing comes up and hides our bright side. By and by we try again but soon fall back once more. But, like the sun, if we keep on with persistent efforts, we may shine for quite a while. Then when a cloud comes, it will be easy to pass. Now, Agatha, it is time for the girls to go out of school and I must close. Some time, when you have time, write me a little answer. If you can come down to play with the girls tonight, come with me and I'll try to keep you from getting into trouble, as you did last night. And when we drill, you must do your best. For you know you make up my company and I want that it should please Miss Eastman. With kindly feeling for you and love, I am one of your schoolmates.

An inmate named Angelina had been previously paroled to forty-two-year-old dry goods shipping clerk George Millikin and his wife, Medora, who resided on Oaklawn Avenue in Cranston with their fourteen-year-old daughter Mary. On March 27 of that year, the Millikins wrote a letter to Mr. Eastman:

Dear Sir, I would inform you that Angelina has made up her mind to come back to the school and is tired of staying with us. She had a letter from her sister last Tuesday and ever since then, she has been anxious to get away. I am sorry to have her leave us but if she will not stay, I cannot help it. I even told her if she would stay and be a good girl as she has been to us, I would give her fifty dollars when her time was out, but that is no temptation. I wish that Mr. Nutting would come down and get her so I could tell him all the particulars about her much better than I can write it.

School authorities felt this failed attempt at parole was the direct result of outside interference by a family member and noted in their written communications with each other:

We must find this sister and have her to be different if possible. Meanwhile, Angelina, we hope will come to her senses and return to a proper appreciation of her home, for her own sake not only, but for the encouragement of others.

Only nine days prior to the date of the Millikins' letter, an agent for the school had visited the Millikin home and submitted a letter to the school: "Visited George Millikin's home, with whom is Angelina. Excellent report."

In April, a man wrote to the superintendent concerning one of his relatives, who was an inmate of Oaklawn School at the time. It appears that some arrangement had been discussed concerning the girl going to live with the relative and decided against. The letter read:

Dear Sir, your favor dated the 22nd was duly received and in reply would state that the interest you have manifested in my niece has impressed me very much. I desire to thank you for all you have done for her and earnestly hope that she may be sustained by the strong arm of God in her every effort to do right. When my wife and I heard of her unfortunate condition through her sister, we decided to extend a helping hand to her at once, in as much as we knew that the home of her father had few, if any attractions, for her. We also concluded that she was living under prison discipline and restraint and would be glad to get the refuge in a home where she could feel the elevating influences of love and kindness, and at the same time move in a purer moral atmosphere. But your kind letters to us, coupled with her description of the school and school life had the effect of banishing the opinion we had formed. We also know that she is being well cared for under your supervision, and we feel much more at ease in consequence. You know what is best for her. Perhaps after all she may do better where she is then to come here to us. I will write to her occasionally and encourage her all I can.

That same month, Angelina wrote to the superintendent from the Millikin family's home:

> We received your letter and were pleased to hear from you. I read the letter you sent, and it has done me lots of good. I am sorry that I was causing you trouble. I thought of what you said, and I wish you could have been here last night to hear Mr. Millikin talk to me. If I tell the truth, I cannot say that they have not been good to me. I am sorry for what I have caused you. I am going to make my mind up to do better, and if I try I can. I have been to Sunday School and to meeting. We had a very good meeting and are going to have a temperance concert tonight. I am glad that Agnes and Catherine have gone out. Summer is coming and it will be very pleasant. I hope you will forgive me for what I have done. Give my love to Mr. Nutting and all the girls. And please give my love to my little brother and tell him I want him to be a good boy, not do as I have done. Please let me know where my other little brothers are. I was surprised to know that Edith and Annie had gone to homes. Are you willing that I should write to them? I cannot think of any more. Give my love to all the teachers. I promise I will do better. Mr. and Mrs. Millikin wish to be remembered in this letter. Mr. Millikin is glad that I have taken your advice and he will try and do all he can for me and make me happy. Please answer. From one of your girls … Angie.

In another letter, Angelina told Mr. Eastman: "Have been doing housework and other kind of work. I was glad to hear from my brother and I hope he is trying to be a good boy. I have not been good and feel as though I don't care."

Mr. Millikin explained the situation to Eastman via letter: "About three weeks ago, she had a letter from her mother. Since then, she has been uneasy, and I fear I can't make anything of her. I try and do the best I can with her."

The school's record of the incident, reported in *The Howard Times*, read:

> We feel sorry to receive such a report. Angelina will do well to brace up, to consider the facts as they are. Her own home is not a suitable place for her or any other child; her brother, for instance, who is now in the Sockanosset School. The condition of that home is no fault of Angelina's. It is the fault of her mother that she uses her influence to upset her where she is. What a contrast the above makes with another

report we have in our possession of the same girl and which reads as follows: "Angelina seems to be happy and at home, so Mrs. Millikin says, and so Angelina says. Mr. Millikin says there never was a better girl made than Angelina. Angelina has improved in the matter of personal appearance, looks wholesome, has gained in flesh, is rosy-cheeked, has an excellent home, and they fully appreciate her." We hope this dear child, after reflection, will not continue in her naughtiness.

Forty-one-year-old Arthur Gilbert Billings of Warwick, whose family had taken in Oaklawn School inmates before, had taken in an inmate named Sadie N. She wrote a letter to the superintendent:

I have occupied my time during the last quarter in helping Mrs. Billings with housework. Have attended church and sabbath school when weather would permit. I am satisfied with my home and like it more and more each day. I am having some clothes made and a nice Easter dress and a number of things more. This is all. Send my love to the girls.

Arthur Billings wrote to the superintendent:

Sadie has proved to be very satisfactory so far. Seems willing, obedient and honest and seems to be contended. We like her very much and hope this feeling will continue. Mrs. Billings thinks she is improving in her work and in time will make a capable housekeeper.

On April 13, an unnamed inmate who had been paroled to a family in Connecticut wrote to the superintendent:

I received your kind letter and *The Howard Times* also, both of which made me very happy. I was glad to see Eliza, Pearl and Clara's names on the Roll of Honor and hope they will try to keep them there until they depart from the school. My home is prettily situated as the Mystic River flows but a short distance below the house. I have a very pretty room, nicely furnished with all I would ask for, plenty of good books to read and also a very good letter which perhaps you would like to hear about. After Mr. Nutting had left me at my new home, I felt just as one would who had lost all her friends and, on opening my trunk, what a pleasant surprise I had. For there in my lap lay a letter and it read thus: "My dear Agnes, Mr. Eastman has got a nice home for you. Now it is your duty when a gift or present is given to you, in some way to show your gratitude for such a benefit as your home will offer you I am sure. Now, Agnes, do this to prove yourself true and faithful in all your ways and works, and with God's help you will more than thank your kind friends and benefactors. Remember us all. Keep kind thoughts of us in your mind, Agnes, and we will remember you."

Also in April, the girls scheduled an entertainment to celebrate Mrs. Forbush's birthday. They each read recitations and performed songs.

That same month, eighteen-year-old inmate Bertha Hart escaped and ran away with an eighteen-year-old boy named George Knowles, who had escaped from the Sockanosset School for Boys. On May 14, they were captured by police and sent back to their respective schools.

On July 8, Mrs. Burdick penned a letter to school authorities, explaining that she was returning Isabel Mont to the school:

> I return Belle with the bearer of this letter. She acts very differently from what she did at first. I find her a very ill-tempered and disagreeable girl and she grows cross, more so, every day. I have neither time nor patience to bother with her longer. She is quick enough and can do her work all right if she likes. It will take a different person from me to make anything out of her. She goes to bed all night at night, gets up in the morning ugly as a bear, especially wash mornings, slams and bangs things around like something wild. I have to have a time with her every few days to keep her within bounds.

In October 28, a girl named Clara Tattersall was committed to the school. Sometime earlier, she had escaped from a reform school for girls in New Bedford, Massachusetts. Receiving information that she was in Bristol, Rhode Island, she was located at a home in Broad Common and captured.

On November 23, Sadie Trainor passed away while on parole after suffering with consumption for about six months. Trainor had been an inmate at the school since at least 1894 and was paroled in 1896. Her obituary in *The Howard Times* stated:

> While in the school, she was distinguished above many for general good conduct. She was obedient, respectful, teachable, and in all things studious to improve herself and to please her teachers. She easily won the confidence and esteem of all who were in any way associated with her. Since leaving the school, she has abundantly met the expectations of those whose charge she was entrusted. Whoever knew her loved her, and those who knew her best loved her most. During her long illness, she was the very pattern of cheerfulness and patience, grateful for each kindness shown her and never uttering a complaint.

An area of about 1 acre was prepared for the disposal of sewage at the school that year. This consisted of troughs and pipes imbedded in concrete and resting upon a foundation of stone 4 feet deep and 4 feet wide. The sewage entered the carrier from a 6-inch pipe leading from the school. Cast iron gates at intervals of 50 feet allowed the sewage to be discharged upon the land at any of the points at which the gates were placed. The field, which sloped away from the carrier, was cleared of stones and stumps and brought under cultivation so that the sewage could be utilized upon it. The pattern for the gates and the machine work upon them was completed by the boys of the Sockanosset School and the cost of the entire project was $54.27.

Other improvements to the property included an outhouse measuring 8 feet by 16 feet, and a 612-foot-long picket fence that partly enclosed the clothes yard and playground. A 50-foot-high flagstaff was erected, made of iron pipe at the Sockanosset School for Boys. Two swings and two seesaws were added to the grounds, and twenty-four double windows were placed on the north side of the building. The outhouse and picket fence were made by inmates at the State Workhouse and House of Correction.

The salary of the staff consisted of $40 per month being paid to Clara Forbush and $25 per month being paid to Emma Silver, Rachel Marwood, Olive Richardson, Agnes McNaughton, Addie Gove, and Jeanette Ramage.

The girls were taken to attend church services at the Rhode Island Hospital for the Insane at 10.15 a.m. on Sundays. At 4 p.m., Sunday School was held at Oaklawn School. It was reported that there were twenty-seven Roman Catholic inmates that year, more than ever before noted at the school.

1898

The salary of the staff consisted of $50 per month being paid to Clara Forbush; $30 per month being paid to Rose Marwood; and $25 per month being paid to Lydia Doe and Agnes Smith.

On Sundays, the girls were taken to the Rhode Island Hospital for the Insane to attend church services in their assembly room at 3.30 p.m.

The physician was called to attend to one abscess, two cases of anemia, one bruise, one case of bursitis, two nasal catarrhs (excessive build-up of mucous in the nose), one case of constipation, one case of coryza, twenty-seven cases of simple diarrhea, one case of enlarged glands, one case of gonorrhea (sexually transmitted disease), one case of hemorrhoids, one case of hip/joint disease, one case of indigestion, one case of leucorrhoea, one case of menorrhagia, one case of pharyngitis, one case of chronic rheumatism, one sprain, one case of acute tonsillitis, and one case of urticarial (hives).

The doctor's report commented that there had been no cases of real sickness, except for a few instances of "summer diarrhea." It is interesting to note that, according to reports, diarrhea seemed to be prevalent in the Rhode Island state institutions year-round. One case of suspected tuberculosis was discovered in an inmate toward the end of the year, and it was feared that the crowded condition of the school might be conducive to the development of additional such happenings in the future.

On July 22, Maria Morena of Bristol was committed to the school for two years, charged with being wayward.

The Rhode Island State Board of Education reported that year that there were fifty-seven inmates remaining at the school as of January 1, 1899. Over the course of the year, twenty-nine had been committed by the courts, five had been committed by the courts awaiting trial, two had been admitted by the Board of State Charities and Corrections, twelve had been returned from homes in which they had been placed, two had returned from the Workhouse and House of Correction, two had returned from the Almshouse, two escaped, one was discharged on bail, and five were released for trial. The Board's report read:

> Thirty-nine of the girls, an unusually large number, were discharged on probation during the year, to go to their homes or to live in families. Of this number, ten were returned to the school for cause, and twenty-nine are believed to be doing well.... One teacher resigned to assume work in the public schools. An additional assistant has been employed to aid the matron of the school, who has charge of the sewing room, thus increasing the number of employees to five. Thoroughness is the motto of the school. Every girl, no matter how small, is taught housekeeping, how to sweep a room, how to make a bed, to cook, to sew and make her own clothes, and to wash and iron. All must be done properly. Machinery is not used in the laundry. Only such conveniences are found there as are in most residences. The health of the girls has continued good, as in past years. This must be attributed to the excellent sanitary conditions of the school, good food, good water and plenty of fresh air. Physical exercise has its due effect too, in keeping the girls healthy. The entire school has been systematically trained in physical culture gratuitously by the daughter of the Superintendent, herself receiving the same instruction at the State Normal School. She appreciates this opportunity of doing good and is happy in the effort. Quarterly reports are required from all girls discharged on probation. They were received regularly during the year. In case a report is not duly received, an inquiry is made, and the reason ascertained for the failure to report. These reports of the conduct of the girls away from the school are generally very interesting and they are made all the more satisfactory by being attested in each case by the parent or guardian of the girl or by the head of the family in whose charge she has been placed. Moreover, Mr. Nutting, the religious instructor of the institutions, under a rule of the Board, visits periodically all the girls who have been discharged on probation and makes a report of his visits, and they are visited too by other officers and are encouraged to correspond with the authorities of the school in addition to making their regular reports. To make their life more pleasant, and to create a home feeling and thus render the girls more susceptible to the efforts made to benefit them, entertainments of an elevating character have been prepared and given by the girls from time to time, to which the superintendent and officers from the other

institutions have been invited. All the holidays are appropriately observed, and special efforts are made to make Easter, Thanksgiving and Christmas bright and cheerful. The exercises prepared for these occasions have been usually repeated at the State Hospital for the Insane. Several of the girls took part in the production of the cantata of "Esther" which was given in the spring at the State Hospital for the Insane, by all of the musical talent to be found among the officers of the several institutions. The girls sang in the chorus and introduced some of their callisthenic exercises and evolutions in marching. Another home should be provided for the smaller or younger girls. In the present building we cannot separate the older from the younger, the most hardened of those from those who are less so. The opinion expressed at conferences of charities and corrections and elsewheres by those who have most earnestly studied the question of the reformation of the young is that children of the characters and ages of those sent to the Oaklawn School should be divided into two classes at least. With the exhibition specimens of the workmanship of the boys of the Sockanosset School, at the fair of the State Fair Association, was an exhibit of articles showing the proficiency of the girls of the Oaklawn School in the sewing room, the laundry, and the kitchen, all of which received much commendation from the public.

Expenses were as follows: salaries, $1,815.64; provisions and groceries, $102.46; meat, vegetables, flour, milk, medical supplies, etc. from Workhouse and farm at market prices, $2,343.52; clothing and bedding, $548.31; fuel $561.84; repairs, $66.25; furniture, $158.40; lights and kerosene oil, $29.24; stationary, $27.49; books, periodicals, etc., $38.82; postage, $37.99; rent of telephone, $75.00; expenses of visiting girls placed in families, and visiting families before placing girls with them, $131.85; and miscellaneous, $93.12. The total was $6,028.85.

Holidays were always celebrated in a grand manner at Oaklawn School, which excited the girls greatly. Decorations, games, activities, music, and a great abundance of food were always part of every holiday celebration. On the Fourth of July, the eleven girls who made up the school's Glee Club performed for the inmates of the State Asylum that year. A big lunch was served in the yard of James Eastman, games and races were enjoyed, and a fireworks show lit up the sky.

On October 4, an inmate referred to as "L. B.", possibly Elizabeth "Lizzie" Bullock, penned the following letter to Mr. Eastman:

> I am trying to be a good woman. I thank God for opening a way for me to the school because I have enough to eat and wear and a good, clean bed to sleep in when it comes night, and that is more than I had at home. Have been here over two years. Mrs. Forbush is just like a mother to me and you are as good as a father to me. I love my teachers very much.

The superintendent, in his yearly report to the state, shared:

> The work of the school has been progressive and, on the whole, satisfactory. Kindness, united with firmness, has prevailed and excellent discipline has resulted. This is remarkable, considering the antecedents of the girls and their previous environment. It is an admitted fact that it is more difficult to reclaim a wayward girl than a wayward boy, and all because of differences in their waywardness. The one has transgressed the moral law as well as the civil, while the other has transgressed the civil law alone. Experience shows that to reform a girl requires more time and patience than to reform a boy and demands the greatest fertility of resource. While being inured to the daily routine and discipline, girls must receive sympathy in the largest possible measure and yet be held to accountability. They are so weak wherein they need so much strength. As an evidence of the sympathy and kindness on the part of the matrons or teachers here, it may be said that for more than two years, no other punishment has been inflicted than sending the girls to their rooms for rest and reflection. Visitors notice the quietness of the home during labor and study hours, the cheerfulness and good behavior of the girls and the excellent ventilation and cleanliness of the whole house. The matron and her assistants continue steadily at their posts of duty, the former instructing the girls in sewing and the latter in the work in the schools and laundry and in other duties. One change occurred in the superintendence in the culinary department during the year and two changes in the school-room. For the supervision of the institution, only four persons, all ladies, are employed. The superintendent's daughter visits the school three evenings or oftener each week. She says "Physical culture and military work, including setting-up exercises or body movements, exercise with the wand, dumb-bell and Indian-club and military drill have been faithfully carried on during the year. The setting-up exercises are performed each morning before breakfast for fifteen minutes, the other exercises three times a week from 6.30 to 8.00 p.m." The girls are organized as a military company, having three girl officers, namely captain and first and second lieutenants who, under the matron, take charge of the morning exercises and of the marching of the girls in line to and from work or recreation during the day. This has proved beneficial to the discipline of the school as shown in strict submission of the girls to commands and in the improvement of their manners. From May until October, the military drill is performed in the open air, where the recreation hours are passed also, which gives the girls all the out-door exercise possible. On Thanksgiving eve, an exhibition drill was given in the armory of the Sockanosset School and the girls were presented with a beautiful national silk flag. On New Year's Eve, they rendered the operetta "Laila" at the same place and, on Monday evening following, the same was given by them in the assembly hall of the State Hospital for the Insane, for the benefit of the inmates there and such of the inmates of the State Almshouse as were able to be present.

1899

Committals that year included two for being idle persons or persons of doubtful reputation, one for assault, five as lewd and wanton persons, two for theft, six for vagrancy, three for truancy, and one for attempted poisoning. At the time of commitment, one was eleven years old, one was twelve years old, one was thirteen years old, six were fourteen years old, two were fifteen years old, six were sixteen years old, and three were seventeen years old. Two were admitted by the Board of State Charities and Corrections upon request of their parents or guardians.

The General Assembly Report that year recommended improvements:

> The heating apparatus will need renewing perhaps before another winter. In the winter of 1898/1899, the apparatus broke down in the coldest weather. It was repaired during the summer but the difficulty was not overcome and we are anxious lest it become disabled at any time. The apparatus, consisting of two Gould's Steam Boilers with twenty-inch fire-pots is located in the basement. The boilers have separate smoke flues, and separate circulation, each heating one half of the building from the basement up.

Many of the inmates who were released or paroled kept in touch with Oaklawn School authorities through letters and visits. One such letter, written by former inmate "A. H.", on June 26, after being returned to her home, read:

> I am sitting up half asleep writing to you to let you know I got up here all right. Oh, dear, how happy I am! But I cried at the supper table and the ladies didn't know what was the matter. I said I didn't know but I told Mamma that I felt homesick for the girls and teachers. I cried in the train and every place. When I reached here everybody was glad to see me, even the birds. I hope every girl will be good. God bless you for all you have done for me! God bless you again and Mrs. Forbush! It took me three hours to eat my supper tonight and Mamma is fast asleep. That means that she is asleep while I am writing but I said I would write and I am going to keep my promise. I want you and Mrs. Forbush to come and spend the day with us. And have everything I can get for you. I want to make you feel happy because you told me to be a good girl. The school has made a good woman out of me. Tell the girls that I will be a credit to them and tell them that I haven't forgotten them. Will write when I can but I wanted to write to you because I knew you wanted me to write as soon as I could. Well, I must close.

In August, inmate Susie Mathewson escaped with inmate Elizabeth Bullock. A description of them was put out to the public as authorities conducted a search.

A girl named Mary Duarte was committed to the school on August 14, for two years, after being brought into court on two warrants and pleading guilty to both charges. The first charged her with the theft of $20 from Mary E. Carmon, and the second charged her with the theft of $9 from Julia Vera.

In September, sixteen-year-old Jane West was found sleeping in outbuildings in Bristol. Brought before the court and charged with being an idle person and a vagrant, she explained to the judge that she had no home. She was committed to the school for six months.

Another recently paroled inmate, "C. M.", penned a letter to school authorities on December 18:

> Arrived here yesterday, safe. Reached here before the letter you wrote did. I came up and my sister was out under the clothesline taking off clothes and when she saw me coming, she dropped the clothes and ran to meet me and such a squeezing as I got you can imagine. And then I wanted to see Mama and May and I started to see her and of course I had to take another hug. I have come home to be a true, noble woman, as I know I can and will be. I think as far as I have seen, I like very much. Mama has a very nice tenement. I think you will be surprised to hear from me so soon, but I couldn't wait any longer before I wrote. I remain one of your sincere girls.

An additional letter, penned by former inmate "N. M. S.", on December 31, read:

> I thought I would write you a few lines, hoping to find you well as it leaves me at present. I enjoyed Christmas day very much indeed. I hung up my stocking Christmas Eve and when I got up the next morning it was full and what do you suppose was sticking out the top of it? Well, it was a doll and its head was sticking out. I have written to some of the girls and they have not answered any of my letters and I wish they would write me a letter, if it is only to write their address. I am just making some clothes for my new doll now. Give my love to all the girls and the teachers. Well, I think I shall have to bring my letter to a close. Your loving friend.

Two inmates who had been assigned to take care of the chickens, work in the gardens, and care for the grounds decided to escape that year. They were located three days later in Connecticut, just over the Rhode Island state line. Both girls refused to return to the school. Since making their escape, one of the girls, who was eighteen years old, legally married a man who was a stranger to her, in hopes the court would not force a married woman to remain at the school. The other was returned to the school by her father a few days later.

The religious instructor communicated in his yearly state report the following regarding the school:

In April last, it was, by your action, made my duty, before a girl from the Oaklawn School should be placed on probation in a home, to visit this home and report to you upon its desirability; to take the girl to the home selected; to visit her and all other girls living in homes with your consent, and to report to you the results. I have given much time and attention to these things and am able to say that I have every reason to believe that all of the girls referred to me are doing well. To the last remark, a single exception must be made, that of a girl nearly twenty-one years of age, who had failed in several homes, who was dismissed to live with her aunt, and who immediately disappeared.

The salaries of the staff that year consisted of $50 per month being paid to Clara Forbush; $43 dollars per month being paid to Mathelia Billsborough; $30 per month being paid to Rose Marwood; and $25 per month being paid to Lydia Doe, Helena Pine, and Agnes Smith.

The physician was called to attend to one case of anemia, two nasal catarrhs, three cases of constipation, two cases of coryza, twenty-one cases of diarrhea, two cases of dyspepsia, three cases of epilepsy, thee cases of enlarged glands, one case of hemorrhoids, one case of herpes, four cases of incontinence of urine, two cases of indigestion, five cases of influenza, one ingrown toenail, one paralysis of the heart, one case of paronychia, three cases of pharyngitis, one case of pleurodynia (sudden chest or abdominal pain), one case of pneumonia, one pregnancy, one case of sciatica (back pain), one case of syphilis, one case of syphiloderma (lesions from the sexually transmitted disease syphilis), one case of trachoma (eye infection), seven cases of tonsillitis, and two cases of tuberculosis.

1900

The two boilers, which had been in service for nearly twenty years, were replaced by a No. 7 Model Steam Boiler, furnished by the Rhode Island Supply and Engineering Company of Providence. The cost was $337.15 and the labor of setting it up was done by men from the other Rhode Island state institutions.

In September, a sixteen-year-old girl named Grace Salisbury was committed to the school for her minority after she and two of her younger brothers were arrested for being disorderly persons and vagrants.

Inmate Elizabeth Judge was taken to the Almshouse upon becoming ill and died there on September 5. Inmate Mary Haskell died of pulmonalis and exhaustion on November 6 and was buried in the school's cemetery.

1901

On May 5, an unnamed inmate who was out on parole wrote a letter to school authorities:

> I write you a few lines as it is quite lonesome here. I miss Mrs. Forbush very much, and the girls, but guess I will overcome it. I wish I had a mother and I would know how to appreciate her. I am going to be a good girl and show the world what the Oaklawn School has done for me. Good night. From one of your girls. Love to all.

On Memorial Day, Mr. Eastman visited the school with bows, arrows, and targets to teach the girls how to shoot them. In the days that followed, during recreation time, this became a popular activity.

When concerns of typhoid arose due to water at the school coming from a main tank that supplied water to buildings in the area, a new windmill was completed on the grounds just after November 23, 1901.

A Rhode Island Board of Education report noted that as of January 1, 1901, there were forty-four inmates at Oaklawn school. Throughout the year, nineteen were committed by the courts, three were committed by the Board of State Charities and Corrections, two returned from trial, seven were returned from placements, one was returned from the State Workhouse and House of Correction, and one was returned from the State Almshouse. Fourteen were discharged on probation to go home, eight were discharged on probation to live with families they had been placed with, one was removed to the State Workhouse and House of Correction, one was removed to the State Almshouse, one was released for trial, one escaped, and three were discharged on the expiration of their sentence. Five had been committed for being idle persons, six as lewd and wanton persons, common prostitutes, or night walkers, five for theft, two as disorderly persons, and one for vagrancy. Three were admitted by the Board of State Charities and Corrections upon the request of their parents or guardians. Of those entering the school, four were thirteen years old, three were fourteen years old, six were fifteen years old, six were sixteen years old, two were seventeen years old, and one was eighteen years old. The report went on to state:

> The Board desire to call your attention once more to certain changes in the law related to the reform school that were suggested in their last report. These suggested changes are that the terms of sentence to the reform school shall be in all cases during minority, instead of as at present 'for a term not longer than during minority nor less than two years' and that no child shall be sentenced to the reform school who has passed the age of sixteen years. The reasons, based upon their experience with juvenile offenders that have led the Board to make these suggestions may be found in their last report. Mr. Eastman calls attention to the need of an additional

building for the girls, to contain the boilers, the laundry, and a hall for exercise. This need was fully set forth in the report of the Board for 1889. Mr. Eastman, after speaking of the disadvantage and unwholesomeness of having the laundry for sixty persons in the basement of the only building of the school says, "Great attention is given to good housekeeping and general cleanliness." Fresh air and sunlight is invited. The exercise the girls get from the routine work of the school is considerable but not enough to satisfy a reasonable solicitude for the children's health in all kinds of weather. There are four employees here, with the matron in charge, five in all. They work harmoniously together. Good discipline is quite easily maintained. The teachers have won their way to the hearts of the girls. Moral suasion has its fullest opportunity. One girl only, in more than five years, has been punished physically. There is seldom a scene. Whatever has been required of any girl in the past year, she has done, not always perhaps with the best grace. Bad temper controls them sometimes but after reflection they acknowledge it.

In that year's Board of State Charities and Corrections report, it was noted:

A girl writing recently says, "I wish I could be as good as some people are. I wish I might control my temper and keep my mouth shut when I should. It is that which gets me into trouble. I know I am trying and saucy and that my teachers put up with

The sewing room within Oaklawn School for Girls. (*Rhode Island Department of State*)

more from me than anybody outside would." Instruction in cooking, laundry and chamber work, the work of the sewing room and in school has gone on from day to day systematically. A summary of the year's results would be hard to make. But in this we are no exception to any other agency whose purpose is the uplifting of society. We find much to encourage. Note the following from a letter written by a girl now in the school who was born in the State Almshouse on December 19, 1886. December 27, she writes, "I wonder if you and all our teachers enjoyed Christmas as much as every one of us girls did! And if there is a girl who thinks that she did not have a nice time, it must be her own fault, for everything was done for us that could be done and every one of us was well remembered. So we ought to feel very thankful and satisfied to know that we have so many nice friends to look out for us. But I believe that there are a great many children somewhere in the world who were not remembered at this time. Santa Claus was very kind and thoughtful to think of us children. We shall not forget his kindness very soon, although we do not know who he is. My present is something very useful to me and will last a long time."

That report went on:

Another girl out in the country at her own request, says in a letter dated November 19, 1901, "I am very happy. I do not think you could have got a place that pleased me any better than this. They are all very good to me. Even the dog is a great friend of mine, for he will come and lay his head on my lap and shake hands with me. I was pleased to hear of R. in your letter. I almost know she will be a good woman because she told me she would do her best and I said I would do my best. So we both made a vow we would do our best when we went out. If it had not been for you and all the teachers being so kind and affectionate to me, I would not have been where I am today. You have helped me to reform. When I was at the school, I learned to love and obey all."

Also in the report was the following:

A.H., who is twenty-one years of age, writes from one of the middle states, "My recent visit to Rhode Island was an enjoyable one. I am sorry I did not meet you. The school looks even better than when I was there. I am enjoying good health. Am to be married January 21, 1902 to a sober, industrious man. He is a foreman over the carpenters of the ice company. I am still one of the old girls." We have sad disappointments, but they are more than counter-balanced by the good work which we have seen done here. The girls work in the gardens as in former years. They have also kept the immediate grounds around the building in tidiness. Physical exercise has been continued as in years past, under the same teacher. Some who have gone out write that they miss their drill, others have formed classes in the neighborhood where they are living. The moral and religious instruction of the girls has been well attended to by the appointed chaplains. The Ladies Board, on the occasion of their visits, have shown especial solicitude. They have always spoken with the girls individually and collectively on these occasions. The Sisters of Mercy have made regular visits to the Catholic girls. The ladies of the Women's Christian Temperance Union of Providence have also shown their interest by twice visiting the school. Such ministrations have our entire sympathy and we crave a continuance of the same. Too much cannot be done for the help of these poor girls by way of faithful watch, care and encouragement. I feel to thank the Board of State Charities and Corrections for their interest in the school.

Expenses that year were as follows: salaries, $1,980.06; provisions and groceries, $107.29; meat, vegetables, flour, milk, medical supplies, etc. from State Workhouse at market prices, $2,277.28; clothing and bedding, $234.96; fuel: $573.16; lights and kerosene oil, $29.98; furniture, $129.17; repairs, $154.52; rent of telephone, $75.00; stationary, $17.95; books, periodicals, etc., $43.11; postage, $17.00; expenses for returning escapees, $6.60; transportation of inmates, $8.00; expenses for visiting girls placed in families and visiting families before placing girls with them, $81.46; and miscellaneous, $90.61. The total came to $5,823.15.

The physician was called to attend to two cases of cellulitis, twenty-five cases of diarrhea, two cases of hysteria, one case of malaria, two cases of syphilis, and one case of tuberculosis of the hip joint.

Inmates working in the garden at Oaklawn School for Girls. (*Rhode Island Department of State*)

Oaklawn Station where trains sometimes arrived carrying a new inmate to Oaklawn School. (*Rhode Island Department of State*)

In September, it was arranged for a train carrying President Roosevelt to slow down as it reached Oaklawn Station so that the inmates of Sockanosset School for Boys and Oaklawn School for Girls could get a glimpse of him. The boys and girls lined up near the station, the girls each holding an American flag.

Over the years, many of the inmates arrived via train at this station to begin serving their terms at Oaklawn School. They were also occasionally allowed to walk to the station where they enjoyed sitting and watching people come and go.

By November, the new windmill for furnishing water to the school was almost completed.

1902

Seven girls were committed to the school by the courts, four were admitted by the Board of State Charities and Corrections, one returned from trial, eleven returned from homes, two returned from the Workhouse and House of Correction, one was transferred from the Workhouse and House of Correction, eight were discharged on probation to go home, eight were discharged on probation to live with families, three were removed to the Workhouse and House of Correction, one returned to the Workhouse and House of Correction, one was released for trial, one escaped, and one was discharged at the end of her sentence. By the last day of the year, there were forty-nine girls remaining at the school.

Of the seven girls committed, one was charged with being an idle person, one with being a disorderly person, two with being lewd and wanton, two for theft, and one as a common nightwalker.

Superintendent Eastman's report to the state that year noted that the training of the girls was all in the line of household work, with three hours of school taught by a normal school graduate and physical culture taught by an expert. The teachers were still unable, due to a lack of rooms, to separate the girls—the larger from the smaller, the older from the younger, the more hardened from the less so—Eastman stated. He added that although they were laboring against great odds in that respect, notwithstanding all obstacles, the girls made fair progress physically, morally, and in their studies. "In our own minds we are sure of this," he wrote. He went on to report:

> The great majority of the girls are intellectually dull and would not go to school from their own choice. Some of them, who could neither read nor write when they came, could at Christmas write a credible letter to Santa Claus.

Teacher Agnes C. Smith taught reading, writing, arithmetic, spelling, geography, language, history, and physiology. Special attention was given to teaching the effects of alcohol on the body. The girls had drills in penmanship and incidental work, such as memorizing selections from various authors, receiving lessons in patriotism, and answering practical questions about the government of the United States. Lessons in housekeeping were taken from textbooks and included building fires, setting tables, washing clothes, washing dishes, making beds, sweeping, scrubbing, and waiting on tables. The following periodicals were regularly received at the school: *Ladies Home Journal, Harper's Weekly, Harper's Monthly, St. Nicholas Magazine, New England Magazine, Youth's Companion, Sunday School Times, Christian Herald, Week's Progress.*

In the sewing room, the girls worked until noon, six days a week. All the sewing for the house was done there. They made the bedding, hemmed towels, and table linen; they also kept them repaired for the inmates as well as the teachers. All of the girls' dresses, aprons, skirts, and underwear were made there. They were also taught knitting, crocheting, and fancy work. Each girl always had a piece of work she could take up at any recreation time or on Saturday afternoons. In the girls' rooms, on each bureau was a muslin cover trimmed with lace, which was crocheted by the younger girls. Their pillow slips were also trimmed with similar handmade lace.

In the afternoon, the sewing room floor was cleaned and bright rugs and table covers were spread out as the room became an assembly room for devotions and

56　　　　　*The Oaklawn School for Girls*

Left: Agnes Smith newspaper clipping from unidentified scrapbook in owner's collection.

Below: The sewing room within Oaklawn School for Girls. (*Rhode Island Department of State*)

social gatherings, a library for those who cared to read, or a music room if anyone chose to play the piano.

That year, the inmates made forty-eight afternoon dresses, forty-eight morning dresses, thirty-six kitchen gowns, forty-eight flannel petticoats, nine cotton petticoats, fifty white aprons, fifty-eight colored aprons, forty chemises, thirty nightgowns, fifty-four pairs of drawers, sixty under-waists, fifteen bureau covers, twenty-five sheets, and forty pillow slips.

The clothing mended consisted of 540 dresses, 750 white aprons, 324 colored aprons, ninety-eight petticoats, 240 nightgowns, 234 chemises, 346 drawers, 228 under-waists, fifty-four sheets, and seventy-four pillow slips.

The laundry instructor was Rose N. Marwood. Nine girls at a time worked in the laundry, and they were changed every three months. Six girls did the rubbing, two worked together at the boiler and the rinsing tubs, and one hung the clothes out to dry. There was no machinery for laundry at the school. With few exceptions, the work was looked upon as drudgery. Eastman's report stated that girls often argued, "I am not going to be anybody's washwoman." The number of pieces washed and ironed that year was 40,521.

Eastman went on to report that corporal punishment was not in favor at the school in any form: "There is no browbeating or threatening or resorting to such methods of punishment as standing on tiptoe, bending over or other like forms of slow torture," he stated. "The treatment is that of moral suasion, of appeals to reason." If those efforts were not effective, the girl might be sent to her room or placed in bed for a few hours or a few days. While there in her room, she was visited often by a matron or a teacher who would provide counsel or advice. "This affords the least ground for a desire for revenge on the part of some girl against a teacher," Eastman went on. "Wordy, saucy outbreaks are frequent, but there not been a case of physical resistance to authority." He noted that when a girl had tantrums, she seemed to get no sympathy from the other girls.

The inmates had their annual outing on September 10 and chose to remain on the grounds of the school rather than celebrate elsewhere. A large number of guests attended and, while dinner was being served, the Sockanosset School Band came marching onto the grounds, lined up, and played several selections.

1903

The Women's Board of Visitors to State Institutions Where Women are Imprisoned visited Oaklawn School that year and compiled the following report:

> We believe that it is not sufficiently recognized that the institution for girls at Oaklawn should be an industrial school for reformatory purposes as well as a home for temporary restraint. In the latter capacity, a temporary home, it is very

The laundry room within Oaklawn School for Girls. (*Rhode Island Department of State*)

good, being clean, attractive, healthy, comfortable and running smoothly. But it returns very few to society better fitted mentally, industrially or morally to support themselves by working for others or to resist evil influences and impulses. We therefore recommend, in order to carry out industrial and reformatory education, that a woman of tact and organizing capacity whom educators themselves recognize as a teacher of superior ability, particularly in the training of peculiar children, in the methods of industrial schools, be appointed visiting supervisor and that the entire direction of the mental, manual and social educational methods be committed to her, subject to the approval of the Board and superintendent. We recommend for the first year an appropriation of $1,000 for the salaries of such a supervisor and of such other visiting assistant teachers as she needs for special lines of instruction.

The salaries of the staff that year consisted of $50 per month paid to Clara Forbush; $30 per month paid to Rose Marwood; and $25 per month paid to Lydia Doe, Alice Reynolds, Abbie Clements, and Agnes Smith.

1904

A silver medal was awarded to the Oaklawn School for Girls for an exhibit of handiwork, needlework, and embroideries at the Louisiana Purchase Exposition. Expenses for that year were reported to be as follows: salaries, $2,115.67; provisions and groceries, $126.48; meat, vegetables , milk, medical supplies etc. from Workhouse and farm at market prices, $2,570.14; clothing and bedding,

$358.03; fuel, $573.38; repairs, $46.96; furniture, $421.64; lights, $49.89; stationary, $26.84; books, periodicals, etc., $110.56; postage, $10.00; farm stock and tools, $12.30; telephone, $75.00; transportation of inmates, $5.25; and miscellaneous, $314.02. The total came to $6,816.16.

As of January 1, 1904, there were forty-nine inmates residing at Oaklawn School. Twelve had been committed by the courts, five had been admitted by the Board of State Charities and Corrections, five had been returned from the homes they had been placed in, one returned from the State Workhouse and House of Correction, one was committed while awaiting trial, and one was committed while being held as a witness. Sixteen were discharged on probation to go home, eight were discharged on probation to live with arranged families, one was removed to the State Workhouse and House of Correction, one went out for trial, one went out on bail, and three were discharged on the expiration of their sentences. Six were committed as idle persons, three as lewd as wanton persons, and six for theft. Five were admitted by the Board of State Charities and Corrections upon the request of their parents or guardians.

The school's yearly report to the state by James Eastman explained:

There have been in the school since the date of its removal, including those brought from Providence July 1882, to December 31, 1904, 490 girls. At the latter date, there were remaining in the school, forty-six, 444 therefore have been released. A careful examination of the record books shows that thirteen of the 444 were subsequently committed to the Jail or the Workhouse and House of Correction. But not any to the State Prison. The books also show during the same period that twenty-five girls were transferred from the school to the Workhouse and House of Correction for incorrigibility. We hear many good things of the girls who have been released in recent years. Some are teaching in public schools of the state, one who graduated the early part of the year being among the number. Excellent health has prevailed, and discipline has been maintained up to the usual high standard. There have been no revolts, individual or collective. Moral suasion is our chief reliance and is nearly always productive of good results. The girls were given their usual holiday with a clambake, August 26th, which occasion was graced by the presence of several members of the Board with their wives, some neighboring citizens, and a few of the former girls of the school, now grown women. It has been the choice of the girls each year, for several years, to spend the holiday given them on their own grounds, in lieu of an excursion such as is given to the boys of the Sockanosset School to Gaspee Point or some other place. This was an extremely happy occasion, quite like those of former years. We are doing the best we can for the mental, physical and moral development and uplifting of the girls with the equipment the State allows us. The one cottage building is good but not adequate for all the purposes of such a school. This fact has been persistently spoken of in former reports. I will but briefly summarize in this. There should be provided another cottage home for the older girls who need to be separated from the younger for obvious reasons. A small plain structure should also be provided which will afford room for the heating plant, laundry and an exercise hall or gymnasium. We must not forget the interest displayed in us and the work we are so devoted to for the reformation of the girls by the Sisters of Mercy, the ladies of the Women's Christian Temperance Union, the King's Daughters, the Thimble Club of Providence and many individuals.

In her own report to the State that year, Clara Forbush noted:

The discipline during the past year has been much the same as in previous years. No harsh measures have had to be resorted to. We appeal to the better nature of our girls, spending much time in talking and reasoning with them. If this proves ineffective, the girl is sent to her room for a time under the observation of the matron or a teacher. In many cases our girls come from homes where cultivated tastes and refinement are lacking, where harshness is the rule. It will be readily seen that the time consumed under the methods pursued, those of moral suasion, must be great. Many of our girls, on leaving us, go to their own homes, where the environment and influences remain the same as previous to their coming. As a consequence, some fall back into the old way of living and doing. We find that where girls are placed in homes where all are strangers, the results are more satisfactory as a rule. Many of the girls say, when they leave the school, that they do not intend to do housework, that they prefer to work in the mills where they may have their holidays, Sundays and evenings free from labor. For this reason, it is hard really to interest some in housework instruction. The health of the girls has been good. For the past few months a dentist has visited the school twice per week professionally. The girl's teeth are now in good condition.

Teacher Agnes C. Smith stated in her yearly report:

The average number of pupils in school for the year is forty-three. These range from nine to twenty years of age. I believe the girls have made good progress in schoolroom work. A change of text books has been made, which certainly has created a deeper interest. I recommend the purchase of new wall maps. Map stencils are in use with us in the study of geography. To cultivate a taste for literature, the advanced class in reading are studying the works of different authors. Each pupil is supplied with a notebook, into which are copied neatly with pen and ink, topics of the lives of the authors studied. When the study of each is finished, a miniature picture of the author is given to the pupil which is pasted into the notebook. We are fortunate in having a few Perry pictures of the homes and haunts of some of the authors and these are used in connection with above work. There have been examinations during the year and the average rank of each scholar has been made out and given to her.

In her own yearly report, sewing room teacher Mrs. Alice D. Reynolds stated:

> From this department girls are drawn to fill vacancies all about the house. As a rule, the small girls are the only ones who stay the full four months, the usual term for special instruction. All new girls begin in the sewing room and others come in if discharged for incompetency or misconduct in other places. After the work of the week is finished in the laundry, girls come from that department. During the time of house-cleaning or any extra housework, girls are taken from the sewing room. Hence the work of sewing is largely done by a floating population. The facilities have been increased by the addition of two Wheeler & Wilson Number 9 sewing machines. The dresses are cut by Butterick patterns and every girl except the very small ones has the opportunity to do some of this work during the year. Our fancy work, samples of knitting, crocheting, drawn and tufted work, making of fine garments and embroidery were sent to the St. Louis Exposition and, with the Sockanosset School exhibit, took the grand prize. Since June 14th, a teacher of raffia work and basket-making has given instruction to a class of ten girls from 10.30 to 12 noon, once a week. Possibly one half of all the number of girls in the school avail themselves of the opportunity to read in the sewing room evenings. The library contains many well-chosen volumes besides magazines and popular weeklies seen on tables of most reading people.

In her report that year, cooking teacher Mrs. Mary P. Dwelley stated: "Five girls are taught cooking at a time, each receiving instruction during four months. They learn to make bread, pies, cake, puddings, etc. and cook for both the teachers and the girls."

Laundry teacher Rose N. Marwood, in her yearly report, wrote:

> The laundry still remains in the basement of our one building. We have no more conveniences in the way of drying clothes than when the school was first opened and when there was half the number now present. There are nine girls detailed to this department and changed every four months. The number of pieces to be washed and dried during the week will range from seven to eight hundred. Most of them require ironing. From the first of December to March, the greater part of these are dried, a few at a time, on ten lines within the ironing room, not more than sixteen feet long. The vapor rising from these wet clothes is passing through the house until the work is finished. This is a branch of household work that does not seem particularly inviting, especially to those who have not the mind to see that honest labor done to the best of one's ability is elevating and ennobling. The following is the number of pieces washed and ironed during the year: For teachers here and female officers at the boys' school: 8,113 pieces. For the girls: 28,015 pieces. Total: 36,128 pieces.

Expenses that year were as follows: salaries, $2,041.91; provisions and groceries, $133.61; meat, vegetables, flour, milk, medical supplies, etc. from the Workhouse and farm at market prices, $2,422.48; clothing and bedding, $514.63; fuel, $619.17; repairs, $87.64; furniture, $116.44; lights and kerosene oil, $43.17; stationary, $24.53; books, periodicals, etc., $163.13; postage, $16.00; rent of telephone, $75.00; and miscellaneous, $203.64. The total came to $6,461.35.

1905

The annual report of the Rhode Island State Board of Education for the year ending December 31, 1905 stated that twenty-three girls had been committed by the courts over the course of the year, one had been admitted by the Board of State Charities and Corrections, three had returned from the homes in which they had been placed, three had returned from the State Workhouse and House of Correction, two had been committed while awaiting trial, one was returned after having escaped, and one was transferred from the Workhouse and House of Correction. Fourteen were discharged on probation to go home, nine were discharged on probation to live with arranged families, one was transferred to the State Workhouse and House of Correction, two went out for trial, one escaped, two were released on probation to go to Sophia Little Home for Unwed Mothers due to being pregnant, and one was released to a probation officer. Five girls were committed as vagrants, eight as lewd and wanton persons, six for disorderly conduct, one for truancy, three for theft, two while awaiting trial, one was admitted by the Board upon the request of her parents, one was transferred by the Board from the State Workhouse and House of Correction, three were returned from homes they had been placed in, three were returned from the State Workhouse and House of Correction, one was returned having escaped. One was eight years old, one was twelve years old, three were thirteen years old, one was fourteen years old, five were fifteen years old, nine were sixteen years old, and three were seventeen years old.

James Eastman's yearly report to the state informed:

> The dividing of the school and the employment of an additional teacher are a decided improvement. It gives double the time to each pupil and a greater interest has been awakened. Some new books and new maps have been provided, as is done every year. These are greatly enjoyed. The sewing room is given another use as an additional classroom. Twenty-four folding tables were made by the class in carpentry at the Sockanosset School. They are folded and set on one side when the room is needed by the sewing class, or for use as a gymnasium, or sitting room, or chapel. All activities of our Oaklawn School home are carried on under one roof. Another cottage should be added to permit of dividing the girls into two classes, with a small building partly for industrial work and partly for a gymnasium. These additions would afford a fair equipment for the school's present needs. Attention has been called to this in the reports for the last eight or more years.

Deputy Superintendent Clara Forbush's yearly report to the state noted:

> The moral tone of the school has greatly improved during the past few years. The teachers (every employee here is a teacher) are untiring in their work for the improvement of the girls and are ready at all times to talk with and to encourage them in their efforts toward a better life. The visits of the Sisters of Mercy every two weeks, and the ministrations of both the chaplains, Protestant and Catholic, are of inestimable worth to us and to the girls. I feel we are a very united family and think the girls appreciate their privileges. We seek to win the respect and confidence of each girl, and in this way to influence them to go right.

Construction finally began on a second cottage on the school grounds. It was to be called "Eastman Cottage," in honor of longtime superintendent James Eastman. The purpose of erecting this cottage was to separate the younger inmates from the older girls.

One of the girls committed to Oaklawn School had just given birth, on November 7, 1905, at the Rhode Island Almshouse. She named the female child Grace Mary Knight. The child died the day after its birth and was buried at the State Farm Cemetery. The mother was transferred to Oaklawn School.

2

THE QUIET HOME-LIKE LIFE THEY LEAD

1906

The annual report of the Rhode Island Board of State Charities and Corrections stated that there were forty-eight girls remaining at the school. Fourteen had been committed by the courts over the next year, two had been admitted by the Board of State Charities and Corrections, eleven had been returned from homes they had been placed in, two were returned from the State Workhouse and House of Correction, seven were committed as they awaited trial, and two had been remanded by the courts. Sixteen were discharged on probation to go home. Thirteen were discharged to live with arranged families, two were removed to the State Workhouse and House of Correction, two were removed to the Almshouse, seven were released for trial, two were released to court as witnesses, and one was discharged on the expiration of her sentence. Two were committed as vagrants, one for assault, five as lewd and wanton persons, one for truancy, three for disorderly conduct and two for theft. Of those entering the school, one girl was eight years old, one was nine years old, one was eleven years old, two were twelve years old, one was thirteen years old, four were fourteen years old, two were fifteen years old, two were sixteen years old, and two were seventeen years old.

Clara Forbush's report to the state that year noted:

> The work of the school the past year has been quite like that of previous years. The employment of an additional teacher was an advanced step and greater progress in the schoolroom has been the result. Mrs. Agnes B. McNaughton has had charge of the girls in physical culture lessons, special drill is given once a week and a period of fifteen minutes each morning before breakfast is devoted to physical exercises. Miss Agnes C. Smith gives instruction in singing and reading music, using the "Natural

Course in Music" and fifteen minutes each day at the beginning of the school session have been given to this work. The girls have made fairly good progress. The conduct of the girls has been generally good and a spirit of subordination has been quite general. The individual girls of an excitable nature have had their tantrums, but they were of no serious moment. The general health of the girls has been good. Early in the spring Mrs. Gustave Radeke, of the Women's Advisory Board, donated flower seeds and plants for the girls' flower beds. A strip of ground on the lawn in front of the school building was prepared and each girl was given a portion as her own. They enjoyed working at the plants and were well rewarded with abundant bloom. The flowers were a source of pleasure to them throughout the season.

Forbush's report went on:

In the fall, Mrs. Radeke also sent bulbs which were planted for spring blooming. On the second Sunday morning of each month, Mass is celebrated by the Reverend Father Buckley. The Sisters of Mercy visited the Catholic girls twice a month and this is a great help to them. October 21st, a class of seven were confirmed at St. Ann's Church in Cranston, with a large class of others of their age residing in that Parish. The usual force at the school remains the same as last year with one exception; Miss Maude S. Howard, a graduate of the Framingham Normal School and Mary Hemenway Department of Household Arts, was placed in charge of the culinary department and is having very good success. As usual, the girls attend Sunday morning exercises at the State Hospital for the Insane. In the afternoon, Sunday school is held in the school room. Chaplain Ewer addresses the girls at the close. Mrs. Ewer has also spoken several times and her talks have been helpful. The holidays have been observed and appropriate entertainments have been given throughout the year. Several instructive lectures from friends outside have also been given.

Her report concluded:

At Christmas time the girls each received a present from a friend in Providence whom they call "Santa Claus" and also from the Thimble Club of Providence. The Catholic girls received presents from the Sisters of Mercy. Work on the new cottage was begun in the summer but had to be suspended during the cold weather. We hope to see the work resumed as soon as spring opens, and the cottage finished, so that our younger girls can be separated from the older. The vegetable garden has been taken care of by the girls after the first hoeing by the State Farm forces, and eighteen girls have been thus employed at times. Four other girls worked about the grounds during the entire season. Over two hundred chickens were raised, the girls caring for them. The girls sent out the past year, indeed for the past ten years, are almost invariably doing well. One only has been committed to the Workhouse or Jail. This record gives us courage for the future.

In James Eastman's yearly report to the state, he penned:

> Mrs. Forbush has omitted to speak of the attempted escape of three girls. On the morning of February 22nd, while the girls were at recreation out of doors, a girl, seventeen years of age, committed two days before, flew down the vista in an effort to escape. All the larger girls started in pursuit and caught up with her before reaching Oaklawn Village. She fell, exhausted by her efforts, while her pursuers seemed fresh and full ready for what might happen. The runaway, after getting her breath, made a desperate resistance, but to no purpose. She was picked up and carried bodily up the hill, through the south gate into the house and laid on the floor by the girls. Again, on October 15th, two new girls, at about the same hour of the morning, made a similar attempt, getting further away from the school than did the other. They ran around neighboring buildings, jumped walls and fences, and hid in the tall weeds and grass, to be captured by the girls and triumphantly returned. These are splendid illustrations of the spirit obtaining at the Oaklawn School and are highly credible to the girls and the management thereof.

1907

Of those committed to the school, one was for vagrancy, one for poor conduct, five for theft, one transferred from the Providence County Jail, and one transferred from the State Workhouse and House of Correction.

Salaries of the staff that year consisted of $50 per month being paid to Clara Forbush; $30 per month being paid to Rose Marwood; $55 per month being paid to Alice Reynolds, Abbie Clements, Agnes Smith, and Agnes McNaughton (who all filled more than one position); and $25 per month being paid to Maud Howard and Annie Burbank.

The annual report of the Rhode Island Board of State Charities and Corrections detailed the construction of the new three-story cottage on the grounds of Oaklawn School. An appropriation had been made at the last session of the General Assembly and the plans had been prepared by architects Martin and Hall. The work was begun late that summer. The construction of the foundations and the basement, to the first-floor level, and excavating, were done by the boys of the Sockanosset School. That part of the work had been finished and a contract for the completion of the building had been made with David J. Barry of Providence for $22,765.00.

It was expected that the cottage would be ready for occupancy in the beginning of 1908. The heating, plumbing, and lighting systems were to be installed by the boys of Sockanosset School, under proper superintendence, the Board providing the necessary materials and fittings. The cottage was located in the grove adjacent to, but across the driveway, from the present cottage. It faced the latter and was so placed that the floor levels of the two buildings were at about the same grade.

The new structure was to be about the height of the other but would differ from it somewhat in appearance, as a less expensive type of building had been decided upon. The walls were to be of red brick and the necessary stonework for sills, steps, etc. of granite. The main building was to have a gable at either end, and a slated pitched roof with wide overhangs. Dormer windows would light the upper story.

The proposed building was L-shaped in the plan. The main portion was to be 79 feet and 6 inches long, and 34 feet and 6 inches wide, with a rear extension measuring 34 feet long and 24 feet wide. The heights of the several stories were to be basement, 9 feet; first story, 11 feet; second story, 11 feet; and upper story 9 feet and 6 inches. A loft running the full length of the building would be located above the upper story. In the basement was planned a large recreation room, laundry, ironing room, general bathroom, lavatory, storerooms, cellars, and a large room in which would be located the heating apparatus, with ample coal storage adjoining.

From the laundry section, a flight of steps would admit directly to the clothes yard, and a flight of steps would be provided for entrance to the cellar from the yard. Both the front and rear stairways would start from the basement and run up

Old school fencing and other debris remaining on the site as of 2019. (*Author's collection*)

through the building to the top story, and the rear stairway would be enclosed in a fireproof shaft from top to bottom. Self-closing metal doors and frames would guard all entrances to this shaft and thus a means of escape would be provided in case of fire. A similarly constructed clothes chute would extend through the stories, by which soiled linen could be sent to the laundry.

In the first story, the building would be divided transversely by a hall 8 feet wide, at one end of which would be the front entrance door and vestibule, and at the opposite end the front staircase. To the right of the front entrance would be the reception room, measuring 14 feet by 16 feet and 6 inches. That room would have a bay window and a fireplace. At the left of the entrance was to be located a teachers' dining room, measuring 14 feet by 16 feet and 6 inches. This room would also have a bay window and a fireplace.

A longitudinal corridor, 6 feet wide, would bisect the main hall, and at one end of this corridor would be placed the sewing or assembly room, measuring 16 feet by 31 feet, with a large bay window and a fireplace. At the opposite end would be the main dining room, of like dimensions and with similar bay window and fireplace. Opening from the passage was to be an office, measuring 10 feet by 13 feet and 4 inches, and a clothes room, measuring 8 feet by 10 feet. The rear stair hall was to connect with the passage and give access to the service room, kitchen, pantry, and storeroom. There would also be a direct entrance from the yard to the kitchen.

The second story was to be bisected by a longitudinal corridor (6 feet wide) with which both stairways would connect. From this corridor would open the schoolroom (measuring 16 feet and 6 inches by 31 feet and 4 inches), two teachers' rooms (measuring 12 feet and 4 inches by 14 feet and 8 inches), and a linen closet, slop closet, and bathrooms. Other storage and linen closets were arranged in the rear extension, and on this floor was to be located eleven bedrooms for inmates, each measuring 8 feet by 12 feet and 4 inches.

Unlike Oaklawn Cottage, which had a dormitory as well as private bedrooms, Eastman Cottage would have only private bedrooms, each with running water and its own wash bowl. The third story was to contain fifteen bedrooms (each measuring 8 feet by 12 feet and 4 inches), an infirmary (measuring 12 feet and 4 inches by 16 feet and 10 inches), a teachers' room (measuring 12 feet and 4 inches by 16 feet and 6 inches), and linen, store and slop closets, a bathroom, and other arrangements similar to those provided for the second story.

A loft, which could be used for storage, would extend over a portion of the third story. The structure, throughout, was to be finished in a plain, substantial manner and furnished with modern equipment. The plumbing system was to be simple and thoroughly sanitary. Ample provision was to be made for heating, and precautions taken to guard against fire and the loss of life from panic. The building, throughout, was to be well-lighted and ventilated. It was not, however, constructed of fireproof materials.

The report of the Rhode Island Board of Education that year stated:

Each girl has a flower bed of her own to care for and disposes of the flowers as she pleases. The seeds and plants for these flower beds are provided by a lady of Providence who is much interested in the girls. The usual Thanksgiving entertainment was given by the girls, also the Christmas entertainment, followed by a Christmas tree. Each girl received a gift from the lady who provides the seeds and plants for the flower beds. The Thimble Club of Providence, as in years past, also sent gifts to each girl.

The Board's report continued:

Two girls ran away December 7th. They were soon apprehended and returned to the school having been at liberty but about two hours. In connection with their running away, the following, as related by the girls upon their return to the school, may be of interest. It seems that they had planned to run away some time previously but there was to be an entertainment on Thanksgiving, and both had prominent parts, so they decided to postpone their departure until after the entertainment, as they did not wish to disappoint the teachers who had worked so hard for its success. The entertainment was given and was a great success and was said to have been the best ever given at the school. Mr. James F. McCusker, Chairman of the Board, was so much pleased with it that he made arrangements to have it repeated on the afternoon of December 7th. The two girls, upon learning this, were very much disappointed, but after talking the matter over, decided that it would not be right to disappoint Mr. McCusker, so they decided to remain over the date set. The entertainment was repeated with quite a number of guests present, and as successfully as before. At its close, after all the guests had departed, the two girls went upstairs, climbed out of a window to the roof of the porch and slid down the grape vine to the ground and to freedom. The alarm was given, and they were soon apprehended and returned to school.

1908

Deputy Superintendent Clara F. Forbush submitted the following Executive Committee report to the Rhode Island Board of State Charities and Corrections:

The work at the Oaklawn School for Girls has been much the same as in former years. At the beginning of the year, there were forty girls at the school ranging from the ages of eleven to twenty years, under the care of five teachers, each earnest, faithful and conscientious in the discharge of her exacting duties. The girls have been employed in the forenoon of each day in the different departments; kitchen, laundry, sewing room, and at general housework. In the afternoon every girl attends school. Two schools of letters are maintained with gratifying results. Four girls are detailed to attend to the work in the garden and to the poultry through the season. The work of the girls is changed every four months, this affording each girl an opportunity to become proficient in the different branches of household duties. No sickness other than now and then an ordinary cold or some slight indisposition occurred during the year.

Forbush's report went on:

The discipline has been excellent. One little girl, when unobserved, walked off the playground and started for home, but was soon returned to the school. This was the only attempt to run away during the year. And we consider this an exceptionally fine record, indicating that the girls are loyal and contented. Mass is celebrated once a month and the Sisters of Mercy have visited the school once in two weeks and have been very helpful to the girls in years past. Instead of attending the Sunday morning service at the State Hospital for the Insane, as formerly, the girls will remain at the school where Sunday school is held for them. In the afternoon a Protestant service is conducted by Chaplain Ewer. Washington's Birthday was observed at the school, as usual, and an entertainment was given by the girls in the evening. Fourth of July was appropriately celebrated. The girls' annual outing was held on the school grounds August 14th and was, as usual, a great success. Thanksgiving was a day of feasting with an entertainment in the evening by the girls. Christmas is the gala day of the year. The turkey dinner, with all that goes with it, fades into insignificance before the gaily decorated Christmas tree loaded with gifts for each girl. A bright, pretty, musical entertainment is given in the evening by the girls. The new cottage for girls, spoken of in our report for 1907 as nearly finished, has been completed during the year and is now being furnished. We expect it will be ready for occupancy very soon. Looking back on the past year we feel that much has been done for our girls and that the ensuing year will find all of us zealous and as determined as ever in our work for these children. We desire to thank those who so generously remembered the girls at Christmas and all other kind friends.

On January 1, 1908, there were forty girls living at Oaklawn School. Over the year, fourteen were committed by the courts, one was admitted by the Board of State Charities and Corrections, four had been former inmates who were returned to the school, one was a former inmate who had been returned from the State Workhouse and House of Correction, two had been committed while awaiting trial, and one had been returned after escaping, bringing the total to sixty-six. Ten were discharged on probation to go home, one was discharged to live with a placement family, one was removed to the State Workhouse and House of Correction, one was removed to the State Almshouse, two were released for trial, one escaped, two were discharged at the expiration of their sentences, and two were returned to the State Workhouse or House of Correction. Of the girls sentenced by the Court to Oaklawn in 1908, two were sentenced for vagrancy, one for night walking, three for theft, two for lewdness, four for disorderly conduct, and one for breaking and entering.

Of those entering the school, one was twelve years old, five were fourteen years old, four were fifteen years old, six were sixteen years old, and two were seventeen years old.

As the campus depended on its gardens and farm to feed the staff and inmates, certain girls were chosen to care for the fruit trees and vegetable plants, as well as the animals. That year, the harvest included 6.5 bushels of apples, 10.75 pounds of asparagus, 8.5 bushels of beans, 17.5 bushels of beets, a third of a bushel of blackberries, 11.5 bushels of carrots, twenty-six heads of cauliflower, 395 bundles of celery, 10 quarts of cherries, forty-seven chickens, 386 dozen sweet corn, 40.5 bushels of cucumbers, 8 quarts of currants, 11.5 bushels of dandelions, 6,759 eggs, 3.25 bushels of grapes, 654 heads lettuce, 116 musk melons, 106 watermelons, 2.25 bushels of onions, 1.5 bushels of peaches, 8 quarts of pears, 13.5 bushels of peas, 3.75 bushels of peppers, half a bushel of quinces, 119 dozen radishes, 12 quarts of raspberries, 88.5 pounds of rhubarb, 12 bushels of spinach, eighty-five squash, 23.75 quarts of strawberries, 69.5 bushels of tomatoes, and 4 bushels of turnips.

Construction of "Eastman Cottage" was completed at a total cost of $28,832.28. Like Oaklawn Cottage, it contained one individual room with a strong door and reinforced window screens.

The salaries of the staff consisted of $50 per month being paid to Clara Forbush and $30 per month paid to Agnes Smith, Agnes McNaughton, Rose Marwood, Alice Reynolds, and Abbie Clements.

1909

The Rhode Island Board of State Charities and Corrections report that year stated:

> The new cottage, begun in 1906 and completed, as to construction, in 1908, was occupied September 20, 1909. It has been named Eastman Cottage in memory of the late James H. Eastman, who was for several years Superintendent of the Oaklawn School for Girls. Fifteen girls were sentenced to the school by the courts in 1909, and two by the department of State Charities & Corrections. One girl was sentenced for vagrancy, three for lewdness, six for disorderly conduct, one for theft, three for truancy, and one for concealing the birth of a child in such a manner that it could not be known whether it was born dead or alive. The ages of the girls at the time of sentence or admission were; one, eleven years; one, twelve years; two, thirteen years; five, fourteen years, three, fifteen years; four, sixteen years; and one, seventeen years.

The report includes Clara Forbush's updates:

> The girls have been employed as usual in the different departments of the school, namely general housework, laundry, kitchen and sewing room, in which last named department an extra amount of work was done preparatory to the opening of the new cottage spoken of in previous reports. This new cottage named in memory of our late Superintendent James H. Eastman, was opened September 20th. It is fitted with all the modern improvements, including electric lights, and the furnishings are in keeping with the building. Quite a number of beautiful, and interesting pictures adorn the walls of many of the rooms and the lower hall of the cottage. In the Eastman room hangs a picture of Mr. Eastman which was presented by Mr. Eastman at Christmas time. An organ has been placed in the Eastman room and an upright piano in the sewing room. The younger girls and those without immoral history were selected and transferred to Eastman Cottage, the number being twenty-three. They are under the care of a matron, Mrs. Frances R. Keene, two assistants and a school teacher, the last mentioned having been transferred from the old building. The religious service, conducted by Chaplain Ewer, is held in the sewing room of the old cottage, on Sunday afternoon, as in the past, and the Catholic girls assemble for Mass at the same place, on the second Sunday of each month. The Sisters of Mercy made their usual visits to the school the past year, and have done a great deal of good, bringing literature and attending to the spiritual needs of the girls whom they instruct. A class in physical culture is still maintained in each cottage. All holidays were observed at the school in much the same manner as in previous years. Under the direction of the teachers, entertainments were given by the girls on Washington's Birthday, Thanksgiving and Christmas. A clam-bake was prepared for the girls on the school grounds, as in past years. Kind friends have donated books, periodicals and gifts during the year. The discipline of the school has been kept up to the usual standard. Each girl has her flower bed, as in years past, money being furnished by a friend in Providence to purchase seeds and plants for these beds. All the vegetables consumed at the school through the summer were raised in the school garden, except potatoes, and the work, except for preparation of the ground, was done by four girls under the direction of a matron.

Oaklawn School's resident physician, Dr. Henry A. Jones, reported to the Rhode Island Board of State Charities and Corrections that year on the health of the girls. His report stated:

> During the early winter months of the past year, the school was visited by an epidemic of influenza that was characterized by unusual severity and accompanied by a bronchial affection that was profoundly prostrating in its effects and most resistant to medication of every sort. The matrons and teachers were much more prostrated than the inmates by this disease, one matron having it in such a severe form that she

The Quiet Home-Like Life They Lead

Above: Oaklawn School for Girls. (*Rhode Island Department of State*)

Right: Francis Redman Keene, the Matron-in-Charge of Eastman Cottage. (*Jennifer Van Ostrand Wilcoxson*)

was compelled to obtain a long leave of absence from duty ere she regained her usual health. One case was transferred to the Almshouse for operation and treatment. This case, a young girl, remained there nearly one month before she was cured. Apart from the epidemic alluded to, the health of the inmates has been good.

The salaries of the staff consisted of $900 for the year being paid to Clara Forbush; $55 per month paid to Mary Dwelley; and $30 per month paid to Agnes Smith, Agnes McNaughton, Rose Marwood, Alice Reynolds, Katherine Pidge, Abbie Clements, Frances Keene, and Joanna Farr.

1910

Dr. Jones's report to the Rhode Island Board of State Charities and Corrections stated:

> During the year, the health of the inmates has been exceptionally good, treatment of minor illnesses only having been required. We believe that the continued good health of the inmates of the school has been due to the quiet, homelike life they lead, and the careful oversight of their food. The lack of cases of anemia among them shows that advantage of the plenteous fresh vegetable diet that is given them. The vegetable salts are needed for the human economy and the indulgence of a capricious appetite supplied with fanciful but poorly nourishing food is detrimental to the proper physical development of the growing girl. One girl suffering from hystero-epilepsy was transferred to the State Hospital for the Insane, from which institution she succeeded in escaping and has not been heard of since. Two girls, both colored, coming to the school in a pregnant condition, were removed to the Almshouse where both gave birth to living children.

The girl who had been sent to the state hospital had arrived at the school, upon committal, in a very nervous condition and it was under the advice of the doctor that she was removed to the hospital.

Committals that year included two as idle persons, two for disorderly conduct, one as lewd and wanton, two for theft, one as a habitual school disturber, one for malicious destruction of property, one as a nightwalker, two for having illicit intercourse with a married man, one for living with a married man, and six for truancy. Of those entering the school, one was nine years old, two were eleven years old, one was twelve years old, two were thirteen years old, two were fourteen years old, three were fifteen years old, eight were sixteen years old, and one was seventeen years old.

The salaries of the staff consisted of $900 for the year being paid to Clara Forbush; $65 per month being paid to Rose Marwood; and $30 per month being paid to Agnes McNaughton, Frances Keene, Mary Dwelley, N. Bently, Joanna Farr, Alice Reynolds, and Abbie Clements.

1911

Eleven girls were committed by the courts: three as lewd and wanton, two for idle and disorderly conduct, one for theft, and five for truancy. Their ages were from eleven to seventeen. Clara Forbush's report to the Rhode Island State Board of Charities that year stated:

> In the laundries, the girls do all the work necessary for the institution. Perhaps it would be well to mention that, as there is no machinery in this department, all the work is done by hand. The girls detailed to the kitchen are taught plain cooking and all that pertains to kitchen work. Under the direction of the teacher, all meals are prepared for the inmates and teachers. Girls appointed for general housework are taught bed-making, care of sleeping rooms and corridors. All girls not otherwise employed are detailed to the sewing room where they are taught to cut, make and mend all garments worn by the girls. At Eastman Cottage, the number being small, those who work in the laundry the first three days of the week spend the rest of the time in the sewing room. In the summer, three girls worked in the garden. A large strawberry bed was made, and a few fruit trees were set out. One girl had care of the hens. The number of visits made by the dental surgeon during the past year was ten. Thirty-three girls received attention, many of whom had several treatments. The eyes of several of the girls were examined. Some received treatment and six were supplied with glasses. The general health of the girls has been good. One girl was suddenly taken ill with Bright's disease. She was removed to the State Almshouse by the advice of the resident physician and died at that institution one month later. Another girl, who was pregnant when admitted to the school, was transferred to the State Almshouse September 3, 1911, and died there December 26, 1911. Two teachers are employed in our school of letters, one in each cottage. They are not only taught what will be of the most practical value to them in life, but effort is made to stimulate an interest in good reading and to have them appreciate the beauties of art and nature. The girls have access to a library containing over nine-hundred volumes, including books of history, biography, fiction, poetry and others. They are also provided with such periodicals as will give pleasure as well as instruction. Through the courtesy of kind and interested friends, the girls have also had the benefit of a traveling library.

A fourteen-year-old inmate named Grace Studley was committed to the school after admitting to police in December that she had kidnapped a ten-month-old female child in the hopes of obtaining money that would be offered as a reward for the child's return.

In mid-November, she had run away from the home of her parents, Orrin and Ella (Chase), on Williams Street in Providence and they had reported her to police as a runaway. Her frantic mother posted ads in daily newspapers, begging her only child to come home as she was sick with worry and promising that she would be forgiven.

On a Saturday afternoon, twenty-nine-year-old Russian immigrant Julius Rubin and his wife, twenty-year-old Dora, who resided on Pine Street in Attleboro, Massachusetts, had come to a Providence department store to do some shopping. When they entered the store, they left their baby outside the door, in her stroller. When they finished shopping and went back outside, the child and stroller were gone. The couple rushed to the police station to report the kidnapping. Days passed as the Rubins desperately searched for their child.

Detectives then discovered that a man and a girl with a baby had rented a room at a boarding house on the night of the kidnapping. The baby had been left in the room alone for most of the next day and its shrieking cries had led neighbors to call police. The detective stayed inside the room with the baby until the girl and the man returned at 2 p.m. that afternoon.

Faced with questions, the girl stated that her name was Helen Chase, that she was from Cincinnati, and that the baby was hers. The man assured the detective that he had just recently met the girl and he was therefore allowed to leave. The girl and baby were transported to the police station for further questioning. While they were there, Ella Studley stopped in to ask if they had received any news concerning her missing daughter. While she was speaking to a police officer, she suddenly saw the girl in another room and cried, "Oh, my Grace!" She ran into the other room where her relief almost immediately turned into anger over her daughter's running away and scaring her so.

The girl admitted to police that her real name was Grace Studley. She then went on to say that she had met the man she was with the previous night in the street, that his name was Walter Johnson, and that he had the baby with him and told her the baby's parents had died so he was taking care of it. She said she offered to help him, and they went and rented a room. When asked about the wedding ring she was wearing, she said some man had given it to her as a joke.

After adhering to her lie for quite some time, she finally admitted that she had taken the baby from the entrance of the store hoping that she would be able to collect a ransom for its return. When the Rubins arrived at the police station to be reunited with their child, the police told Studley, "Now tell the mother and father what you took their baby for."

"I thought I'd get a reward," she replied. Police were stunned to witness such a young innocent-looking girl answer to these horrific charges in such a calm, unconcerned manner. After pleading guilty to the charges, she was arraigned in juvenile court and sent to Oaklawn School as the youngest girl ever held on a kidnapping charge in Rhode Island.

A Rhode Island Board of State Charities and Corrections report read:

> The number of girls at the Oaklawn School is smaller than for some time past. During the fall term the school had the privilege of using the State traveling library. Two libraries were sent, and the pupils derived much pleasure from the books. The Board was pleased to learn that a direct telephone service is now installed for the use of the Superintendent at Oaklawn. The Board is glad to report the good health of the girls. The Superintendent has kept up her high standard of discipline while at the same time exerting a motherly influence. The teachers are to be commended for their untiring efforts in the interests of the girls.

1912

Special Easter exercises held at the school included a program of recitations that was given by the girls.

Of those committed to Oaklawn School that year, one was a sixteen-year-old girl who was found guilty of theft, by the Third District Court, on September 25, 1912. After violating the conditions of her suspended sentence and probation, she was brought into court and sentenced to Oaklawn School. She was charged with stealing money from a Mrs. Thompson while in the employ of a Dr. Webster, as well as stealing women's wearing apparel from the residence of Louis Silverstein. She was arrested in the vicinity of Watch Hill.

When she had previously stood before the court, she had pleaded for leniency and promised to behave better. However, she had been leaving home repeatedly without permission and became so disobedient that her mother considered it her duty to put her under restraint. To the court, she expressed the desire to be sent to the reform school rather than live under the conditions in which she claimed she had been living for two years.

It was noted in a report by the Advisory Board of Visitors that teachers were experiencing a great deal of difficulty in grading inmates school work as their progress was slow and their education level far behind that of "normal girls of the same age." The Board recommended that the teachers be assisted in their work by the aid of lantern slides, a method being used in many public schools "where pupils are backward or, for other reasons, require special attention."

There was one escape that year, and one death, following a short illness due to Bright's disease. The annual State report of Dr. Henry A. Jones read:

> During the past year there has been little illness among the inmates of this institution. There have been diseases incident to climate changes and these have responded to treatment. No epidemics have appeared nor has there been any serious accidents. The death of one of the larger girls in the Eastman Cottage, from an attack of acute

uremic poisoning, was not looked for as the patient did not complain but an hour or so before she was stricken down, nor did she exhibit any of the characteristic symptoms of kidney disease. It is rather a strange coincidence that this death, and the one occurring last year, should have happened in the new cottage, the inmates both working at the same form of employment in the kitchen, and both dying of kidney disease.

Eastman Cottage was closed for occupancy on July 1, 1912.

1913

Superintendent Clara Forbush presented a report to the Rhode Island Board of State Charities and Corrections:

Gentleman, I have the honor to present a report of the Oaklawn School for the year ending December 31, 1913. The number of inmates at the school for the past year has been small especially during the first six months. There was an increase toward the end of the year. On July 1, Eastman Cottage was closed and the girls, sixteen in number, were transferred to the old building, making the total number of inmates in the school at that time forty-two. In the closing of this cottage, the number of employees was reduced to six, the school teacher being retained to carry on the work with the girls transferred from Eastman Cottage. The sewing room in the old building was fitted up with tables in the afternoon for this purpose, so that two schools have been maintained as before. In the morning the girls have been employed in the different departments, namely laundry, kitchen, sewing room and at general housework under the instruction of those employed for that purpose. Five girls are detailed to the kitchen where all the cooking for officers and girls is done except the making of the girls' bread. In the laundry there are eight girls who do all the work for officers, girls and a small amount for Sockanosset School.

Forbush's report went on:

There are ten girls employed at general housework and are taught bed-making, care of sleeping rooms and corridors. Those who are not employed elsewheres are detailed to the sewing room where they are taught cutting, making and mending all garments worn by the girls. Through the summer four girls attend to the flower and vegetable gardens, pick the fruit and care for the hens. A piece of land has been cleared and fruit trees set out. A new strawberry bed has been made and raspberry and blackberry bushes reset to which were added some new stock. The garden furnishes all the fresh vegetables consumed by both officers and girls at the school during the summer. There has been one change in school teachers and one in kitchen matrons during the year. Repairs inside and out on the old cottage are very much needed, both from an economical and sanitary point. There is also great need for a store house with a place for cold storage.

The report continued:

The old cottage is lighted by kerosene lamps which furnish insufficient light for reading, working or studying, therefore electric lights are very much needed. During the past year the Sunday services have been held as usual; Protestant services every Sunday afternoon at 3.00 and a Catholic service the second Sunday of each month. Sabbath School is held every Sunday morning at 10.00. The Sisters of Mercy have made occasional visits throughout the year. The usual holiday entertainments have been given by the girls under the supervision of the teachers. The girls have had physical culture every morning and special lessons once a week. The general health of the girls has been good with the exception of colds. One girl was removed to the State Almshouse for an operation for appendicitis and two were sent there for treatment for a short time. All returned in good health. I wish to thank the honorable Board for the kind consideration and support extended to me in carrying on the work for the school during the past year.

Special Christmas exercises included the inmates being given the liberty of the yards and play rooms on Christmas Day. Three special meals were served that day. Breakfast included cold meat, hot biscuits, potatoes, and doughnuts with all the fixings and coffee. Lunch consisted of roast turkey, squash, mince pies, pickles, fruit, candy, nuts, and cranberry sauce. Supper was bread and butter, peach preserves, two kinds of cake, and tea.

The number of inmates at Oaklawn School as of January 1, 1913, was forty. Over the year, nineteen were committed by courts, two were committed awaiting trial, one was admitted by the State Board of Charities and Corrections, eight were returned to the school while on parole, one was transferred from the jail to await trial, and one was returned after having escaped, bringing the total to sixty-seven. Fourteen were released on probation to go home, two were released on probation to live with arranged families, one was released for trial, one was released on bail, and one escaped, bringing the total remaining at the school on January 1, 1914 to forty-eight. Of the nineteen inmates sentenced by the court, three were for truancy, seven were for being idle and disorderly persons, five were for being lewd and wanton, three for being common night walkers, and one for fornication. One of the girls was eleven years old, three girls were twelve years old, two girls were thirteen years old, one girl was fourteen years old, three girls were fifteen years old, five girls were sixteen years old, and four girls were seventeen years old.

A report later that year, by school authorities, presented to the General Assembly, read:

At present time there are forty-nine girls at the school. During the last year, when for a time the number was much smaller, the Board of State Charities and Corrections deemed it advisable as a matter of economy to close Eastman Cottage. The services of the teachers in this building were dispensed with, the girls transferred to the old building and the schools consolidated. Since the girls who are allowed to enter Eastman Cottage are more promising than those of lower moral standard who are detained at the old cottage, the Advisory Board earnestly desires that this distinction and segregation be maintained. The overcrowding of the old cottage by reason of increasing number of inmates and the necessity for keeping Eastman Cottage heated, though unoccupied, have resulted in the prompt decision by the Board of State Charities and Corrections to reopen Eastman Cottage and to procure the necessary teachers. It is with marked pleasure and satisfaction that this Board contemplates the restoration of the better girls to their former school surroundings.

The report continued:

Eastman Cottage, being the newer building, is in fairly good condition, but the older building and its furnishings are decidedly dilapidated. While it is freely admitted that immediate repairs are imperative, demands from other sources for available moneys have resulted in delaying the work at this building, and the Advisory Board regrets to report that it is obliged to content itself with the promise of early attention to the needs of this place. Generally speaking, the girls at Oaklawn School are industrious, neat and well-behaved, and to the Superintendent and teachers we give unstinted praise for their careful and efficient work. The question of industrial training, which is being so generally discussed as desirable for inmates at these institutions, has been carefully considered by the Advisory Board and in this connection a visit was paid to a nearby institution where such instruction is being given. The members of this Board examined and investigated the plan and its result in detail and after due deliberation and study, have decided to recommend the teaching of rug and towel weaving, also basket weaving at Oaklawn School.

The report went on:

We would recommend that for such girls as show ability and aptitude for the course we heartily recommend instruction in stenography and typewriting. A proper training would afford a practical means of support to those who attain proficiency in the work. The girls have again, as in the previous year, received from this Board copies of the weekly edition of a school paper on current events which serves to keep them informed regarding the world's events of interest and educational value to them. At the time of the Annual Conference of State Charities, a very large number of delegates visited the State Institutions, members of the Advisory Board assisted in conducting them through the buildings. On all sides were heard words of praise for the immaculate order and cleanliness which was everywhere so evident.

The exterior of Oaklawn School was painted, the veranda repaired, the interior fully renovated, the walls and woodwork painted, and new floors laid. Slate blackboards were put up around the school room, electric lights were installed, and a telephone extension to Eastman Cottage was put in.

The yearly medical report of Dr. Jones to the Board of State Charities and Corrections stated that there had been five inmates transferred to the State Almshouse for treatment. The causes for their transfers were one case of chronic suppurating sinus of groins (persistent or recurring discharge from the groin cavity), one case of acute specific conjunctivitis, and three obstetric cases (pregnancy). The pregnant girls were fourteen, fifteen, and seventeen years old. Shortly after delivery, one girl and her baby contracted scarlet fever while at the Almshouse. This had a devastating effect on the girl, and she developed choreiform movements (repetitive involuntary movements) and a tendency toward hysteria when fatigued. It was stated that she had a "defective parent history." Both she and the baby died.

Another pregnant girl developed puerperal eclampsia (seizures, convulsions, high blood pressure, organ dysfunction, and coma following the act of giving birth) at delivery and both she and the child died. The report stated, "This case also had defective parentage and developed a peculiar mental condition, due perhaps to the puerperal state, in which prevarication was a most astonishing feature."

In November, a very thorough laboratory examination was done on the urine of all inmates, as there had been deaths within the institution that year due to Bright's disease and acute nephritis. No positive cases were discovered but the physician was astonished to see:

An old Mazda lightbulb from the school, still intact in 2019. (*Author's collection*)

The high specific gravity of the greater number of specimens. This leads us to suspect that the diet is too heavy in proteids (pertaining to proteins) or the exercise is not vigorous enough during the cold weather to assist in elimination of the waste products of the body. It has been commented on how rapidly the inmates put on flesh after they have been at the school a short time.

The report went on to say that the weight gain was not muscle and may have attributed to the kidney complications that had been occurring. There was also an Influenza epidemic among the inmates as well as the staff.

1914

Nineteen girls were committed by the courts: two for truancy, two as vagrants, three for theft, eight as idle and disorderly persons, three as lewd as wanton, and one for illicit intercourse with men. Two were eleven years old, one was twelve years old, one was thirteen years old, one was fourteen years old, five were fifteen years old, seven were sixteen years old, and two were seventeen years old. One girl died that year at the Almshouse of convulsions following childbirth.

In her yearly report to the State, Clara Forbush commented:

> Considering the mental incapacity of many of the girls sent to this institution, as much progress has been made in the school of letters as could be expected. Aside from the regular course, which includes the common branches, much time is spent in teaching the pupils that which would tend to lift them to a higher standard. To make them acquainted with the best literature, works of art and lives of those who have made life worthwhile, is to put into their minds something new and lasting. Such plan is carried out in this department. Much time and attention is given to music. All girls attend school in the afternoon from 2.15 to 5.30 o'clock. The teachers are given the privilege of attending the Rhode Island Institute of Instruction for Teachers, held in Providence each year.

Eastman Cottage reopened for occupancy on February 5, 1914.

1915

Of those committed that year, one had been transferred from the Rhode Island Almshouse after giving birth on June 14, 1914, to a child she named William Tyler Sherman. The child died in May 1915 and was buried in the State Farm Cemetery. The mother was then transferred to Oaklawn School. The medical report submitted to the Rhode Island State Board of Charities and Corrections that year by Dr. Jones stated:

There were several cases in both cottages treated for climatic diseases such as sore throats, bronchitis, pleurisy and one pneumonia which was of the characteristic type. Several girls having ocular trouble have been visited by Dr. Harvey and their faulty vision corrected, in these instances we have found that this is indeed a minor matter, nor does it cause the institutional officials concern as does the faulty mental vision that is sometimes manifested in these psychopathic children. The anxiety to be noticed to evoke sympathy and attract attention so far as to feign severe pain and desire operations is characteristic of some of them. One such instance is worthy of record. We were greatly concerned over one girl who had injured the knee while playing and even long after swelling and all signs of inflammation had subsided, she insisted that the knee was too painful to be without her crutches. A relative who visited her, stating that he would remove her from the institution as soon as she could walk without crutches, resulted in her immediately throwing them away and no further signs of lameness were shown. No reflection is cast on the acumen of officials who had the case in charge and who felt that exaggeration was a natural attribute of this girl's nature and who, having been operated on once or twice in a general hospital before committal, had as her stock in trade her operative scars to deliver her from much needed discipline. The Wasserman reaction was made on all the girls and many cases of inherited or congenital syphilis were found and treatment instituted.

Elsie Witherell, who was an Oaklawn School inmate in 1915. (*Crystal Trementozzi*)

A cement storage building was constructed that year over the vegetable cellar for the refrigeration and storage of meats and groceries. In addition, Eastman Cottage underwent repairs and painting.

It was discovered that most of the chestnut trees upon the grounds were diseased and their immediate removal was advised.

1916

In the sewing room that year, the girls repaired 805 white aprons, 816 gingham aprons, ten bureau scarves, 795 corset covers, 539 chemises, fourteen coats, two sash curtains, three carpets, 1,903 gingham dresses, six laundry dresses, seventy-three lawn dresses, forty-six wool dresses, 857 pairs of drawers, five flags, forty-five holders, 1,034 night dresses, fifty-six table napkins, 248 pillow slips, 267 sheets, 173 wool skirts, 227 gingham skirts, three gingham shirt waists, 2,589 pairs of stockings, 121 towels, and eight table cloths.

In addition, they made eighty-eight white aprons, ninety-six gingham aprons, five bureau covers, two bread cloths, twenty-four corset covers, three cabbage bags, fifty-one chemises, 116 gingham dresses, five wool dresses, seven laundry dresses, sixty-one dusters, eighty-five pairs of drawers, seventy-five dish cloths, eleven pairs of garters, sixty-one holders, eighty-one night dresses, 124 pillow slips, five pairs of gingham sleeves, twenty gingham skirts, nine white skirts, forty-three wool skirts, two sleeve-board covers, eight ironing board covers, five sprinkling cloths, fourteen sheets, ten sanitary bands, seventeen gingham shirt waists, 123 sanitary napkins, thirty-eight huck towels, eighty-eight crash towels, twenty-three tray cloths, ten table cloths, ten tea bags, and one laundry table cover.

1917

The school's annual report to the Rhode Island Board of Education stated:

> The Oaklawn School for Girls is an institution for the confinement, instruction and reformation of juvenile offenders and of young persons of idle, vicious or vagrant habits. It is maintained by the state and is under the care of the State Board of Charities and Corrections. While it has been anticipated that the operation of the Juvenile Court Act would tend to decrease the number of inmates, it has been found during the past year that, while sentences have been shorter, the number committed has not been smaller. Under the law as previously administered, the short sentence was two years. Under the Juvenile Court Act, the sentence is much shorter. Age of girls at Oaklawn School range from twelve to twenty years. A classification is made

according to the nature of the offense charged, and the classes are separated and live apart in two cottages. In each cottage a school of letters is conducted every day, except Saturday, with three-hour sessions from 2.15 to 5.30 p.m. including a fifteen-minute recess. These schools are in charge of Miss Agnes C. Smith and Miss Clara F. Forbush, both women are graduates of the normal school at Castine, Maine. The results here are fairly good, considering the low mental capacity of the girls received, and the comparatively short time the girls remain at the institution. Many are below the average pupil in the public schools and have had little school training. The common school branches are taught, and quite a little time is given to music and drawing. The girls have access to the library, which contains volumes of history, poetry, biography, and fiction. They are also provided with periodicals received during the year.

On July 17, a fire broke out in the third-floor dormitory, believed to have been due to a short in the electrical wiring. Much of the furniture and bedding was thrown from the windows. The damage was not extensive and the slate on the roof prevented the flames from spreading.

Old pieces of slate and brick the school was constructed from. (*Author's collection*)

1919

The report of The Rhode Island Penal and Charitable Commission that year stated:

The Oaklawn School richly justifies its existence and its methods by pointing to its graduates. On May 29th, three girls graduated from the eighth grade. They successfully passed the tests given pupils of the same grade in the Providence public schools. This did not represent, however, the maximum of their requirements. Each of the girls could cook and serve a meal and wash and iron fine fabrics and each had made her own graduating dress. After commencement, all were released on parole. One is attending a business college, one is married, and the other is a maid in a family, giving such good satisfaction that the woman she works for writes to the superintendent of the Oaklawn School that she is the best trained maid she has ever employed. A ten-weeks course in infant hygiene was given in the spring. Thirty-two girls passed the test and received diplomas. Girls thus trained are in demand for the position of a child's nurse.

The report noted that there had not been an escape for fifteen months. It went on:

The average membership of school room classes is close to twenty-five. Graded classes are practically impossible. Very much of the work of the teachers is confined to individual instruction, which while effective is uneconomical. In some instances, the girls committed are illiterate, although beyond school age, progress is generally slow. On the other hand, occasionally, a precocious child receives in this school her first experience of kindly, interested instruction and makes rapid progress. The small size of the school limits the possibility of industrial and vocational demonstration. Domestic science is taught however, principally by participation in the household work required at the institution. In this respect very little change in the routine of the institution has been made from previous years. Work in the different departments is done by the girls under the direction of teachers employed for that purpose. In the laundry of the old cottage seven girls are detailed to do the work. All of the laundry for the officers and girls of this building, the heavy washing from Eastman Cottage and a small amount from Sockanosset School is done here. At Eastman Cottage where the younger girls are, a small number of girls spend three days of each week in the laundry and the rest of the time in the sewing room. Four girls are appointed to do the work in the kitchen at each cottage. They are taught to prepare meals, to serve them and all that pertains to kitchen work and care of dining rooms.

The report continued:

In each cottage seven girls are appointed to do general housework. They are taught bed-making, care of sleeping rooms, corridors. All girls who are not employed elsewhere are detailed in the sewing room. Here all the mending of garments for the institution is done and the girls are taught to cut and make all garments worn by them. Girls are changed about from the different departments that they may have an opportunity to learn the different branches of housework. During the summer months five girls work at gardening. Weeding the vegetable garden, caring for the flowers and lawns, picking the fruits and gathering the vegetables come under this head. As hens are kept on the place, a girl is appointed to care for them. The health of the girls has been good, the only serious illness being a case of pneumonia. The dental surgeon gives two days each month to the school. This seems very little time to accomplish much yet the work is appreciated, and the results are satisfactory.

The report concluded:

The girls have had physical culture in the open air during the summer and in the play room during winter months. In line with this idea, long walks have been taken. The Thimble Club of Providence sent gifts as they have done for many years. The Camp Fire Girls of Newport sent each one a stocking filled with various things which interested and pleased all. Two ladies of Providence, interested in the school, sent presents as they have done for the past few years. Such kindness and attention are heartily appreciated by the inmates of the institution. Through the efforts of members of the Ladies Advisory Board, a talking machine and a number of records were donated by two ladies of Newport. This has been greatly enjoyed. Ladies of the Women's Christian Temperance Union of Providence made their annual visit to the school bringing fruit and candy which was enjoyed by all. The entertainment furnished by them was of a pleasing nature.

Inmates enjoy time outdoors on the school grounds. (*Rhode Island Department of State*)

The Advisory Board of Visitors to Institutions where Women are Imprisoned reported their suggestion that yet another cottage be constructed on the grounds for unmarried mothers and their children. They believed that mothers who were inmates, along with their babies, should have a cottage more suitable to their needs.

1920

There were several escapes from the school that year. It was believed by school authorities that the occurrence was so high due to the fact that there were a lot of new girls that year and they were not yet drilled in the school's standards.

The coming decade would see the blue uniforms of the inmates discarded or cut up for making aprons. It was decided by school authorities that each girl wearing the same plain blue dress probably did little to build up any sense of personal pride or concern for appearance. Each girl would be allowed to select three patterns and three different colored print materials to sew herself a trio of new dresses.

In addition, all of the institutional bench-like tables and stools in the dining room would be removed and replaced with actual sets of tables and chairs. The thick, hospital type dishes would be disposed of and a set of modern restaurant-style dishware would be brought in. The tables would be set with tablecloths and more attention placed on teaching the girls proper dining manners.

1922

The report to the Rhode Island State Board of Education, by Acting Superintendent Agnes C. Smith, stated:

> Work in grades from one to eight inclusive was carried out much as in the public school. There were no commencement exercises at the close of the year as in the past, owing to the fact that those in the eighth grade did not complete the work required.

1923

In August, legislature decided that no more federal prisoners would be taken in by Rhode Island State institutions. The adult female prisoners within the Howard complex numbered sixty that year and it was suddenly desired to reduce that number by half. As there were only eighteen inmates residing at Oaklawn School, and there were two buildings on the property that could each accommodate fifty

The Quiet Home-Like Life They Lead

Stella Douglas, who was an Oaklawn School inmate in 1920. (*Linda Pearson*)

Remains of dishes once used by inmates at the school. (*Author's collection*)

women, it was decided to move thirty of the adult inmates from the Howard complex to Oaklawn Cottage.

Agnes Smith was instructed to vacate the cottage of its inmates and transfer them to Eastman Cottage. It was planned that bars would be erected over the windows of Oaklawn Cottage to keep the women from escaping, suitable barriers would be erected between the two cottages to keep the women from intermingling with the young girls, and other safety provisions would be made.

1924

In December, the Wild Rose troop of Girl Scouts wrapped gifts and put them into stockings to be sent to the inmates of Oaklawn School.

Eastman Cottage was employed that year as a place to house female delinquents considered 'misfits' for the other institutions in the state. Some of these new inmates were as old as forty years and had come from the Exeter School for the Feeble-Minded and the Rhode Island State Home and School. Many had been paroled from state institutions only to return again and again. Collectively, they were referred to as the 'Colony' during their time at Oaklawn School, and a high-wire fence was put up to separate them from the regular inmates on the grounds. The last inmates of the 'Colony' were released from Oaklawn School in 1936.

Building debris that has been left behind acts as gentle reminders of the long-gone school. (*Author's collection*)

1926

Friends who wished to visit an inmate at the Oaklawn School were invited to do so any day of the week, between the hours of 2 and 5 p.m., except for Saturdays, Sundays and holidays. Saturdays were reserved for visits from family members of the inmates, between the hours of 1 and 5 p.m.

A report submitted to the Rhode Island Public Welfare Commission by superintendent Louis Heizer stated:

> We feel the need of a good library, perhaps not large but at least a goodly number of selected books, chosen by the teacher who is working with the girls and realizes their needs. Books that will be helpful both morally and intellectually. We have no library fund so have depended on donations from various societies and individuals We are most grateful but too often the donated book does not meet our needs. A small amount yearly spent for replacing the good ones that will wear out and securing the ones of value to us would aid materially in character-building and be of untold value. Training in weaving and millinery, hairdressing, typewriting and shorthand are dreams of the near future. An occupational teacher is a necessity.

1929

One sixteen-year-old girl was committed that year when it was discovered that she was prostituting herself, alone and along with other girls, to customers inside taxi cabs. She remained at the school until her release at age eighteen and went on to have two illegitimate children, of whom the state took custody. She was then committed to the Rhode Island School for the Feeble-Minded in Exeter where she gave birth to a third illegitimate child, Frederick, in 1943. The baby was judged to be mentally challenged, described as having an odd-shaped head and exhibiting feeding problems. He did not talk, did not sleep well, and was unable to sit up at the age of one-year-old. It was noted that the child continuously pushed his hand down his throat, causing vomiting, and that his hands had to be restrained. As the feeble-minded school did not house children under the age of five, he was placed in the State Home and School for a term of his minority.

1930

On May 12, the fire local department spent hours battling a fire near the school. The area had blazed up a few days before and now began raging again just after 11 a.m. that morning. Inmates from Sockanosset School for Boys used shovels and brooms to try and beat out the flames. The heat was intense. Burning embers rose high into the air, with a recently plowed field between the fire and Oaklawn School keeping it from spreading in that direction.

1932

In September, many displays created by inmates were for sale at the Newport County Fair. These included embroidery, cutwork, dresses, tatting, drawings, cut-outs, preserves, flowers, and fruits, all made and grown by the inmates. The proceeds from the sale of these items were used to purchase more material for their use.

It was announced by school authorities that inmates would no longer be allowed to attend the Catholic Sunday services at the Women's Reformatory. The Public Welfare Commission made the decision as a way of preventing contact between the wayward young girls and the hardened adult criminals. Some Catholic organizations were upset and confused by this, as they noted that the girls were free to visit the other institutions on the Howard complex during the week to attend entertainments. Reverend John Quinn decided to begin visiting Oaklawn School every Monday to give a Catholic Mass to the girls.

1933

Eighteen girls were committed to Oaklawn School that year. All of the girls were Caucasian with seven being under the age of sixteen, ten being sixteen- and seventeen-year-olds, and one being eighteen years old. The total number of girls within the facility in December 1933 was thirty-one.

A 1935 fire hydrant on the school grounds. (*Author's collection*)

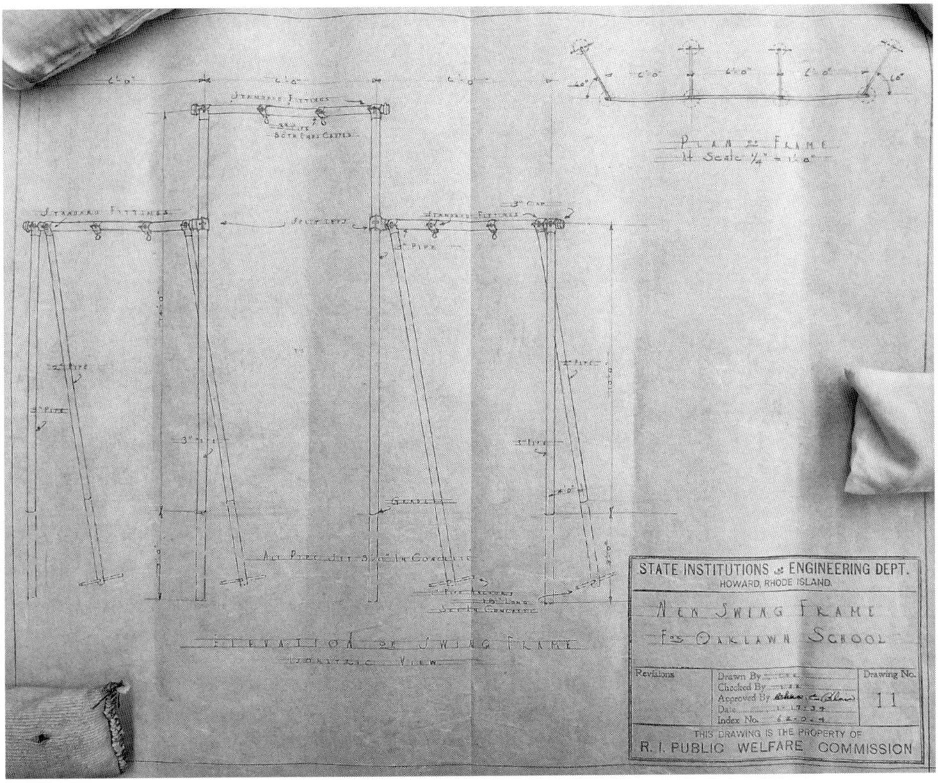

The Quiet Home-Like Life They Lead

Above and below: Swing-set plans for the school's playground. (*Rhode Island State Archives*)

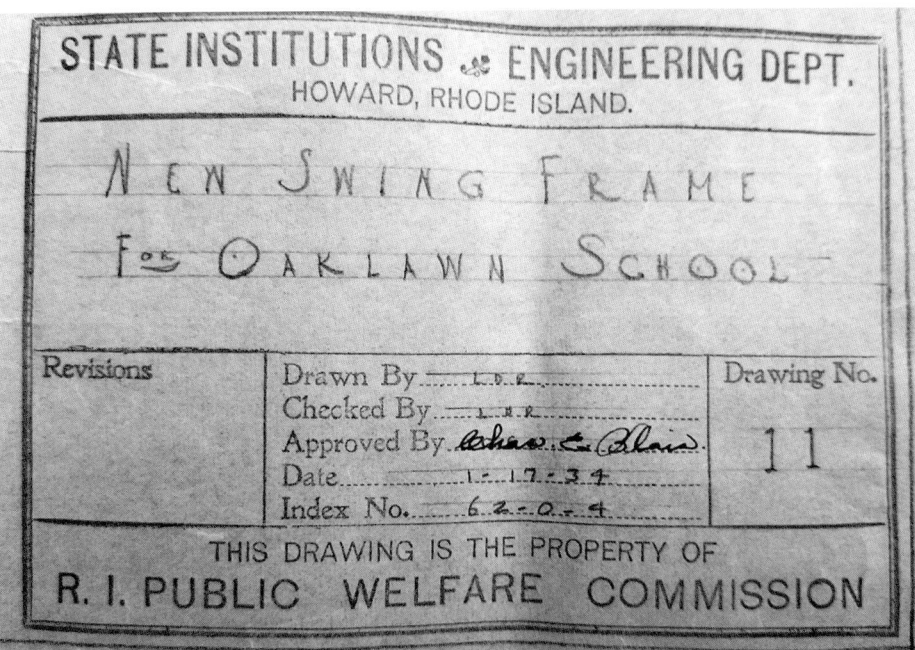

1943

A report issued by the State Home and School that year demonstrated the horrific conditions which some of these girls were removed from. A fourteen-year-old girl who was born in 1929 was placed there after the death of her mother and the desertion by her alcoholic father. She had been residing with an older sister but was committed when she kept running away. She had four older brothers and four older sisters. It was noted that one brother was married to a woman he had two illegitimate children with. The whereabouts of the other three brothers was unknown, but two of them had a history of sexual relations with their sisters.

One sister was happily married with a family and it was this sister with whom the fourteen-year-old girl resided. Two other sisters had illegitimate children and one of them was a professional prostitute. The fourth sister had been committed to Oaklawn School, escaped, and was never located.

1945

The population of Oaklawn School would reach its highest number ever, with seventy-three inmates. An inspection of the school showed that the buildings were not fireproof; however, precautions had been taken in the form of access to both a front and back staircase, a sprinkler system in every room, and regular fire drills.

1946

A fourteen-year-old girl admitted to the school that year had been committed to the Rhode Island State Home and School as a child after the death of her mother, due to her becoming dependent. She was placed in a foster home for two years where she exhibited severe temper tantrums for no apparent reason. Due to this, she was referred to a psychiatrist who determined she had an IQ of sixty-four, attributing the behavior to that. There was a consideration of committing her to the Exeter School for the Feeble-Minded, but conditions there were overcrowded so she was transferred to a children's center.

She lived in two additional foster homes before being sent to live with an older brother who was married with one child. He had also been committed to the State Home and School after the death of his mother and had exhibited disruptive behavior there. After being charged with stealing, he had been transferred to Sockanosset School for Boys.

The girl became pregnant at the age of fourteen and gave birth to a child identified in records as "Ernest" around April 1946. When the baby was two and a half months old, the State Home and School took him into their care and the girl was committed to Oaklawn School. It was alleged that the girl's brother was Ernest's biological father.

A medical exam on the baby showed him to be healthy and he was immediately placed in a foster home. He adjusted and appeared happy for a while but soon his demeanor changed, and he was examined again. Medical personnel explained to the foster mother that the child was in great need of love, attention, and understanding. She stated that she believed he acted this way due to a low IQ and was informed the child's IQ was ninety-four. Disappointed with the baby's continual crying and constant desire to be near her, she asked that the baby be removed from her home and care.

By the age of two, the baby was placed in his third foster home. There, the foster parents loved and cared for him and he was very well-behaved and affectionate unless he was confronted with strangers or new situations. On those occasions, he became fearful and emotionally unstable, crying incessantly and exhibiting temper tantrums.

He continued to progress and then it was arranged for him to visit with his birth mother on two occasions. After those visits, he began to regress. His foster parents declared great love for him and a desire to legally adopt him, as he had become extremely attached to his foster mother. The state would not approve of an adoption as the foster mother had been diagnosed with multiple sclerosis and they did not feel that contributed to good adoptive parent material.

At the age of three, the child was examined again in preparation to put him out for adoption. His IQ was 104 and he was found to be healthy. However, because of his emotional sensitivity and insecurity, it was decided to wait at least another year.

In the meantime, his alleged birth father had served three months for being a common drunk and then gone on to murder a married couple (who had befriended him) and their three children. The psychiatrist who examined the child did not feel his alleged father's behavior suggested possible inherited traits and should not have any effect on readying the child for a legal adoption.

That year, the name of the school was changed to the Rhode Island Training School for Girls. However, it was often still referred to as Oaklawn School.

1948

A thesis completed by Marguerite Daniels Armstrong, at the Boston University School of Social Work, detailed the lives of several inmates of Oaklawn School. "A Study of Forty-One Mentally Deficient Girls Placed on Probation by The Rhode Island Juvenile Court From July 1, 1944 to July 1, 1947" showed that a large number of girls declared to be delinquent had endured great loss early in life or came from homes that induced great emotional hardship. The study included the following teenagers.

Wanda was a seventeen-year-old girl brought before the court on the complaint of her mother on the grounds of waywardness, legally defined as "disobedient to the reasonable and lawful commands of her parents." Her mother complained that Wanda had not worked in seven months and spent most of the day sleeping. In addition, she stated, Wanda would go out at night and not return home until 3 or 4 a.m. During the two weeks prior to the complaint being filed, she had only slept at home for two nights and refused to tell her mother where she was staying when she was gone.

It was determined that Wanda spent most evenings at a local café with her younger sister, Stella, and an older sister. The café was notorious for staying opened beyond legal hours of operation. She had been warned twice by police officers about being out late. All three girls admitted that they were in the habit of "picking up sailors." When charged with waywardness, Wanda maintained that she felt she "didn't do anything wrong" and so it was none of her mother's business where she went.

Described in the thesis as being a "not too attractive girl" whose "mental deficiency was not apparent in her appearance," Wanda was said to be of a quiet disposition. Her mother reported that she had been no trouble in her younger years and had been very obedient and more helpful around the house than her sisters were. Additionally, she had experienced no behavioral or attendance problems while in school, although she was two grades behind the other children her age.

After leaving school, her employment record was good for about a year, but nine months before her mother filed the complaint, she had quit her job and not worked steadily since. Her friends consisted almost exclusively of her two mentioned sisters and other girls they met at the café.

Wanda lived at home with her parents, two older sisters, and two younger sisters. Her parents had both been born in Poland and were described in the report as hardworking "simple, peasant-type people." It was noted that her father showed no interest in the waywardness of Wanda or the other girls, all of whom had been in trouble except for the youngest girl, who was eight years old. The oldest daughter had been committed to Oaklawn School after being found guilty of larceny and running away when was she was fifteen years old. Every time she was let out of the school on parole, she violated the rules and was sent back. She was finally ordered to remain at the school until her eighteenth birthday.

The second oldest daughter had left home many times without her parents' permission but had never been in any legal trouble. Stella had been before the court on a truancy charge and put on probation. By the time their mother's complaint against Wanda was filed, Stella had violated her probation and been sent back to Oaklawn School.

There was a history of marital discord between Wanda's parents due to her father's drinking and keeping company with other women. It had reached a point where her parents simply ignored each other's presence. Shortly after her mother filed the complaint, her father left the home and was never heard from again.

The report noted that it seemed the parents only concern toward the girls regarded how much money they were able to bring to the household. When they were not working and would come home late, their mother would lock them out of the house and explain it by saying, "They don't bring any money in. Why should they eat and sleep here?" When a probation counselor advised her against doing this, she reportedly acted unconcerned about putting their safety in jeopardy and simply wanted them to be forced to obtain jobs.

While Stella was at Oaklawn School, Wanda was placed on probation. She then ran away from home and, when she was apprehended, she was taken in for mental and physical examinations. Two doctors diagnosed her as being "feeble-minded" with an IQ of sixty-two, which qualified her committal to the Exeter School for the Feeble-Minded. However, when it was determined that she was a virgin, one of the doctors suggested she be given "a second chance" away from her family.

Wanda was placed in a foster home, but under a month later, she returned home by her own choice. Again, she refrained from working and began staying out late. When authorities discovered she was spending time with girls who were known to be "sex delinquents", she was committed to Oaklawn School as well. She remained there for a year and made good progress, so she was given a choice of returning home or being placed with a family. She chose to return home.

By this time, Stella had also been released from the school. A probation officer had been working with their mother and the situation within the home was greatly improved. Wanda obtained a good job in a mill near her home where she steadily advanced in responsibility as well as pay. She was earning $35 per week and, a year later, she had been advanced to boss doffer and was earning $50 per week. She had managed to save $600 in her bank account.

Marian was a seventeen-year-old girl brought before the court on a charge of being wayward by "associating with dissolute persons." She had been picked up by police after midnight in an intoxicated condition. She admitted that she drank and became intoxicated frequently, both while at home and while away, and that she saw nothing wrong with that. She had given birth to an illegitimate child two years earlier.

Of African-American descent, Marian was described as being in good physical condition and a "short, not unattractive youngster, quite dark in coloring." It was also noted that "with her deceptively sweet and innocent appearance, she gives the impression of shyness and reticence rather than mental deficiency." She was said to be compliant and accepting of "whatever comes her way" but apparently had no sense of right and wrong.

Her school history was poor in that she did not attend regularly. While her teachers described her as being polite and cooperative, there were frequent complaints from the school about her interest in boys. By the age of fifteen, she was still in the fourth grade. That year, when it was discovered she was pregnant, she was excluded from the school.

Her poor behavior at home and within the community began at an early age and, by the time she was thirteen, a statutory rape charge was brought against a man living in the family home whom she'd had sexual relations with. The man was not indicted due to her reputation being questionable.

Marian lived with her father, her older sister Lucy, her younger brother George and her son. While she appeared to be very fond of her child, she had little understanding of the care he needed and never let his needs interfere with her desires.

When she was nine years old, her mother had died as a result of shock. The report stated that "all of family definitely appeared mentally deficient" and that Marian's father was a "quiet, slow-witted, agreeable person" who was unable to distinguish between right and wrong himself. He informed authorities that he found some of Marian's disturbing experiences "amusing." She paid absolutely no attention to what little direction her father attempted to give her.

It was noted that while he seemed fond of his children, he had no control over them. Four years earlier, he had suffered a cerebral hemorrhage which had left him partially paralyzed. Since that time, the family had been completely dependent on financial assistance from Aid to Families with Dependent Children.

A female cousin of Marian's father, who was also financially supported by Aid to Dependent Children, lived in the home as a housekeeper. A former inmate of the Exeter School for the Feeble-Minded, she had two illegitimate children and was said to have a poor reputation in the community. Many of the local and state agencies who had come in contact with this family suspected there may have been an inappropriate relationship between the father and his cousin.

Marian's sister, Lucy, had two illegitimate children and her brother, George, had been committed to the Exeter School for the Feeble-Minded at the age of ten for "exposing himself and bothering girls." The home was said to be in a "poor section" of the state and "absolutely filthy." The report stated that what little housework was done was completed by Marian.

Marian made no constructive use of her free time but loitered at the homes of various people in the community who had poor reputations. One of the homes she often visited was known to be not much better than a house of prostitution with servicemen coming and going at all hours.

After being declared wayward by the court, she was put on probation. Soon, she was discovered to be frequenting a neighborhood house of prostitution, sometimes staying away from home all night. In under a month, she was charged with breaking probation and committed to Oaklawn School. She did very well at the school and was well-liked by the staff and the other inmates. She remained at the school for one year and was then sent back home on probation. Once home, her "sexual delinquencies" resumed, and four months later, she was again charged with breaking probation and sent back to Oaklawn School. Upon an exam there, it was discovered that she was three months pregnant.

Marian remained at Oaklawn School and when her baby was born, it was committed to the custody of the State of Rhode Island. She remained at the school for at least two more years and her behavior was noted as being wonderful. She became a willing and cheerful worker and one of most-liked girls within the facility.

Anna was a fifteen-year-old girl brought before the court by police on a charge of being wayward for "deserting her home without good and sufficient cause." She had been missing from home for a week and when police located her in a nearby town, she admitted to engaging in misconduct with three different men during that time.

The fifth child in a family of eight children, her mother was from Scotland and her father was from Armenia. When her father learned of her actions while gone, he refused to let her return home. She was thereby sent to Oaklawn School, pending physical and mental examinations and an investigation of the case.

Anna was described in the thesis as being "rather attractive" and "unusual" in that she "had the features of the Armenian with the blond coloring of the Scotch." She was said to have a quiet and seclusive personality and her parents reported that they had no idea why she decided to leave home.

Referred to as a "lone wolf" with few friends, she had a record of poor work performance in school but exemplary behavior there. She spent most of her free time at home but seemed to have no interests.

For a month prior to the complaint of waywardness, she was staying away from home from the time she left for school in the morning until about 10 p.m. Her father had been employed for a year but stated that in the thirteen months previous to that, he had been unable to work due to "ill health." During that time, the family was supported by various state agencies. It was reported that conditions within the home were not good and that the father's "ill health" was actually mostly mental. While the father was said to be very strict, the mother was described as being too lenient.

One of Anna's younger sisters had a serious history of truancy and had run away from home on several occasions. After the conditions of the home were investigated, she was committed to the State Home and School by Rhode Island Child Services. Anna's brothers had also been before the court for truancy and larceny.

Following the complaint of waywardness, Anna was committed to Oaklawn School for one month then returned home and placed on probation. Two months later, she left home and was gone for three days. After she was apprehended and questioned by a probation officer regarding where she had been, the officer reported, "I could get nothing but a very rambling, disjointed statement about her whereabouts while away and she contradicted herself many times during her story." Her IQ was reported to be sixty-four.

Anna was committed to Oaklawn School again, where her transition was said to be very poor. The superintendent reported that she acted "vacant most of the time", that she did not mix well with the other inmates, and that she would laugh "quiet foolishly every so often at nothing at all."

After spending a year at the school, she was returned to her home. For the next six months, she adjusted very well and worked regularly. She was closely supervised by her mother and her behavior was good. She then began displaying very abnormal behaviors. It was reported that she began playing the radio "all day long at full blast," explaining that she had to do this because she was "pregnant by a famous band leader" and he and President Truman were sending her messages through the radio.

Anna began having many additional strange delusions and was sent for observation at a psychopathic ward. She was then committed to the Rhode Island State Hospital for Mental Diseases with a diagnosis of schizophrenia.

Gracia was a seventeen-year-old girl brought before the court for being wayward after a complaint by her mother. The seventh of nine children, her mother had been born in America and her father in Italy. During the month prior to the complaint, she had stayed away from home a few days at a time on seven occasions. Her explanation during these absences was that she was either walking the streets or sitting in the waiting room of the railroad station.

A physical examination showed that she had already had "considerable sex experience." She was described as being "tall and well-built" and "rather attractive." She was reported to have a "mental deficiency not apparent in her appearance" and an IQ of seventy-three.

Said to be "defiant, aggressive, emotional and uncontrolled," she had been in trouble during her last three years of school due to truancy and leading others to engage in disturbing behavior. She was diagnosed as being a "borderline mentally defective child" with "neurotic or psychopathic behavior."

She progressed slowly at school and had to repeat the fifth, sixth, and seventh grades. Her IQ had reportedly dropped ten points within the previous four years.

A year before the complaint was made, her father had died after being ill for a year and her behavior became increasingly worse at that time. She had been very fond of him and his death was a great shock to her. Following his death, she was put under the care of a physician for issues with her nerves. Since leaving school, she had been unable to hold a job for any length of time. At the time of the complaint, she had not attended church for a few months.

It was reported that Gracia came from a good family who were respected within the Italian community they lived in. Her parents had once owned their own home but had lost it during the Depression years.

One of her sisters was part of a religious order and her mother was very fearful that any scandal arising due to Gracia's behavior would be humiliating for them all. She was said to be a very nervous person and strict with all of her children.

The only other child in the family who had exhibited delinquency was one of Gracia's brothers. Reported as having an acute behavior problem, he had previously been committed to Sockanosset School for Boys.

Upon the complaint being made, Gracia was committed to House of the Good Shepherd, a religious institution for wayward youths in Rhode Island. When she first arrived, she was said to be emotional and cried a lot but finally settled in and stayed a year.

When she returned home, she found employment at once. The probation officer stated that it appeared that Gracia was really trying to do what was right but that her mother was much too strict. It was noted that despite her having reached the age of eighteen, her mother expected her to be home in bed by 9.30 p.m. In addition to her mother's strict rules, she was continuously told what to do by her siblings.

Eventually, she began coming home late or staying out all night. It was learned that she had stayed at a hotel with a married man with whom she had known and been intimate with before she was committed to House of the Good Shepherd. She was reportedly very dramatic in admitting to this, almost as if "she enjoyed telling it" and had the attitude that any confinement of her to an institution was all "in the cause of love." As she had violated her probation, she was committed to Oaklawn School.

Gracia made an excellent adjustment at the school and exhibited no belligerent or antagonistic behavior. She was an exemplary inmate and soon was given charge of work in the superintendent's apartment. She was described as being a very willing worker and would often volunteer to do things that were not even not required of her. The superintendent and matrons felt that she was "starved for affection."

She was released to go home after one year, although an exam showed that her IQ had dropped eleven points while she was there. No one in her family had visited her even one time during her confinement and they stated they did not want anything to do with her, nor did they want her to even come home for a visit. Unwelcome to return home, arrangements were made for her to work and live at a nearby hospital. She did very well and after a while some of her family members agreed to let her come and visit them. This pleased her greatly.

Two months after her release, a married brother agreed to let her come and live with him and his family. A few months later, however, it was discovered that she was pregnant. While she claimed that the father of the baby was a co-worker at the hospital, she told a friend that the father was the married man she had been keeping company with.

After being sent to the Sophia Little Home for Unwed Mothers, in Providence, she gave birth to a baby boy who was placed with a foster family. Despite her mother previously stating she wanted nothing to do with her, she now agreed that Gracia could return home. She obtained a job and paid her board as well as ten dollars per week to the family boarding her baby. She worked for several months and appeared to be doing well but then began coming home late and acting argumentative, and disagreeable in her brother's home. After leaving the home and failing to return for two weeks, she was apprehended. Her family had definite information that her affair with the married man was continuing. She was returned to Oaklawn School, pending commitment to the Exeter School for the Feeble-Minded.

Jennie was a fifteen-year-old girl sent before the court on a complaint by police of being a wayward child associating with immoral persons. The youngest in a family of five children, her parents were natives of Italy. She and her cousin, Marjory, had been apprehended by police while wandering the streets late at night. An investigation into the matter showed that both girls had allowed themselves to be picked up earlier that night by two young male strangers and taken to a nearby wooded area where they had sexual relations with them. When questioned by authorities about her behavior, she admitted that she had had sexual relations with at least six other boys within the past year. She also admitted staying away from home on two occasions, once for three days and once for five days. Both times, she stated, she had been in the company of Marjory. Jennie was very frank in her admissions, stating that she knew her sexual behavior was wrong but that she "just didn't want to refuse when the boys insisted."

After examinations for venereal infections and to determine her mental condition, it was noted that she had an IQ of sixty-eight, and she was committed to Oaklawn School. Described as being "short, pleasantly rounded and rather attractive," she was said to have a "mental deficiency not apparent in her appearance." She was also recorded as being a "quiet, compliant girl with a pleasing personality."

Jennie's mother stated that her development had been normal and her school attendance and behavior good although she was two grades behind others her age. She got along well with her family and admitted that they had always been good to her and given her everything she wanted. Most free time had always been spent with them, but for the past year, she had had been spending her time with Marjory instead. Her parents did not approve of the influence Marjory had on their daughter but, in order to keep family relations peaceful, they had not forbidden Jennie to see her.

The family was respected within the Italian community where they resided, and were known as decent, hard-working people. They owned their own cottage and it was observed that the family was close-knit and that the parents got along well with each other and with the children. Jennie's three older sisters took great interest in her. While all members of the family were said to have normal intelligence, her older brother had been committed to Sockanosset School for

Boys in the past, charged with truancy. He was released before his sixteenth birthday and allowed to get a job. He then joined the Army.

It was apparent that Jennie's mother was the dominant person in the household as well as the breadwinner. She had been employed, even before marriage, in the same local mill for thirty years. Jennie's father had never worked consistently and had reportedly "retired" when his children became old enough to work.

Jennie was close to her mother, who provided firm but fair discipline. Jennie did not seem to have any problem with discipline until she began keeping company with Marjory.

Committed to Oaklawn School, Jennie underwent physical and mental examinations which showed that she had had "considerable sex experience" and indicated that she suffered from emotional instability as well as mental retardation. Due to the seriousness of her offense and her alleged mental condition, she was ordered to remain at the school for another two months.

Upon her release, it was suggested that she be placed at House of the Good Shepherd due to her limited mentality and possibility of emotional instability. Her father and sisters were in favor of this idea but her mother was adamantly against it, stating, "Jennie is not that kind of girl."

The family was assured that Jennie would need close supervision if she was allowed to come home. Her older sisters therefore made it a point to take her out with them on weekends, dancing and to the movies. She was delighted they wanted to spend time with her. After her sixteenth birthday, she left school and secured a job working in the mill alongside her mother and one of her sisters. She earned about thirty dollars per week. After a year had passed and she had exhibited no other disturbing behavior, she was released from probation. Happy at her job and within her home, a check on her two years later showed that she had encountered no further difficulties.

Carolyn was a fifteen-year-old girl brought before the court on a complaint by the school truant officer charging waywardness. She had been refusing to go to school for three months and had taken money from her family as well as $75 from a neighbor. In addition, in the company of another girl, she stayed out late at night and "picked up" servicemen.

Described as being "very unattractive" and "looking much younger than her fifteen years," Carolyn was also said to be "sullen, dirty, dejected and unloved." Despite acting shy around strangers, she was said to be very belligerent at home, threw temper tantrums, and was suspicious of adults. Her parents were natives of England and she had one older brother and one younger brother.

An examination showed her to be in poor physical condition. The year prior, she had been diagnosed with juvenile hypothyroid and backwardness. Her IQ was determined to be sixty-eight.

While in the first grade, she had been referred to a clinic due to the fact that she was unable to adjust to school, could not learn, was always alone, and cried easily. Her behavior, however, was good and the doctor felt that her problems were the result of deplorable home conditions.

Several years earlier, before the complaint was made, authorities had attempted to have Carolyn removed from her home and placed in a foster home. When the placement agency said there were not enough foster homes available, a child protective agency was notified and informed that Carolyn was a victim of "psychological neglect" within her home. The agency responded that it was not possible to remove her from the home on those grounds.

She lived with her mother, her two brothers, and her maternal aunt and uncle. Her father had been committed to the Rhode Island State Hospital for Mental Diseases when she was three years old. He had remained there for nine years and when the time came for his release, he elected to remain there, working as an attendant. He came home one day a week but was not able to live at home because he claimed the children "made him nervous."

Carolyn's mother was described as being "very unattractive, dismal, emotionally and intellectually inadequate" and someone who had "no real love or affection for her children."

The dominant person within the home was Carolyn's aunt, who had herself been committed to the mental hospital six years earlier, suffering from depression. It was reported that she nagged Carolyn continually and made life miserable for her. The aunt worked during the day and when she returned, Carolyn would leave and stay out all evening. The family lived in an eight-room cottage in a very desirable neighborhood. It was said that while the exterior of the house was nice, inside was "dark, drab and sparsely furnished."

When the court decided to commit Carolyn to Oaklawn School, her mother was in full agreement. She remained there for a year and a half. The housemother at the school reported, "This girl tries very hard but gets nowhere fast."

Upon returning home, she was placed on probation. She showed no interest in finding employment, explaining that she was "afraid to meet people." Once again, she began staying away from the house, reportedly going to the movies and staying to watch two or three shows. Her family continued to push her toward finding a job and, after six months, she was charged with violating probation and sent back to Oaklawn School pending commitment to the Exeter School for the Feeble-Minded. She remained at Oaklawn School for at least a year.

Alma was a sixteen-year-old girl brought before the court on a complaint by her father of waywardness. He stated that she was staying out at night and sometimes coming home as late as 4 a.m. or even later the following day. She refused to work regularly and was associating with undesirable female companions with whom she would "pick up" servicemen. Alma admitted these accusations were all true but did not seem particularly concerned that a complaint had been filed.

She was described as being a "tall, rather stocky youngster, untidy and unattractive in appearance." She was said to have a pleasant personality but appeared lazy and indifferent in her attitude and "her dullness was somewhat apparent in her facial expression."

She had never had behavior or attendance problems in school but did not like school and was two grades behind others of her age, still being in eighth grade when she dropped out of school that year.

Her father appeared very anxious and worried about her. She had been exhibiting troublesome behavior at home for two years and paid absolutely no attention at all to her father's attempts at disciplining her. She stated that he had threatened her so often, she knew he never meant it. She was usually fond of her father and got along with him unless he acted disagreeable to her. He was described as being respected in the neighborhood and a hard-working man who had been at the same job for thirty-seven years. However, because he worked from 3 p.m. until 11 p.m., Alma was unsupervised during those hours. While he was very fond of his children and showed great responsibility for them, it was noted that he was far too lenient.

Alma's mother had died when she was twelve years old and, although she had never been in trouble before, she was spending her free time with girls who were known to the police as sex delinquents. In their company, she attended movies, cafés, and public dance halls to "pick up" servicemen. Alma admitted she had had intercourse with one sailor.

She had one older brother and one younger brother. The younger brother had been involved in several larcenies. The home was located in an undesirable neighborhood and despite comfortable furnishings, it was "dirty and dingy." Alma's father took on what little housework was done.

After the complaint was made, a probation counselor went to the house to investigate. It was immediately noted that Alma's father's attitude was much too lenient and overprotective as he had decided not to go through with court proceedings but simply wanted the counselor to "give her a talking to." The counselor told him he could contact the probation office again if he changed his mind.

Less than a week later, he called to report that Alma had come home at four o'clock in the morning and he wanted the proceedings to resume. Two weeks later, when the case hearing came up, he changed his mind again, stating that he only wanted to make her "scared" not have her sent away. The judge did not comply with his wishes, however. He declared Alma to be wayward and ordered she be committed to the Catholic Training School.

During the month she spent there, her father repeatedly visited the court and pleaded with the judge and the probation counselor to let her come home as he was sure she had "learned her lesson."

She was released to go home but only a week later, she left and remained gone for two weeks. When she was apprehended, she explained that she had been staying at a local hotel with a married woman whose name she did not know. She admitted that while at the hotel, a sailor she had met stayed there with her while he was on leave. She admitted having intercourse with him several times.

The probation counselor brought Alma back to court and she was committed to the House of the Good Shepherd. Again, her father continued to visit the court, begging and pleading for her to be allowed to return home. After two months, she was released.

Less than two weeks after returning home, she left again. Two weeks later, she was apprehended by police at a local hotel. She was again committed to the House of the Good Shepherd, where she remained for a year. Her father visited the courts, begging for her release and stating that he was "dying of grief."

Authorities felt that Alma was doing so good at the institution that she probably would have been content to stay there "indefinitely" if not for "her father's attitude."

When she was released and returned home, arrangements were made for her to be supervised evenings by an aunt who lived downstairs. Her behavior, however, continued on as it had previously. Within four weeks of her return, she had left home three times. The last time, she was gone for almost three weeks when she was apprehended by police in a café.

The following day she was taken to court and ordered detained at Oaklawn School pending commitment to the Exeter School for the Feeble-Minded. It was determined she had an IQ of sixty-four. She remained at Oaklawn School for a year before being transferred to Exeter.

1950

Anna Moroney, who was superintendent of Oaklawn School, was attending the Boston School of Social Work and did her thesis on the comparisons between the facilities at Oaklawn School and accepted standards. Moroney explained that as each new inmate came to the school, she was given a medical exam and a psychometric exam, then isolated in her own bedroom for seven to ten days until it was certain she carried no infectious diseases.

Inmates were provided with wearing apparel consisting of Navy pea-jackets, kerchiefs, mittens, cardigan sweaters, woolen skirts, cotton blouses, overshoes, girdles, pajamas, and housecoats. All other clothing was made by the inmates, as original as one wished to get. Combs, toothbrushes, and disposable sanitary napkins were also provided.

As per the daily schedule, the inmates awoke at 6.15 a.m., those on kitchen duty reported to the kitchen at 6.45 a.m., breakfast was served at 7.30 a.m., inmates cleaned their bedrooms at 8 a.m., all inmates who were above the legal school age of sixteen reported to their work departments at 8.30 a.m., all school-aged inmates reported to the classroom at 10.30 a.m., lunch was served at 11.30 a.m., the first bell signaling inmates to return to work and school rang at 12.45 p.m., inmates reported to the classroom and their work areas at 1 p.m., recreation time began at 4.30 p.m., those on kitchen duty reported to the kitchen at 5 p.m., supper was served at 6 p.m., evening recreation began at 6.30 p.m., inmates retired to their bedrooms at 8.30 p.m., and lights were to be out at 9.30 p.m. A state dietician visited the school several times a week to plan the menus and order food. Meals were served family-style at tables of four.

Both cottages had a shower room in their basement, consisting of four individual showers. The inmates were required to shower three times a week and undergo a complete change of clothing each time. During the summer months, they were allowed to shower every day if they wished. Porcelain toilets, without lids, were also housed in each cottage's basement.

A store-room in the basement of Oaklawn Cottage was clean and well-stocked and contained an electric walk-in refrigerator for the storage of meats and vegetables.

Inmates under the age of sixteen were required, by law, to attend school. The school had a single classroom for academic studies, with one teacher leading a class comprised of those in first through ninth grade. Each inmate received individualized instruction based on her grade level, but those with special needs or learning disabilities were given simple tasks, such as coloring, unless the teacher had time to devote to their unique needs.

In the recreation leader's office, shelves placed around the walls were referred to as the school's "library." The room measured 9 feet by 12 feet and approximately fifty books per year were purchased for the shelves. In addition, the Junior Literary Guild had been providing the school one book a month since around 1939. The school also subscribed to a number of magazines for the inmates' reading enjoyment, including *Ladies Home Journal*, *Good Housekeeping*, *Mademoiselle*, *News Week*, *Time*, and *Reader's Digest*.

Much entertainment was provided for the girls at the school. They were transported to the Sockanosset School for Boys twice a week to use that facility's swimming pool, once a week to use its bowling alley, and one evening per week to use its gymnasium. Inmates were also provided the use of the roller-skating rink in the community one afternoon per month. During the summer, beach parties for the girls were held every other week at Scarborough Beach, where they would spend the entire day and enjoy a picnic. An annual clambake was held every August, and some of the inmates were members of an organized softball team that played against other female softball teams in the community. Every Saturday night, the inmates were permitted to watch current movies on a 35-mm projector. Dances, shopping trips into town, overnight camping trips, and numerous other activities were planned throughout the year to keep the girls busy and happy.

A fully equipped beauty parlor within the school was under the direction of a licensed beautician. There, the inmates were taught how to wash and wave hair, as well as how to give permanents, manicures, and facials. The inmates were allowed to have visitors every Saturday and were allowed to write home twice a month. The girls participated in regular fire drills and the buildings were equipped with fire escapes. Each cottage had its own radio and phonograph for the enjoyment of the inmates. Each also had a recreation room.

Moroney's thesis went on to describe the medical services provided to the inmates. No ear or eye exams were given, but annual x-rays and immunizations were administered. A dentist visited one day per week. Until recently, Moroney explained, pregnant inmates had been kept at the school until they went into labor and were then transferred to the Rhode Island State Hospital for Mental Diseases for delivery. The new process was to remove the girls from the school at least two months before their due date and transfer them to a private agency that cared for unwed mothers, most likely the Sophia Little Home. A female physician visited the school every Tuesday and, along with general doctoring, provided pre-natal care to those girls who needed it. A male doctor visited the school twice a week.

Religious services for Catholic and Episcopalian inmates were held at an alter which had been improvised from a closet at the front of the classroom. Other religious services were held in the recreation room.

In all, the thesis showed that the school was above accepted standards in some areas, below in others, and, in additional areas, average.

Anna Moroney, a teacher and superintendent at Oaklawn School. (*Kathan Lambert*)

1951

On May 10, three girls escaped from Oaklawn School and decided to hitchhike down the road. That night, in the location of the Point Street Bridge, about ten minutes from the school, they were offered a ride by twenty-one-year-old Everett Francis Amaral. A landscaper and the son of Jose and Emilia, Amaral resided on Transit Street in Providence with his parents and was on his way to do some fishing at Narragansett Pier. He later described two of the girls, in his report, as "very pretty, one with red hair and the other a brunette." Once he arrived in Narragansett, he stopped to let the girls out and later reported that one of the attractive girls pulled out a long-bladed Boy Scout knife. "The short, dumpy one jumped on me while the knife girl held the weapon almost to my face," he stated. They then ordered him into the back seat. The *Newport Mercury Daily News* gave Amaral's account:

> I was forced to go because the one in the back pulled my hair. When they told me what I was going to have to do, I told them I didn't want to. They said, "you have to." I decided it was very dangerous to argue. I decided I'd keep my head and try to please them. I was afraid that knife would come through me at any time.

The third girl got behind the steering wheel and drove the car to Charlestown where she turned down a side, dirt road. While the girl with the knife held the weapon to his back, the girls forced Amaral to have sex with the "dumpy" girl. They then robbed him of $10 and drove to Westerly where they stopped at a pharmacy and ordered him to go inside and buy them some peroxide for their hair as they had decided they wanted to be blonde. Amaral got out of the car and slipped into a telephone booth where he called police.

When the officers arrived, the girls were still waiting outside the store. They identified themselves as Eileen Harop Reposa, Barbara Raposa, and Eunice Miller, stating they were all twenty-one years of age and that two of them were from Fall River and one was from Newport. Police later learned the girls were all seventeen years old and the names they gave were fictitious. They were arrested and taken to the Hope Valley State Police Barracks. After being unable to make the $1,000 bail set for each of them, they were transported to the Women's Reformatory on charges of disorderly conduct and lewd and lascivious behavior. They pleaded not guilty.

When it was discovered that the girls were not, in fact, adults, they were transferred to the juvenile court and the charge was reduced to waywardness. During the court hearing, the girls loudly protested being restrained while being walked from their cell to the courtroom. They elbowed court attendants, shouted at spectators, and caused total bedlam. When the first two were returned to their cell they were in tears, however when the third girl joined them, they began yelling insults at the deputies, pounding on the walls, singing love ballads, and repeatedly yelling, "We're going back to Oaklawn!"

1953

On March 23, two girls escaped from the school by making a rope out of bedsheets which they lowered out a small ventilator window in a third-floor room. One of the girls was from Woonsocket and the other from Providence. It was believed that one of the girls may have gotten injured during the escape as the rope had broken about thirty feet above the ground.

In April, a public welfare committee visited Oaklawn School and noted their recommendations. They stated that they had watched a typing class in progress and were very disappointed in the age and poor condition of the typewriters and felt they should be replaced. They also felt the washing machine at the school needed to be replaced due to its poor condition. Inside Oaklawn Cottage, they noticed that the toilet room was poorly located. It was also damp, as were the walls of the commodities room. The tread on the basement stairs, according to their report, also needed replacing. The school's classroom, they noted, was unusually cold due to the inadequate heating system within the building. In addition, the committee felt that the school should employ a full-time social worker for the inmates who suffered with emotional problems. At that time, the only such professional for the girls to talk to was a psychiatric physician who visited the school for just four hours each week.

On the night of April 28, four girls escaped from the school after staging what was called the worst riot in the history of the school. The riot began just after evening prayers had been said and the girls began yelling, "Let's go home!" An elderly supervisor who was present was unable to prevent the ensuing smashing of windows and furniture, the act of a water pipe being ripped out and flooding the room, and massive destruction done to the floors and ceilings of the forty-person dormitory. Estimates of damage were at several thousands of dollars.

A fifth girl, who was fourteen years old and described as being "quite attractive," was captured as she attempted to flee with the others that night. Police throughout Rhode Island searched for the group of four the following day, capturing one, who had just turned sixteen, around noontime as she was walking along a downtown street.

1955

The local fire department was called out to fight a brush fire in back of the school at 7.17 p.m. on December 30, 1955. On several occasions over the years, fire-fighting apparatus and the use of the school's hydrants were used in fighting blazes upon the grounds, including a mattress fire inside the school.

Another old fire hydrant still standing on the property. (*Author's collection*)

1958

On the weekend of December 26, nine girls escaped from Oaklawn School, angry that inmates were not being allowed to go home for Christmas. Acting superintendent Hazel Geran told authorities that it had been decided to keep the girls at the school over the holiday because they feared they would not return, and because there was likely to be considerable drinking of alcoholic beverages at their homes during the celebrations. One of the girls was apprehended by police shortly after she fled. Five others voluntarily returned. As of December 29, three of the inmates had not yet been found.

1960

During the summer, applications were being taken for the positions of superintendent and assistant superintendent of Oaklawn School. The pay for superintendent was to be between $102.50 and $130.50 per week. The pay for assistant superintendent was to be between $85.00 and $107.50 per week.

Eventually, both positions were filled by residents of Cranston. Donald MacDougald and Esther Reali were selected from civil service lists. MacDougald started on August 29 and Reali started on September 1.

On September 15, a fifteen-year-old girl gave birth to a son while an inmate at the school. Custody of the child was assumed by Child Welfare Services. In 1964, custody of the child was returned to the mother and, two months later, when the state claimed that the switch in custody was only on a trial basis and she must return the child to their care, the mother filed suit in court. It was determined that the mother had not initially been afforded proper legal representation and that the court had acted in excess of its rights.

1961

Six girls, ranging in age from eleven to sixteen, were arrested for breaking and entering, as well as stealing and tampering with mail. They were sent to a variety of institutions, with one being sentenced to Oaklawn School.

It was announced in August that construction of a new training school for girls was being planned at a different location. The grounds would include a main administration building, a service building, and three single-story cottages, one acting as a security cottage and one as a transition cottage. Each of the three cottages would accommodate up to thirty girls in single rooms and small dormitories.

1965

On December 21, two teenaged girls were picked up by authorities from a restaurant in Newport. One of the girls was seventeen years old and had run away from Oaklawn School on November 28. She claimed that she was from Middletown and had been sleeping in cars since her escape. The other girl was a sixteen-year-old resident of Massachusetts and had run away from home the previous week.

1966

In April, the Rhode Island Council of United Church Women presented the school with an extended library. The project they had undertaken included raising nearly $1,000 to fill the library shelves with a selection of 162 different books and magazines. The organization continued toward their goal of raising funds to accomplish a total of 1,000 books. The Reverend Raymond Dyer contributed forty additional books and a set of Catholic encyclopedias.

In December, the Women's Auxiliary of Trinity Church packed gifts for the twelve inmates of Oaklawn School.

1973

The arrival of a certain girl at Oaklawn School caused national publicity. The fifteen-year-old was the daughter of a woman who came from wealthy parents, and a man who, like his father, was a multi-millionaire. The girl's parents divorced in 1959, when she was a toddler, and her mother was given legal custody and moved with her to Texas. She would not be in contact with her father again for over ten years. Her mother married again in 1960 and, five years later, her stepfather legally adopted her. In 1969, the marriage crumbled, and another divorce took place. The girl's mother sent her to live with her maternal grandparents in Connecticut. Over the next four years, she would be sent to live in eight different locations, staying anywhere from one week to one year in each place. She was shifted around from maternal and paternal grandparents, aunts and uncles, to homes in Texas, Connecticut, Florida, and the Midwest.

In 1971, legal custody of the girl was signed over to her paternal uncle, a cattle-rancher worth $7 million. The following spring, she was sent to live with her birth father and his second wife in Rhode Island. Eventually, some began to feel that the girl needed psychiatric care, but, allegedly, her father refused to obtain the help she needed. One day, the girl's stepmother took it upon herself to deliver the girl to a Providence Hospital. The girl spent the next ten weeks at the Rhode Island State Institute for Mental Health. The state of Rhode Island took over legal custody of her that July and she was placed in a boarding home. As a ward of the state, the cost of supporting the girl was $59 per day. The state attempted to bill her family for the care she was being provided, but they refused to cover the charges.

In November, the girl ran away from the boarding home. For this, she was placed in Oaklawn School in December. In February 1973, she was released to live with foster parents. Choosing a blue-collar couple in Rhode Island, the authorities at the school felt they had made a good match. School officials took the girl on visits to their home before finalizing the exchange and the girl seemed to want very badly to stay with them. "She used to cry all the way back to the training school," after visiting her new foster parents, a school employee reported, according to an article in the *Amarillo Globe Times*.

The publicity surrounding the predicament of the poor little rich girl in Rhode Island brought a multitude of phone calls to Oaklawn School from all over the country. So many people had inquired about taking the girl into their home that Superintendent Esther Reali urged them to turn their attention to other needy juveniles around the country as, except for her family's finances, her story was the same as that of many other children.

1974

In September, three women employed by the Oaklawn School were transferred to Sockanosset School for Boys due to a decrease in the number of female inmates. The male employees of Sockanosset were not happy with this arrangement, which caused the three women and a number of other people to protest their work options being based on sex. The matter was taken up by the Rhode Island Commission for Human Rights.

Escapes had become so common that new security measures had to be undertaken. There were twenty-four escapes from the girls school that year, with five of the girls never having been located.

Today, in 2019, the grounds that once held Oaklawn School for Girls is a softball field called Brayton Park. Oaklawn Cottage and Eastman Cottage are gone. The outbuildings, the windmill, the playground and gardens have vanished into the past, as has any trace of the school's cemetery.

The Brayton Park ballfield, now where Oaklawn School once stood. (*Author's collection*)

3

THE STAFF

The following individuals were employed at Oaklawn School, during different periods of its existence. This is not a complete list of all school employees, just a sampling of the staff over the decades.

Fanny May Arnold was employed as a teacher in 1926. Born in Rhode Island on October 30, 1878, she was the daughter of Joseph Spink Arnold and Hannah Bissell (Allen). In 1910, she was employed as a school teacher in North Kingstown. She was unmarried at the time of her employment and died in 1972.

Edward Andrews was born in Rhode Island on March 10, 1869, the son of William Andrews and Ann (Tarbox). He was married to Carrie (Armstrong) and employed as a janitor in 1930 until at least 1941. He died on November 26, 1941.

Guida Laurel Allen was employed as a teacher in 1913. She was born in Maine on April 26, 1890, the daughter of George Allen and Flora (Webster). She was unmarried at the time of her employment and had previously been employed as a drug store saleslady.

Minerva Abbie (Smith) Aldrich was employed as a supervisor in 1941 until at least 1952. Born in August 1881 in Florida, she was the daughter of Josephine Smith Randall and the step-daughter of Albert Randall. At the age of eighteen, while living in Florida with her mother and stepfather, who married in 1896, she was employed as a rubber worker. In 1902, she married construction worker and sewer contractor Allen Aldrich. They resided in Providence and, in 1920, she was employed as a dry goods saleswoman. By 1940, she was widowed and employed as a live-in housekeeper for a widower in Providence.

Anna C. Anderson was employed as a matron in 1920. A native of Sweden, she was born in 1886 and unmarried at the time of her employment. In 1930, she was superintendent at the Rhode Island Reformatory for Women.

Harriet Anderson was employed as an instructor in 1926; she was married at the time of her employment.

Ella Mortimer Armes was employed as a matron in 1882 until at least 1883. She was born in Massachusetts on March 21, 1847, the daughter of clergyman Josiah Armes and Marcia (Keith). She had previously worked as a school teacher in New Hampshire. She was unmarried at the time of her employment and, by 1900, she was again working in New Hampshire as a school teacher.

S. C. Atwood was employed as a kitchen matron in 1891.

Ella R. Brown was employed as a teacher in 1896.

N. Grace Bently was employed as a matron in 1910.

A. M. Barber was employed as a matron in 1884.

Annie Burbank was employed as a matron in 1907.

M. A. Baker was employed as a matron in 1885 until at least 1886.

H. L. Bullard was employed as a laundress and music teacher in 1884 until 1887, and a teacher in 1888.

W. A. Bennett was employed as a kitchen matron in 1891.

Catherine Bryant was employed as a matron in 1925; she was born in Massachusetts in 1880.

K. C. Buckelew was employed as a teacher in 1896.

Mary Harris (Miller) Boomhower was employed as a sewing room matron and substitute teacher in 1896. Born in Rhode Island in 1875, she was the daughter of Edmund Miller and Lillie (Demarra). In Massachusetts, on July 22, 1909, she married carpet salesman Archibald Boomhower.

Ada L. Batchelor was employed as a housekeeper and matron from 1922 until at least 1926. She was born in Maine in 1866 and was widowed at the time of her employment. She had previously been employed, in 1900, at the Reformatory Prison for Women in Sherborn, Massachusetts as a matron and in 1920 as an instructor. In 1940, she was living at the Home for Aged Women in Auburn City, Maine.

Mrs. R. S. Butterworth was employed as superintendent upon Oaklawn School's opening on July 13, 1882. She was initially paid $50 per month. She resigned in August 1895. Previously, she had been in charge of Allyn House, a department of the Connecticut Industrial School for Girls and had worked at the Rhode Island Almshouse.

Mary "Molly" Celestine (Murphy) Bergmann was employed as an attendant in 1956 and, by 1964, had been named a dormitory supervisor. She was married at the time of her employment to Emil Bergmann, a fire insurance adjuster. She was born in Rhode Island in 1897, the daughter of Daniel Murphy and Mary (Lynd). She died on October 22, 1970, after a two-month illness.

Hope (Kendall) Bourne was employed as an assistant superintendent. Born on February 26, 1883, she was the daughter of Hiram Kendall and Lydia (Kilburn). A long-time social worker, she died on March 17, 1951. She was married at the time of her employment.

Susan E. Black was employed as a sewing matron in 1925 and 1926. She was born in Massachusetts in 1879.

H. H. Buffington was employed as a matron in 1882.

E. S. Bacon was employed as a matron in 1882.

Annie M. Brown was employed as a teacher from 1913 until at least 1918.

H. Brayton was employed as a teacher in 1896.

Mathelia J. Bilsborough was employed as a matron in 1898 until at least 1900.

Rebecca Bliss was employed as a matron in 1886 and 1887.

Susie E. Curtis was employed as a matron in 1891.

C. R. Cheney was employed as a kitchen matron in 1888.

Emily M. Cope was employed as a kitchen matron in 1891.

Annie Crowell was employed as a matron in 1893.

Pearl M. Christie was employed as a matron in 1925 and 1926. She was born in Rhode Island in 1895.

Laura C. (Rogers) Conlon was employed as a teacher in 1956 until at least 1961. She was born in Rhode Island on December 29, 1896, the daughter of Thomas and Ellen Conlon. Before and after her employment, she worked as a public school teacher. In 1943, she was a teacher for The Works Progress Administration adult education program. She was also employed as a teacher at the Sockanosset School for Boys in 1947 until at least 1954. She was married at the time of her employment to Thomas Conlon, a chain store manager.

Elizabeth H. Chrosby was employed as a matron in 1925. She was born in Massachusetts in 1882.

Abbie Jo (Clary) Clements was employed as an assistant matron in 1903, and a kitchen matron in 1907 until at least 1910. She was born in Maine on May 9, 1859, the daughter of James Clary and Matilda (Ellis). She was married to farmer Frank Clements and had been widowed by her first husband, William Cunningham. In 1900, she had been employed as an attendant at the Rhode Island State Almshouse.

Edna M. Carlson was employed as a sewing teacher in 1920. A native of Nova Scotia, she was born in 1877 and was unmarried at the time of her employment.

Angelina Jane (Brown) Chandler was employed as a kitchen matron in 1930 until at least 1934. She was born in New York in 1869 and was a widow. Her husband, Orrin Chandler, had been an attendant at the Rhode Island State Hospital.

Annie Cameron was employed as a matron in 1920. She was born in Rhode Island in 1896 and unmarried at the time of her employment.

Janie Catherine Cameron was employed as a sewing teacher from 1922 until at least 1924. She was born in Nova Scotia, Canada on April 22, 1871. She came to America and arrived in Maine on March 14, 1913. Standing 5 feet and 5 inches tall, she weighed 138 pounds and had light brown hair and gray eyes. She was naturalized in 1924 while employed at the school.

Lizzie T. Conley was employed as a laundress in 1885 and as a laundress and music teacher in 1886.

J. A. Durant was employed as a matron in 1894.

Eleanor Alice Donahue was employed as a teacher in 1935 and 1936, and as superintendent from 1936 until 1940. She was born in Rhode Island on September 25, 1909, the daughter of Cornelius Donahue and Susanna (Murphy). At the time of her employment, she was unmarried.

Mabel S. Dexter was employed as a sewing instructor and laundry matron in 1930 until at least 1948. She was born in Rhode Island in 1888 and was unmarried at the time of her employment.

Marion E. Doyle was employed as a teacher in 1930. She was born in Connecticut on December 15, 1904, the daughter of Patrick Doyle and Mary (Kelly).

Lydia Emma Doe was employed as assistant matron in 1896, sewing room matron in 1901, and assistant matron in 1903. Born in Maine in October 1851, she was the daughter of Hiram Doe and Lydia (Pierce). At the time of her employment, she was unmarried.

Mabel C. (McKenney) Danvers was employed as a social worker from at least 1915 until at least 1926. Born in Rhode Island in 1874, the daughter of James and Phebe McKenney, she married Andrew Danvers in Massachusetts on November 10, 1894. She was widowed by 1930. She was employed as a Rhode Island police matron in 1911, and as a Rhode Island Court probation officer for women and girls from 1915 until at least 1923.

Mary (Phelps) Dwelley was employed as a cooking instructor in 1902 until 1904, as a teacher in 1909, a sewing teacher in 1910, a kitchen matron in 1913, and an assistant matron in 1918. She was born in Virginia in 1854 and married Dr. Gustuvas Adolphus Dwelley, who died in 1914. She was employed as an attendant at the Rhode Island Asylum for the Insane in 1894, then as an attendant at the Rhode Island Almshouse in 1904. The daughter of John Phelps and Mary (Matcher), she died of angina pectoris on October 10, 1930, in Virginia.

Iva Dixon was employed as a teacher in 1924.

Nellie May (Rogers) Dean was employed as a matron in 1887. Born in Rhode Island in 1855, she married William Dean in Massachusetts on June 15, 1875. In 1920, she was head matron at the King's Daughter's Home in Hartford, Connecticut.

Carrie Dana was employed as a teacher in 1891. Born in Rhode Island in April 1841, she married Jesse Dana in 1867. He was a janitor and she was widowed at the time of her employment.

Emma Dutton was employed as a matron in 1893 and substitute matron in 1894.

Eva Downs was employed as a matron in 1886.

James Henry Eastman was born in Hanover, New Hampshire on May 31, 1842, the son of Larnard and Lucy Eastman. He attended the New Hampshire

Conference Seminary and Wesleyan University and served in the Civil War. His work history included superintendent of the Reform School for Boys on Deer Island, instructor of the Industrial Department at the Connecticut State Reform School, superintendent of the State School for Girls in Middletown, superintendent of the State School for Boys in New Jersey, superintendent of the Sockanosset School for Boys in Rhode Island, superintendent of Rhode Island State Institutions, superintendent of the Rhode Island State Workhouse, and superintendent of the Oaklawn School for Girls, which he took charge of on October 31, 1895. He remained in that position until 1907 and would posthumously have a new cottage built on the grounds named in his honor. He married Francis Elizabeth Finley in Connecticut on October 10, 1862. His wife and his daughter Grace also worked at Oaklawn School. He died on August 22, 1907.

Molly Evangelista was employed as a clerk and stenographer in 1952 until at least 1973. She was a graduate of Lockwood High School in Warwick, Rhode Island.

Francis Elizabeth (Finley) Eastman was employed as a matron in 1910. She was the wife of superintendent James Eastman. Born in Connecticut on February 9, 1844, she was the daughter of George Finley and Rachel (Kelsey).

Grace Eastman was employed as a physical culture instructor in 1901. Born in New Jersey on December 12, 1876, she was the daughter of superintendent James Eastman and Francis (Finley).

Gracia C. (Luce) Erskine was employed as principal in 1922. Born on March 21, 1894 in Saco, Maine, she was the daughter of Frank Luce and Agnes (Parks). She married Herden Erskine in Maine on March 29, 1916. He was employed as a guard at the Rhode Island State Prison. By 1930, the couple had moved back to Maine and were living with Herden's parents and she was employed as a public school teacher.

Ermina Eiler was born in Connecticut in 1863, the daughter of Heinrick Eiler and Mary (McCall). She was employed as a laundress in 1882 and 1883 and as a laundress and music teacher in 1884. She later married and went on to become a professional artist. She died in 1905 at the State Hospital in Tewksbury, Massachusetts, after having delirium tremens for more than three days, at the age of forty-one.

Kittie Eiler was employed as a matron in 1883.

Ida M. Elden was employed as a teacher beginning on April 5, 1893. Born in Maine in December 1864, she was the widow of Paul Elden. By 1900, she was boarding with the Anderson family on Patten Street in Watertown, Massachusetts, employed as a public school teacher. In 1910, she resided on Susan Avenue in Old Orchard Beach, Maine, and was employed as a school teacher. In 1920, she was still working as a teacher and had two boarders living with her as companions; a divorced female pianist, and the woman's daughter, who was a theatrical performer. By 1930, she had retired. She died on March 27, 1951, in Maine.

Clara Myrtice (Potter) Engley was employed as a supervisor in 1954 until at least 1961. She was born in Providence, Rhode Island, on March 25, 1912, the daughter of George Potter and Bessie (Fiske). She was married at the time of her employment.

Harriet J. Engley was employed as a supervisor in 1948 until at least 1961. She was born in Rhode Island on February 22, 1909, the daughter of William Engley and Charlotte (Fanning).

Rosa Bell (Prentiss) Eames was employed as a kitchen matron in 1891 and as a teacher until at least 1894. She was the wife of Albert Eames, who she married on May 1, 1875. Born in Massachusetts in 1852, the daughter of Benjamin Prentiss and Susan (Johnson).

Joanna Stults (Dey) Farr was employed as a housekeeping matron in 1909 until at least 1910. She was born in New Jersey on October 25, 1845, the daughter of William Dey and Hannah (Mount). She married farmer Vincent Farr in New Jersey in 1870. He died in 1875 at the age of thirty-three. In 1880, she was employed as a matron at the New Jersey State Reform School. In 1900, she was employed as a housekeeper at the Rhode Island State Workhouse. She spent over three decades employed at the Home for Boys in New Jersey. When James Eastman secured a position as superintendent at the Rhode Island State Reformatory, she accompanied him to Rhode Island and spent fifteen years employed at the Workhouse. She died of a heart attack in New Jersey, while visiting her daughter, on January 27, 1920.

L. A. Foster was employed as a sewing room matron in 1893.

Clara Francis (McFarland) Forbush was employed as matron in charge in 1896, deputy superintendent and sewing room instructor in 1897, matron in charge in 1903, and deputy superintendent in 1907 and 1908. She was appointed superintendent on January 15, 1909, and remained in that position until 1918. She was born in Maine in April 1851 and married railroad clerk William Forbush on November 18, 1869. He died in 1888. She died on April 18, 1924, in Belfast, Maine. She had previously worked as a matron at the Rhode Island Almshouse and was described as being "a large, motherly woman."

Harriet French was employed as a housekeeper in 1926.

Beatrice Beach (Baxter) French was employed as superintendent until 1926 when she resigned on account of a physical breakdown. Born on October 15, 1886, in Apponaug, Rhode Island, the daughter of Elijah Baxter and Izetta (Pierce). On October 3, 1908, she married farmer Horace Wells French. They divorced in 1921. By 1940, she was living with her son on a farm they operated in Massachusetts. She died in that state on October 9, 1971.

Hattie M. (Holmes) Furbish was employed as a matron in 1916 until at least 1918. She was born in Maine on January 4, 1865, the daughter of James Holmes and Harriet (Gilbreth). She was married to Harry Furbish who was employed as a blacksmith at the Rhode Island State Workhouse. Her daughter Clara also worked at Oaklawn School.

Clara Francis Furbish was employed as a teacher in 1913 until at least 1918. Born in Maine on December 26, 1892, she was the daughter of Harry Furbish and Hattie (Holmes). Her mother also worked at Oaklawn School. She later married Angelo Mackey. By 1920, she worked as a stenographer for a Rhode Island heating company.

Ella L. Foote was employed as a sewing room matron in 1891.

Myra E. Flynn was employed as supervisor in 1947 and 1948. She was employed as a cook at the Rhode Island State Home and School in 1942 and 1943. From at least 1950 until at least 1957, she was employed as a house mother at Sockanosset School for Boys and then went on to become a house mother at the Rhode Island Hospital from at least 1960 until at least 1962. Born in Rhode Island on December 14, 1892, she was married at the time of her employment to Henry Flynn, a machinist. In 1930, they resided on Sampson Avenue in Providence and she was employed as a manufacturing assistant. In 1940, they resided on Chambers Street in Providence and she was employed as a restaurant cook.

E. N. E. Gibson was employed as a matron in 1883.

Eliza G. Goodman was employed as a matron in 1885 until at least 1888.

A. Gaskill was employed as a matron in 1884.

Floraine Grosloius was employed as a laundry room supervisor in 1954 until at least 1959. The inmates called her "Mrs. G." Born in Canada in 1903, she was the wife of Aime Grosloius.

Florence Garrett was employed as a house mother in 1930. She was born in New Jersey in 1886. At the time of her employment, she was a widow.

Addie M. Gove was employed as a teacher in 1897. She resigned in December that year due to ill health and her work was taken over by Miss Ramage.

Henry Allen Guile was employed as a janitor in 1952 until at least 1956. He was born in Scituate, Rhode Island, on July 23, 1885, the son of Henry Guile and Hannah (Bacon). He stood 5 feet and 9 inches tall and had brown eyes. Late in his life, he was described as having a ruddy complexion and a scar on his forehead. His first wife was Winnifred, and his second wife was Lillian. In 1907, he worked as a teamster. In 1924 until at least 1932, he was an iceman. In 1934, he was employed at a dairy. In 1940, he was a laborer working on a city sewer project.

Hazel I. Geran was employed as assistant superintendent in 1954 until 1956, as acting superintendent in 1957 until 1959, and as a supervisor/superintendent in 1959. She was born in Massachusetts in 1897 and was the wife of Timothy Geran.

M. E. George was employed as a sewing room matron in 1891.

A. M. Holmes was employed as a laundry matron in 1889 and as a substitute matron in 1891 until at least 1893.

Orminda "Minnie" (Sherman) Hodgins was employed as a matron in 1925 until at least 1928. She was born in East Greenwich, Rhode Island, on May

26, 1876, the daughter of Frank Sherman and Alvira (Lewis). She married William Henry Hodgins in 1900 and was divorced in 1905. In 1910, she lived in Providence with her widowed father and her eight-year-old daughter. In 1920, she was employed as an attendant at the Rhode Island State Hospital. By 1930, she was living in New York and was employed as an attendant at the Manhattan State Hospital.

Louise (Koelble) Heizer was employed as superintendent from 1923 to 1926. She was born in Ohio on July 2, 1869, and was the wife of Dr. Edgar Heizer, a Pawtucket, Rhode Island dentist. She had been employed elsewhere as a teacher, and as a matron at the Ohio Industrial School. She died on July 3, 1942, following a stroke.

Lillie C. Hollister was employed as laundry matron in 1891 and as a teacher in 1892.

Annie R. Hackett was employed as a teacher in 1891.

Ethel M. Hazard was employed as a matron in 1939. She was married at the time of her employment.

Agnes V. Higney was employed as a house mother in 1930 and as a matron from at least 1934 until at least 1939.

Elizabeth Hewitt was employed as a social worker in 1930. She was born in New York in 1881 and was a widow at the time of her employment.

Lena E. Horne was employed as a teacher in 1893. In 1900, she was employed as a teacher at a county school in Alabama.

Maude S. Howard was employed as head of the culinary department in 1904 until at least 1907. She was a graduate of Framingham Normal School and the Mary Hemenway Department of Household Arts.

Nellie Heath was employed as an instructor in 1930. She was married at the time of her employment.

Margaret S. Harbourt was employed as a kitchen teacher in 1901. She was born in Pennsylvania on November 30, 1861, the daughter of Uriel and Marcianna Harbourt. She was unmarried at the time of her employment. In 1900, she worked as a dressmaker. She went on to work as a matron at the Indignant Widow and Single Women's Home in New Jersey, from at least 1910 until at least 1930. She died on March 16, 1940.

E. D. Hinman was employed as a sewing room matron in 1891, remaining until at least 1896.

A. F. Helfin was employed as a matron in 1894.

M. F. Hopkins was appointed superintendent on August 16, 1895, replacing Mrs. Butterworth. She resigned on October 31, 1895, and was replaced by James Eastman. She was married at the time of her employment.

Alithea M. (Hutchins) Hubbard was employed as a teacher in 1882 until 1885, as a teacher and laundress in 1886, as a teacher in 1887, as a teacher and substitute superintendent in 1888, as a teacher and sewing room matron in 1893, and as a substitute teacher in 1895. Born in Massachusetts in 1859, the daughter of Augustus Hutchins and Lavinia (Pitman). In 1880, she was a school teacher in New Hampshire. On September 17, 1887, in Boston, Massachusetts, she married Frederick Plumb Hubbard. Her husband was a manufacturer of tin boxes and, by 1910, they had removed to Durham, Connecticut.

E. L. Hopkins was employed as a teacher in 1896.

H. S. Hutchinson was employed as a matron in 1894.

F. G. Howe was employed as a sewing room matron in 1891.

Edith L. Irwin was employed as a farmer in 1928.

Mina Jones was employed as a teacher in 1916. She was married at the time of her employment.

Winifred Jones was employed as a kitchen matron and instructor in 1930 until at least 1932. She was born in Connecticut in 1894 and was unmarried at the time of her employment.

Rita F. Janson was employed as assistant superintendent in 1943. She was born in Rhode Island in 1908 and was the wife of Nicholas Janson. In 1940, she was the educational director of a Rhode Island public school. Her husband was the business manager at Rhode Island State Hospital.

Jennie A. Jones was employed as a laundry matron in 1895 and as a substitute laundry matron in 1896.

Stella (Rogers) Johnson was employed as a teacher in 1922 until at least 1924. Born in Rhode Island in 1886, she was married to Norman Johnson, a physician. In 1940, she was employed as a public school teacher.

Florence Knowles was employed as a matron in 1920. She also worked as a matron at the Rhode Island State Infirmary in 1919 until at least 1922. She was born in Vermont in 1893 and was unmarried at the time of her employment.

Ethel Kenney was employed as a laundress in 1893.

Isobel M. Knipe was employed as a secretary from at least 1934 until at least 1940, then as superintendent from 1940 until 1945. She was born in Ohio on March 15, 1906, and was unmarried at the time of her employment. In 1948, she was assistant superintendent at the Maine State School for Girls and was superintendent at the Montrose School for Girls in Maryland in 1951. In 1930, she worked as a public school teacher in Vermont.

Kate B. Kobelsperger was born in Columbus, Ohio, in 1875, the daughter of Andrew Kobelsperger and Sarah (Birmingham), natives of Germany. After graduating from the Ohio State Normal School with a teacher qualification, she taught at institution schools for four years before becoming an instructor at the State School for Girls in Ohio. She was then employed as a matron, inspector, and general assistant at Sleighton Farm in Pennsylvania. She became employed as superintendent at Oaklawn School on January 1, 1917, and remained in that position until 1921. Unmarried at the time of her employment, she worked as a matron at the Rhode Island House of Correction in 1925.

Virginia L. Kelly was employed as a supervisor in 1959. She was the widow of salesman William Kelly at the time of her employment.

Francis Berenthia (Redman) Keene was employed as matron in charge of Eastman Cottage in 1909, then employed at the school until at least 1913. Born in Maine on August 29, 1857, she was the daughter of Erastus and Sarah Redman. In 1884, she married Dr. George Frederick Keene, superintendent of the Rhode Island State Hospital. She died in Rhode Island on February 2, 1929.

May Kerr was employed as an instructor in 1928. She was married at the time of her employment.

Lillian Kane was employed as a supervisor in 1943.

Mary I. Kinnicutt was employed as a substitute teacher and laundry matron in 1895, then as a substitute teacher in 1896. She was born in 1862, the daughter of George and Sophia Kinnicutt.

Margaret Lasson was employed as an instructor in 1928. She was married at the time of her employment.

May Lawrence was employed as a laundress in 1891.

Mary A. Lamb was employed as a laundress in 1886 and 1887, then as a substitute teacher in 1889.

Nellie M. Lewis was employed as a laundry supervisor from 1939 until at least 1950. A native of Ireland, she was born in 1889 and was married.

Rita Lennon was employed as a teacher in 1936.

N. Leighton was employed as a matron in 1893.

Elizabeth Lennon was employed as a clerk in 1948.

Rose N. Marwood was employed as laundry matron, assistant matron and instructor from 1896 until at least 1924. She was also matron of outside farm work from 1920 until at least 1926. She was born in Vermont in June 1860 and was unmarried at the time of her employment. She died in Rhode Island in 1929.

S. A. Main was employed as a kitchen matron in 1888 and 1889.

Emma Victoria McAuliffe was employed as assistant superintendent in 1950 until at least 1952. She was born on September 16, 1911, the daughter of Frederick McAuliffe and Emma (Bernier). Unmarried at the time of her employment, she worked as a clerk for the United States Selective Service in 1953 until at least 1959. She worked as a cashier in 1932, as a saleswoman from 1934 until at least 1939, and as a stenographer for a real estate company in 1940.

S. McDonald was employed as a substitute sewing room matron in 1891.

Jane/Jennie E. Moss/Morse/Mors was employed as superintendent from 1927 until 1940. She was born in New Hampshire on December 14, 1898, and was widowed at the time of her employment. In 1940, she was employed as a matron at the Lyman School for Boys in Westborough, Massachusetts.

Donald D. MacDougald was employed as superintendent after placing first in state examinations for the position; he started on August 29, 1960. A native of Pennsylvania, he attended Classical High School, Holy Cross College, Rhode

Island College of Education, Boston College School of Social Work, Providence College, and the University of Rhode Island. He began work in his field as a public assistance caseworker in Providence and Newport. He went on to work as a psychiatric social worker with mental hygiene services, classification counselor at the Rhode Island Adult Correctional Institution, chief casework supervisor in the Rhode Island Bureau of Probation and Parole, and assistant superintendent of the Sockanosset School for Boys. In 1967, he served as director of the Youth Development Center in Pennsylvania.

Agnes B. McNaughton was employed as a teacher in 1897, a teacher of physical culture in 1907, and a grammar teacher in 1910. A native of Scotland, she was born in 1873 and was unmarried at the time of her employment. In 1920, she was employed as superintendent at North Carolina State House and Industrial School for Girls in Bensalem, North Carolina.

Susan C. Malley was employed as a matron in 1939 and as a kitchen supervisor in 1940. In 1935, she worked as a pastry cook at the Sockanosset School for Boys. The wife of William Malley, she was born in Ireland on January 23, 1888, and died in 1970.

May C. McDonald was employed as an instructor in 1928.

A. M. Mason was employed as a laundry matron in 1887 until at least 1895.

Rae Evelyn Mills was employed as a teacher from at least 1919 until at least 1932. She was born in Massachusetts on January 11, 1888. Unmarried, she lived with her widowed mother Carrie Mills on Montgomery Avenue in Cranston and remained at that location for most of her life. From at least 1941 until at least 1952, she was employed as principal of Cottage Street School. In 1956, she was employed as principal of Highland Park School.

Anna Mary Moroney was employed as a teacher from 1938 until 1942, as assistant superintendent from 1943 to 1944, and as superintendent from September 1945 until at least 1950. She was born in Rhode Island on May 11, 1911, the daughter of Maurice Moroney and Annie (Mahon). She was unmarried at the time of her employment. In 1935, she was employed as a public school teacher. She had earned a bachelor of education degree at Rhode Island College. In 1950, she enrolled at the Boston School of Social Work to obtain her master of science degree. She was a member of numerous social welfare organizations and worked as a guidance counselor at a high school in Warwick in 1960.

Bessie Mabel McNab was employed as a matron in 1895. Born on July 20, 1877, in Nova Scotia, Canada, the daughter of Alexander McNab and Mary (MacCallum). She married Melvin Curtis Paul on June 23, 1897, in Rhode Island. She died in Minnesota on October 24, 1955.

Mary Merrill was employed as a matron in 1884 until at least 1885.

Catherine McCann was employed as a cook in 1935, then as a matron in 1938. She was born in Rhode Island on July 20, 1890, and was widowed at the time of her employment.

Elizabeth Maguire was employed as a teacher in 1916.

M. E. Mills was employed as a substitute matron in 1896.

Irene J. McDonnell was employed as a teacher in 1936.

James Hill Nutting was employed as the religious instructor for Rhode Island State institutions. He was born in Rhode Island in May 1841 and, on May 8, 1862, married Frances L. Herman. He was employed as a teacher in 1861 and 1862, then as a Methodist pastor in 1884. The son of Joseph Nutting and Priscilla (Hill), he died very suddenly of a heart attack while driving through Wickford Junction on February 23, 1906. Just prior to this, he had recovered from a long and critical bout with double pneumonia.

Florence K. Parkhurst was employed as a farm matron in 1930 until at least 1935. She was born in Massachusetts in 1896 and was widowed at the time of her employment. In 1940, she was employed as a private family companion in Bushnell, Florida.

Jennie Parker was employed as a matron in 1894.

Katherine A. E. Pidge was employed as a matron in 1909. Born in Rhode Island in 1874, she was the daughter of Edgar Pidge and Katherine (Mellahan).

L. K. Phillips was employed as a matron in 1893.

Florence Pierce was employed as a relief matron in 1930. She was born in Rhode Island in 1907 and was married at the time of her employment.

Beatrice Hannah (Bowman) Pierce was employed as a supervisor in 1945 until at least 1961. Born in Rhode Island in 1898, she was divorced at the time of her employment. In 1920, she worked as a switchboard telephone operator and, in 1940, as a filing clerk for the State of Rhode Island. She was married to and divorced from insurance salesman Galan Pierce.

M. E. Pierce was employed as a sewing room matron in 1893.

Lily M. Platt was employed as a matron in 1935, as a supervisor in 1938 and 1939, as a house mother in 1940, and as a supervisor in 1941 until at least 1943. She was born in Rhode Island on March 5, 1895, the daughter of Wright Platt and Mary (Horsfield). She was unmarried at the time of her employment.

Helena Grace Pine was employed as a teacher in 1896. She was born in Canada in 1875, the daughter of Philip and Fannie Pine. In 1900, she was residing with her parents and six siblings on Pine Street in Providence and she was employed as a public school teacher. On September 23, 1903, she married William Homer Smith. She died in Rhode Island on August 28, 1954.

Olive N. Richardson was employed as a teacher in 1896 as well as matron in charge of halls and dorm work.

Alice D. Reynolds was employed as a replacement sewing teacher after the resignation of Lydia Doe, in 1903. She held that position until at least 1916. She was born in New York in 1851 and was married to Walter Reynolds. In 1935, she and her husband were both employed at the Sockanosset School for Boys, she as a matron and he as a military drill instructor. She had also worked at Sockanosset School prior to her employment at Oaklawn School.

Aldea D. Racicot was employed as a teacher and a clerk in 1930. She was born in Massachusetts on May 17, 1908, the daughter of Alex Racicot and Anna (Lamothe). She was unmarried at the time of her employment. In 1940, she was employed as a public school teacher.

Jeanette Haig Ramage was employed as a teacher in 1896. She resigned in 1897, after less than a year, to accompany her sister and brother-in-law to South Africa. She died in Indew, South Africa, on January 13, 1901.

Dorilla A. Rivard was employed as a teacher in 1922. Born in 1898 in Massachusetts, she had moved to Vermont by 1931. She lived in a tourist lodge there and was employed as principal of Lyndon Graded School. She was unmarried at the time of her employment and, in 1939 until at least 1948, she was working in Vermont as a public school teacher.

Esther A. (Castelli) Reali was born in Providence, the daughter of Mauro Castelli and Madalena (Romano). Employed as a recreation supervisor in 1954 until January 1957, she was married at the time of her employment. She graduated from Rhode Island College of Education and Providence College. In 1957, she was employed as a social worker by the Rhode Island Department of Public Welfare. In 1958, until at least 1960, she was employed as a social case worker by the Rhode Island Department of Social Work. On September 1, 1960, she took on the position of assistant superintendent at Oaklawn School, where she remained until at least 1973. In all, she served more than thirty years at the school.

Phebe Robinson was employed as a teacher in 1922.

Ruth Riley was employed as a recreation leader in 1959. She was married at the time of her employment.

Cora Ray was employed as a laundry matron in 1896.

M. Rhodes was employed as a matron in 1891. She was married at the time of her employment.

Hannah Rowand was employed as kitchen matron in 1896.

Lucy R. Swift was employed as a sewing matron in 1925 and 1926. A native of Canada, she was born in 1870.

Ella M. Smith was employed as an instructor in 1930.

Agnes C. Smith was employed as a teacher in 1898 until 1916, then employed as a matron from 1917 to 1921. In 1907, she was the instructor of singing and reading music. On September 20, 1921, she was elected acting superintendent after the resignation of Kobelsperger. She was briefly replaced when Miss Catherine Tobin took over the position of superintendent, but Tobin soon resigned. Agnes served as acting superintendent until elected superintendent in 1924. She was born in Maine in November 1879, graduated from the Eastern Normal School in Maine, and was unmarried at the time of her employment. In 1930, she was employed as a matron at the Reformatory for Women in Framingham, Massachusetts.

Mildred R. Smith was employed as a matron in 1924. She was married at the time of her employment.

Charlotte (Stone) Straub was employed as a teacher 1935 and 1936, then as a matron and house mother from 1938 until 1943. She was born in Rhode Island on August 3, 1904, and married Earl Straub.

Ida Smith was employed as laundry matron and kitchen matron in 1896.

Mary J. Smith was employed as a sewing room and laundry matron in 1930. She was born in Massachusetts in 1875 and was a widow at the time of her employment.

E. M. Sheldon was employed as a teacher in 1889, and as a teacher, a kitchen assistant, and a substitute matron of the sewing room in 1891.

Millie E. Shildon was employed as a teacher in 1892 until at least 1894. At the time of her employment, she was unmarried.

Emma A. Silver was employed as kitchen matron, sewing room matron, and assistant matron in 1896 until at least 1900.

Margaret B. Starratt was employed as superintendent in December 1926, taking the place of Beatrice French, until at least 1928. Formerly, she had been superintendent of the Home for Delinquent Children and Women in New Haven, Connecticut, and employee of the John Hancock Mutual Life Insurance Company. During World War One, she organized 300 employees of the insurance company into a branch of the Special Aid Society of American Preparedness. She resigned from her position there to serve with the storage committee of the War Industries Board of the Council of National Defense. She was also chairman of the home hospitality committee of the Boston branch of the War Camp Community Service, director of the Boston branch of the Katherine Gibbs School, and organizer of the National Federation of Business and Professional Women in New York.

Jennie S. Sherman was employed as a teacher in 1887.

E. A. Smith was employed as a matron in 1895.

Miss Spears was employed as a kitchen matron in 1896.

Miss Searle was employed as a kitchen matron in 1896.

Ruth S. Taylor was employed as principal in 1936 until at least 1943. She was born in Rhode Island on June 9, 1896, and was married at the time of her employment.

M. B. Tilotson was employed as a matron in 1894.

M. D. Tyler was employed as a laundry matron in 1895 and 1896.

Barbara Earle (Vogler) Tower was employed as principal in 1924 until at least 1928, and as a teacher in 1930. She was born in New Hampshire on March 14, 1877, the daughter of John Vogler and Lillian (Downes). She married William Tower on October 3, 1900. Previously, she was employed as a teacher at Washington Street School and Highland Park School in Rhode Island. She would go on to work as a teacher at Meshanticut Park School in Rhode Island. She died in April 1933.

I. S. Van Riper was employed as a matron in 1887.

Jessie A. Webster was employed as a teacher and head of the sewing and laundry department in 1920. A graduate of Columbia University, she was unmarried at the time of her employment.

Mae Wigmore was employed as supervisor in 1947 until at least 1959. She was born in Rhode Island on March 10, 1890.

Nellie L. White was employed as a matron in 1887 and a kitchen matron in 1888.

Lena Welton was employed as a substitute teacher in 1893.

Grace Webb was employed as an instructor in 1928. She was married at the time of her employment.

S. P. Wardwell was employed as a matron in 1893.

Lillian Walker was employed as a teacher in 1895 and 1896.

Alice M. Wilder was employed as a laundress in 1891, a matron in 1894 and 1895, and as kitchen matron in 1896.

Dora Williams was employed as a teacher in 1896.

Mrs. Welch was employed as a kitchen matron in 1896.

Emma M. Young was employed as a matron in 1940, then as a supervisor in 1941 until at least 1943. A native of Canada, she was born on August 10, 1881, and was unmarried at the time of her employment. In 1935, she worked as a governess at a private Children's Home in Newport, Rhode Island.

Mac A. Young was employed as a teacher in 1893 until at least 1895.

4
OAKLAWN GIRLS

The following individuals were inmates at Oaklawn School during different periods of its existence. This is not a complete list of all inmates, just a sampling of the girls who were housed there over the decades.

Francis Abbie Alfonso was born in Rhode Island on March 14, 1922, the daughter of Antony Alfonso and Sarah (Woodson) and of African-American descent. In 1935, she resided on North Main Street in Providence and was in the fourth grade at Thomas A. Doyle Public School. She was an Oaklawn School inmate in 1940.

Margaret Alves was born in Massachusetts on December 29, 1920, the daughter of Theopolus and Lucy Alves. In 1925, she resided on Pike Street in Providence with her parents (natives of Cape Verde, Portugal), a twenty-year-old Portuguese male boarder, and her siblings—Anthony (nine), Domingoes (eight), George (six), and Walter (one). Her father was a seaman on a barge. By 1920, the family was residing on Second Street in New Bedford, Massachusetts. She was an Oaklawn School inmate in 1935.

Alice Anderson was born in Rhode Island in March 1892, the daughter of John Theodore Anderson and Selma Charlotte (Bingstrom), natives of Sweden. In 1900, the family resided on Wilson Avenue in East Providence. She had six younger siblings and one older sibling. Her father was employed as a laborer for a chemical company. She was an Oaklawn School inmate in 1910.

Freida Anderson was born in 1891, a native of Finland. She was an Oaklawn School inmate in 1910.

Mary Angolia was born in Massachusetts in 1905. She was an Oaklawn School inmate in 1920.

Reta Abraham was the daughter of Charles and Ellen Abraham. During the school's play *Old Times Made New*, which was performed at the Hospital for the Insane in May 1897, she played Sappho. She was an Oaklawn School inmate in 1896 until at least 1897. While there, in November 1896, she wrote to the superintendent, "I enjoyed the day very much at your house and thank you for letting us do it. I am going to do the best I can. In this way, I will please the teachers and you too. I hope that you will have a good report at the end of each month of each girl. I am working in the dining room. When I get through, I ask Mrs. Forbush to come and see it and she said it was very nice indeed and I know that you would be pleased with it. I remain one of your girls." During the school's Thanksgiving entertainment of 1896, she publicly recited "Four Things."

Angelina Aycot was Oaklawn School inmate in 1896. During the school's Thanksgiving entertainment of 1896, she publicly recited "The Baby's Mistake." During an entertainment in April 1897 to celebrate Mrs. Forbush's birthday, she did a recitation of "The Little French Poodle."

Eunice Ainsworth was an Oaklawn School inmate in 1897.

Angelina B. (surname unknown) was an Oaklawn School inmate in 1897. Out on parole in April 1897, she wrote to the superintendent, "Have done housework and different things during the last quarter. Have been regular in attendance at church and sabbath school. Have been careful regarding my habits and associates. Am satisfied and contented with my home. I was happy to hear from you and your letter has done me lots of good and when I think of what you said it makes me feel better. Give my love to all the girls."

The man of the home in which she had been paroled to, Gurden A. M., wrote to the superintendent, "We feel satisfied with Angie and she is doing well."

Rita Mary Bessette was born in Rhode Island on October 28, 1923, the daughter of Hormisdas Bessette and Mederise (Giroux). Her father was from Canada and her mother from Rhode Island. She had two younger siblings and four older siblings. In 1925, she resided with her family in Warren, Rhode Island. In 1930, they lived on Bagley Street, in Central Falls. In 1935, they lived on Mt. Pleasant Avenue in Providence and she attended Nelson Public School. She was an Oaklawn School inmate in 1940.

Elizabeth Bronson was born in Massachusetts in 1893. She was an Oaklawn School inmate in 1910.

Annie Bethea was born in Rhode Island in 1893. She was an Oaklawn School inmate in 1910.

Carrie Bingham, during the school's Christmas cantata *The Capture of Santa Claus* in 1897, played a frost fairy. During an entertainment in April 1897 to celebrate Mrs. Forbush's birthday, she did a recitation of "Parody on Old Oaken Bucket." During the school's play *Old Times Made New* in May 1897, she played Martha Washington. An Oaklawn School inmate in 1897, she was admitted to the school in January that year.

Mattie J. Bilsborough was born on January 2, 1877, in Rockport, Massachusetts, the daughter of John Bilsborough and Jessie (Conroy). In 1880, she was a boarder in the Rockport home of Albert and Eliza Pittee. Her father, a native of England, was widowed by that time and living in a boarding house in Rockport. A brother, Benjamin, had died at the age of four years and ten months on December 17, 1872. During an entertainment in April 1897 to celebrate Mrs. Forbush's birthday, she did a reading of Mark Twain. During the school's play *Old Times Made New* in May 1897, she played a genius of the tenth century. She was an Oaklawn School inmate in 1896 and 1897. While there, in November 1896, she wrote to the superintendent, "My dear friend, for such I feel you are and will be as long as I try to do as you and your assistants would have me do. I wish to help both teachers and scholars all I can and to do just what is required of me and to do it cheerfully. Again, let me renew my promise of the first part of this year to you. In all sincerity the above shall be kept as thoroughly as I am capable of doing. With many good wishes for your health, comfort and prosperity, and that all will be pleasant for you and your assistants, I am sincerely one of your mean-to-be helpful girls."

It is possible this is the "Mathalia J. Bilsborough" who was later employed at Oaklawn School from 1898 until at least 1900. On February 14, 1904, she married John McCann in Rhode Island. They were later divorced and on March 7, 1911, she married William Lothrop in Massachusetts. She was working as a stenographer at that time.

Elizabeth "Lizzie" Richmond Bullock was born on November 19, 1880, in Bristol, Rhode Island; she was the daughter of James Booth Bullock and Sarah (Lake), both of Rhode Island. The family lived in Bristol where her father was employed as a rubber worker. Her siblings included Lillian (born 1878), Robert (born 1883), Emma (born 1887), James (born 1890), Josephine (born 1893), Arthur (born 1896), and Walter (born 1907). Of the eleven children her mother had, only eight survived childhood. She was committed to Oaklawn School on August 8, 1896, after being arrested for and pleading guilty to being an idle person of dissolute habits. Having only a fifth-grade education, she was sentenced to remain at the school for her minority. While there, in November 1896, she wrote to the superintendent, "I take pleasure in writing these few lines to tell you I will be a good girl and try to do better in my work and be kind to all. I hope that when my mother comes out to see me that my teachers can tell her that I have been a good girl and I hope you will forgive me if I did anything that I hadn't ought to yesterday. I will close with love." In August 1897, she escaped with inmate Susie Mathewson. She had a dark complexion, dark hair, and dark blue eyes. She married road worker Frederick Essex and died on September 17, 1942, in Rhode Island.

Edith May Bailey was born in December 1880. She was an Oaklawn School inmate in 1895 and until at least 1897. While there, in November 1895, she wrote to the superintendent, "I enjoyed myself very much looking at the pictures at your house. I thank you for giving us the privilege of coming over today. From this day I have fully made up my mind to serve the Lord. I will help the teachers all I can, and I will do my work well each day. Since you came, I have just made up my mind to do what is right. Mr. Eastman, I am glad that you are our superintendent. You haven't had the school but one day and a half, but the girls have felt happy ever since you took the school. You made every girl happy yesterday and what you said will not be forgotten by them."

During the school's Thanksgiving entertainment of 1896, she and Amelia Charbello performed a duet of the song "Softly Over Bethlehem." She escaped from the school in July 1896 and was located less than an hour later at the home of George Shields in Lippitt, Rhode Island.

In 1897, she was on parole with the family of twenty-nine-year-old Melvin Wood in Foster, Rhode Island. She lived with him, his wife Harriet and their children—George (four), Florence (one), and newborn Howard. In April of that year, she wrote to the superintendent, "I have attended school a few weeks and have helped Mrs. Wood with the work. Have attended church whenever the weather was suitable. Have been careful regarding my habits and associates. I am very much pleased with my home and find no fault at all."

Mrs. Wood wrote to the superintendent, "Edith is doing quite well. She is willing to help about the work. I think she is careful in choosing her associates and hope she is trying to do right in every way." She was still living with the Wood family in 1900, along with her one-year-old baby Frank R. Bailey.

Elizabeth Brozinski was born in Massachusetts in 1893. Her parents were natives of Poland. She was an Oaklawn School inmate in 1910.

Elizabeth D. Brophy was born in Rhode Island on April 2, 1918, the daughter of Domenic Brophy and Mary (O'Brien). In 1925, she resided on Putnam Street in Providence with her parents and siblings—Mary (fifteen), Helen (thirteen), and Anna (eight). The family resided at the same location in 1930. Her father owned a tinsmith shop. She completed three years of high school. She was an Oaklawn School inmate in 1935. In 1940, she was employed as a private governess and was living in the home of William Martin, who was a steeplejack for a painting company, and his wife, Delores, who was a hosiery inspector, on Chestnut Street in Providence.

Doris L. Butler was of African-American descent, born in Rhode Island on January 28, 1916, the daughter of Emeline Frances Butler. Her mother was unmarried. She had three siblings—Agnes Butler, born in 1900; Wilhelmina Butler, born in 1904; and Everett Butler, born in 1923. In 1925, she resided at Codding Street in Providence as a boarder in the home of sixty-three-year-old Jane Clark who also had two other young African-American girls boarding there. In 1930, she was an inmate at the Rhode Island State Home and School. She was an Oaklawn School inmate in 1935. Her mother died in 1938 at the age of fifty-eight.

Josephine Emilie Broussard was born in Providence, Rhode Island, on February 21, 1921, the daughter of Marshall Broussard and Emily (Freeman). She was an Oaklawn School inmate in 1935.

Aldea Beaudoin was born in Woonsocket, Rhode Island, on September 3, 1919, the daughter of Louis Beaudoin and Eva (Meunier). She is recorded as being crippled. She completed the third grade and is recorded as being unable to read or write. In 1920, she resided on Social Street with her parents and her brother, Alpherie (one). Her father was a native of Canada and was employed as a laborer. In 1930, she resided on West Street in Woonsocket with her mother and her siblings, Alice (nine) and Charles (seven). Her father was not living in the home and her mother was employed as a private housekeeper. She was an Oaklawn School inmate in 1935, while her mother resided on Bernon Street in Woonsocket with her siblings, Alice and Charles. Her mother was still employed as a private housekeeper and her father was still not living in the home. In 1940, she was an inmate at the Exeter School for the Feeble-Minded. At that time, her mother was residing on Lavab Street in Woonsocket and still working as a private housekeeper. Charles lived with her and, although she was still married, there was no husband living in the home. Her mother lived to be ninety-nine years old.

Marie Helen Beaulieu was born in Rhode Island on November 25, 1918, the daughter of Charles Beaulieu and Helen (Thomas). Her mother was a native of Wales. In 1920, she resided with her parents and her brother Thomas (four) on Washington Street in Attleboro, Massachusetts. Her father was employed as a twister tender in a cotton mill. In 1925, she resided on Cedar Street in Providence with her parents and her siblings Thomas, twins Edward and Edmond (both four), and Madeline (eleven months). In 1930, she and her sister, Madeline, were Rhode Island state wards residing in the home of John and Johanna Cullinan on Atlantic Avenue in Warwick. John was employed as a carpenter and the couple had several other state ward children residing with them also. She was an Oaklawn School inmate in 1935.

Viola Beaulieu was born in Rhode Island on August 8, 1918, the daughter of Eva Beaulieu, who was a twenty-four-year-old divorcee serving a sentence at the Rhode Island House of Correction in 1920. She was an Oaklawn School inmate in 1935.

Mary C. Bielusiak was born in Massachusetts on November 22, 1918, the daughter of Jozef Bielusiak and Katarzyna (Skupien). Her father was from Poland and her mother from Galicia. She had sisters born in 1913 and 1921 and brothers born in 1914 and 1916. She was an Oaklawn School inmate in 1935.

Hannah Banks was born in New Jersey in 1896, of African-American descent. She was an Oaklawn School inmate in 1910.

Jeanette Braudette/Beandelte was born in Canada in 1891. She was an Oaklawn School inmate in 1910.

Laura Burkman was born in 1895. She was an Oaklawn School inmate in 1910.

Annie M. Berchen was born in Rhode Island in January 1881. She was an Oaklawn School inmate in 1900.

Mary Bowen was born in Rhode Island in 1895. She was an Oaklawn School inmate in 1910.

Edith Brouilette was born in 1894. Her parents were natives of Canada. She was an Oaklawn School inmate in 1910.

Mary Billings was born in Rhode Island on July 6, 1892, the daughter of James Billings and Lillian (Miller). Her mother died on August 17, 1903 at the age of thirty-seven. In 1900, she was an inmate of the Rhode Island State Home and School, along with her sister, Harriet (ten), and her brother, Thomas (fourteen). Her sister, Annie (thirteen), was a boarder in the home of the Peckham family of South Kingstown. Her brother, James (thirteen), was an inmate at the State Almshouse. She was an Oaklawn School inmate in 1910 along with Harriet. Thomas was still an inmate at the State Home and School and James, who was reported to be able to read and write and attended school, was now at the State Home and School as well.

Harriet Madeline Billings was born in Rhode Island on May 29, 1890. Her sister and family are discussed above. She married in 1911. Her husband died in Vermont on December 4, 1913, at the age of twenty-five, from a hemorrhage caused by typhoid fever. She died in Vermont on January 29, 1914, at the age of twenty-four, leaving a two-year-old daughter.

Caroline E. Bingel was born in Germany in February 1883, the daughter of Moritz Bingel Anna (Rosler). Her father was a native of Griegshein, Germany. In 1900, before being committed to the school, she resided on Faith Street in Providence, Rhode Island with her parents and siblings—Henry (nineteen), Ludwig (eleven), and Frederick (one). She was an Oaklawn School inmate in 1900.

Emma Benaway was born in Connecticut in July 1887. She was an Oaklawn School inmate in 1900.

Violet M. Brown was born in Rhode Island in 1911, the daughter of Arthur Brown and Bertha (Smith). In 1915, she resided in North Kingstown with her parents, brother Alfred (two), and maternal grandfather Samuel Smith. Her father was employed as a weaver at a tape mill. In 1925, she resided on Post Road in North Kingstown with her mother, stepfather Albert Taylor, siblings Alfred and Arthur (nine), grandfather Samuel Smith, and half-siblings Leslie (three), Samuel (two), and Lillian (nine months). A half-sister, Florence, was born in 1926. A half-sister, Helen, was born in 1929 and died in 1930. She was an Oaklawn School inmate in 1925 and 1930. She worked as a laundress within the facility in 1930.

Isabella E. Brown was born in Rhode Island in 1909. She was an Oaklawn School inmate in 1925.

Catherine Buski/Burke was born in 1881. She was an Oaklawn School inmate in 1900.

Pearl Booth was born on April 10, 1924, in Rhode Island, the daughter of Richard Booth and Helen (Whitaker). Her father was from Connecticut and her mother from New York. In 1925, she resided on Blackstone Street in Providence, Rhode Island, with her parents and siblings, Edward (five) and George (two). Two siblings had died young—Beatrice at less than a year of age in 1925, and Arthur at less than a year of age in 1921. In 1930, she was a ward of the Rhode Island State Home and School and remained there until at least 1935. By 1940, her mother was married to John Kirby and lived in Providence. She was an Oaklawn School inmate in 1940.

Dora Brais was born in Central Falls, Rhode Island on October 20, 1902, the daughter of John Brais and Eliza (DeRoy). In 1910, she resided on John Street in Pawtucket with her parents and siblings—George (twenty-one), Frank (seventeen), Eliza (fifteen), Joseph (twelve), Alphons (nine), Eva (five), and Louise (three). Her father was employed as a loom fixer at a silk mill. Only nine children survived of the eighteen her mother had given birth to. In 1915, she was an orphan residing at St. Francis Orphanage on St. Joseph Street in Woonsocket. She was an Oaklawn School inmate in 1920.

Theodora Bolis was born in Rhode Island in 1906, the daughter of Russian natives George Bolis and Petronella (Westfield). She was an Oaklawn School inmate in 1920, at which time her parents and siblings—Polikarpa (fourteen), Regina (twelve), and Dominick (ten)—resided on Valley Street in Providence.

Marion Blanchard was born in Rhode Island in 1914. An Oaklawn School inmate in 1930, she did farm work within the facility.

Eva Z. Berry was born in Maine in December 1884. She was an Oaklawn School inmate in 1900.

Florence May Bender was born in Rhode Island on July 27, 1883, the daughter of Charles Bender and Annie (Jordan). She was an Oaklawn School inmate in 1900. Prior to becoming an inmate, in 1900, she had resided in Johnston with her grandparents Henry and Mary Jordan and her siblings, Lillian (nineteen) and Clara (eleven). Her grandfather was employed as a day laborer. In 1904, she married Arthur Grover. She died in 1941 at the age of fifty-eight.

Helene E. Burdick was born in Rhode Island January 10, 1909. In 1915, she resided with her grandparents, Dennis and Josephine Glavin, in the village of Kenyon in Richmond, Rhode Island. Her grandfather was employed as a retail grocery salesman. She was an Oaklawn School inmate in 1925.

Bertha Brunelle was born in Massachusetts in 1908. She was an Oaklawn School inmate in 1925.

Bertha M. Brown was born in Connecticut in 1883. She was an Oaklawn School inmate in 1900.

Margaret N. Baker was born in Rhode Island in 1903. She was an Oaklawn School inmate in 1925.

Mary Barrett was born in Massachusetts in 1910. She was an Oaklawn School inmate in 1925.

Florence M. Borden was born in Massachusetts on April 1, 1911, the daughter of Clifford Borden and Edith (Austin). In 1915, she resided in Providence, Rhode

Island, with her parents. In 1920, she resided with her parents and siblings on Abbott Street in Providence. Her father was employed as a hotel porter. In 1925, she resided in Providence with her father and siblings—Gladys (eight), Ralph and Marlan (both one). An Oaklawn School inmate in 1930, she cooked within the facility.

Clara May Broome was born on August 8, 1911, the daughter of Thomas Broome and Gertie (Broadfield). Her father died on December 15, 1914, at the age of thirty-nine. Her siblings included Thomas (born 1903), Florry (born 1898), Carrie (born 1900), Martha (born 1906), Rose (born 1909), Walter (born 1914 and died 1915 at the age of ten months), and Isabel (born 1912). In 1915, she resided in Providence, Rhode Island, with her mother, Florry, Carrie, Thomas, Martha, and Isabel. Her mother was employed as a mill spinner. Later that year, she was placed in a Rhode Island orphanage with Isabel. In 1920, Clara, Isabel, and Martha were inmates at the Rhode Island State Home and School. An Oaklawn School inmate in 1930, she worked as a waitress within the facility. In 1930 and 1940, Isabel, who reportedly had a third-grade education, was an inmate at the Exeter School for the Feeble-Minded. In 1935, Clara resided on Princess Street in Cranston and, in 1940, resided in a lodging house in Palm Beach, Florida and was employed as a private maid. She died on June 14, 1965, and was buried with her sister Isabel in Highland Memorial Park in Johnston, Rhode Island. Isabel died in 1975 and neither ever married. Gertie Broome, their mother, died in 1945.

Agnes Bannon was born in England in 1882. She migrated in 1889. Her parents were natives of Ireland. She was an Oaklawn School inmate in 1900.

Adella May Bailey was born in Rhode Island on November 17, 1923. In 1925, she lived with her parents and her siblings, one older and two younger, on Buttonwoods Avenue in Warwick, Rhode Island. The family was at the same address in 1930 and her father was employed as a dairy farmer. Still at that address in 1935, she attended Buttonwood Public School. She was an Oaklawn School inmate in 1940.

Pearl Etta Boyd was born in Rhode Island in September 1882. During an entertainment in April 1897 to celebrate Mrs. Forbush's birthday, she performed a solo of "Lock on the Chicken Coop Door." During the school's Christmas cantata *The Capture of Santa Claus*, in 1897, she played a fruit fairy. She was an Oaklawn School inmate in 1896 and until at least 1900. While there, in November 1896, she wrote to the superintendent, "I thought I would write a few lines to let you know I am well. I am going to be a good girl so I can get home. But that is not why I am going to be a good girl, just to get home, I am going to be good for it is right. I am glad I came here. It has done me good. I did not know how to read or write. I did not care to read or write, but now I like to. The girls say that they like Miss Grace Eastman and Mrs. Eastman and, Mr. Eastman, for they are so good to them. From one of your girls."

Annie Bogan was born in Rhode Island in September of 1891. By 1900, she was an inmate at the Rhode Island Catholic Orphan Asylum. She was an Oaklawn School inmate in 1910.

May Lawrenz/Burton was born in 1871, the daughter of James and Margaret Lawrenz. In 1876, she was living in Brockton, Massachusetts, with her parents and siblings, Frank (seven) and Joseph (three). That year, she and her siblings were handed over to the Home for Destitute Children in Brockton when her father could no longer support the family. She was adopted by a Mrs. Burton of Providence and later committed to the Oaklawn School. Her brother searched for her and located her there in 1888. She was an Oaklawn inmate until at least 1888.

Mary Casey was an Oaklawn School inmate in 1897.

Noella Loretta Cote was born in Woonsocket, Rhode Island, on December 24, 1919, the daughter of Theodore Cote and Marie (Thibeault). In 1925, she resided on Winthrop Street in Woonsocket with her parents and siblings—Doris (six), Evelyn (three), and Theodore (one). In 1930, she resided on Paradis Avenue in Woonsocket with her parents and siblings—Doris, Evelyn, Theodore, Rita (one), and Leo (newborn). Her father was employed as a worsted mill watchman. She later resided on Elm Street in Woonsocket and attended Hudson Academy Senior High School. She completed the eighth grade. She was an Oaklawn School inmate in 1935. In 1940, she was an inmate at the Rhode Island State Reformatory for Women.

Katherine J. Cheevers was born in Rhode Island in 1892, the daughter of John Cheevers and Katie (Calhoun), natives of Ireland. In 1900, she lived in Manhattan, New York with her parents and two younger siblings. She was married for the second time in 1925. She was an Oaklawn School inmate in 1910.

Louisa E. Capwell was born in Massachusetts in April 1884. She was an Oaklawn School inmate in 1900.

Virginia Weeden Craighead was born in Rhode Island on February 14, 1919, the daughter of Christopher Craighead and Mabel (Johnson), and was of African-American descent. In 1920, she resided on Halton Street in Providence with her parents, brother Christopher (four) and her mother's siblings, Mildred Johnson (seventeen) and Harrison Johnson (twenty-one). Her father was employed as a mill laborer. In 1925, she resided on Benedict Street in Providence with her parents and siblings, Christopher and Althia (three months). In 1930, she resided on Walds Street in Providence with her parents and siblings, Christopher, Althia, and Edward (two). Her father was employed as a furniture mover. Prior to becoming an inmate, she resided on Salem Street in Providence. She was an Oaklawn School inmate in 1935.

Jessie M. Cornell was born in Rhode Island on March 15, 1906, the daughter of Frank Cornell and Louisa (Hunt). In 1910, she resided on Bayside Annex Street in Warwick with her parents and siblings—Walter (eight), Grace (six), and Sarah (two). Her father was employed as a teamer. In 1920, she resided with her parents on Rugby Street in Providence and had additional siblings—Harriet (eight), Mildred (five), Catherine (three), and Frank (one). Her father was employed as a switchman at an electric car company. Additional siblings included Gertrude (born 1920 and died 1921), Gertrude (born 1922), and Doris (born 1925). She was an Oaklawn School inmate in 1925.

Mabel Chandler was born in Rhode Island in November 1881. She was an Oaklawn School inmate in 1900.

Thelma E. Cain was born in Rhode Island on January 12, 1911, the daughter of Louis Cain of Virginia and Mary Lavinia (Freeman) of Rhode Island and was of African-American descent. In 1930, she resided on Glen Drive in Warwick, Rhode Island, with her mother, her stepfather Warren Boyd, and her step-siblings from her mother's second marriage, her step-father's previous marriage and the baby the couple had just had together: Warren Boyd (twelve), Harold Boyd (ten), Walter Scott, (ten), Gertrude Scott (seven), and Barbara Boyd (one). Her stepfather was employed as a cook at a boarding house, and her mother was employed as a private cleaning lady. An Oaklawn School inmate in 1930, she did cleaning within the facility.

Winifred Marguerite Canty was born at the State Infirmary in Tewksbury, Massachusetts, on July 29, 1912, the daughter of Martin Canty and Gertrude (Coveny). At the time of her birth, her father was employed as a furniture polisher. Prior to her birth, her parents had a stillborn infant on October 6, 1910. In 1920, she was an inmate at St. Vincent De Paul Infant Asylum. An Oaklawn School inmate in 1930, she did cleaning within the facility.

Beatrice Corbeille was born in Rhode Island in 1915, the daughter of James Corbeille and Rose (Frigon). In 1920, she resided with her family on King Avenue in Stafford Springs, Connecticut. In 1925, the family lived on Clinton Street in Woonsocket, Rhode Island. Her father was employed in a woolen mill. She had two older siblings and four younger. One of her brothers died at the age of sixteen on June 14, 1929. In 1930, her parents and siblings were residing on Boydon Street in Woonsocket. Her father was employed as a trucker. An Oaklawn School inmate in 1930, she did cleaning within the facility.

Olivia Connoly was born in Rhode Island in 1913. An Oaklawn School inmate in 1930, she did cleaning within the facility.

Floridine Commean was born in Rhode Island in 1904, the daughter of Henry and Roseanna Commean. In 1910, she resided on Diamond Street in Providence with her parents and her brother Felix (three); her brothers Joseph Genton (twenty-one) and Henry Genton (nineteen) from her mother's first marriage; and brother Fred Commean (sixteen) from her father's first marriage. Her father was employed as a house carpenter. Of the nine children her mother had given birth to, only four were still alive. She was an Oaklawn School inmate in 1920.

Rose Chaput was born in Canada in 1902. She was an Oaklawn School inmate in 1920.

Lilian Coleman was born in Canada in 1893. She was an Oaklawn School inmate in 1910.

Lillian Cook was born in Rhode Island in 1906. She was an Oaklawn School inmate in 1920.

Lena Cook was an Oaklawn School inmate in 1897.

Ella Chin was born in Rhode Island on February 20, 1923. In 1930, she resided on Warners Lane in Providence with her parents, who were natives of China, and siblings Mary (eight), Emma (six), Anita (four), and Rose (three). Her father was employed as a salesman for a noodle manufacturer. In 1935, she resided with her family on Oak Street in Providence and attended Gilbert Stuart Public School. She was an Oaklawn School inmate in 1940 along with her sister, Emma.

Emma Chin was born in Rhode Island on August 11, 1924. She was an Oaklawn School inmate in 1940 along with her sister, Ella (above).

Gertrude Evelyn Cavanaugh was born in Foster, Rhode Island on May 22, 1909, the daughter of Owen Olney Cavanaugh and Cora Evelyn (Hopkins), who were Rhode Island natives. In 1910, she lived in Foster with her parents and siblings Flora (nine), Annie (seven), John (six), Earl (five), and Edward (three). Her father worked as a blacksmith. She was an Oaklawn School inmate in 1920 until at least 1925. In 1930, she was living in Providence with wholesale paint salesman Edward Langlois and his wife, Mazie, as their maid. On June 30 of that year, she married George Usher in Rhode Island.

Margaret Jennie "Maggie" Cullerton was born in Ireland in March 1886, she immigrated in 1887 and was the daughter of William Cullerton and Ann (McCassey). Siblings included James, Bridget, Elizabeth, Patrick, Katherine, Joseph, and Annie. Her father died in Woonsocket, Rhode Island, on January 1, 1902, at the age of fifty-seven. Her mother died on February 11, 1889, in Woonsocket at the age of thirty-six. She was an Oaklawn School inmate in 1896 and until at least 1900. Her sister, Annie, was also an Oaklawn School inmate. During the school's Thanksgiving entertainment of 1896, she publicly recited "Little Bess."

Beatrice N. Cournoyer was born in Canada in 1909. She was an Oaklawn inmate in 1925.

Annie L. Cullerton was born in Ireland. She migrated in 1887 and was the daughter of William Cullerton and Ann (McCassey). Siblings included James, Bridget, Elizabeth, Patrick, Katherine, Joseph, and Margaret. Her father died in Woonsocket, Rhode Island, on January 1, 1902 at the age of fifty-seven. Her mother died on February 11, 1889, in Woonsocket at the age of thirty-six. She was an Oaklawn School inmate in 1897 until at least 1900. She died in Rhode Island on June 18, 1908, at the age of twenty-one. Her sister, Margaret, was also an Oaklawn School inmate.

Lillian Mae Cleveland was born in New Hampshire on September 17, 1921, the daughter of Frederick Elma Cleveland and Emma Jane (Hunt). In 1930, she resided on Blackstone Street in Providence, Rhode Island, with her parents and siblings Fred (two) and Evelyn (one month). Her father was employed as a painter. In 1935, she resided with her family on Fillmore Street in Providence and attended Esak Hopkins Public School. She was an Oaklawn School inmate in 1940.

Mary E. Conley was born in Scotland in October 1883. She migrated in 1897. She was an Oaklawn School inmate in 1900.

Amelia Charbello was born in Italy in 1881. During the school's play *Old Times Made New*, in May 1897, she played Pocahontas. She was an Oaklawn School inmate in 1896 and until at least 1897. While there in November 1896, she wrote to the superintendent, "I will write you a few lines to let you know that I am going to be a good girl and help all the girls all I can. When I go to school will try to learn all I can. Mr. Eastman, I want to do right because it is right and because God wants us to do right. I am sure I will enjoy all the good times you will give us. I will close now."

During the school's Thanksgiving entertainment of 1896, she and Edith Bailey performed a duet of the song "Softly Over Bethlehem." During an entertainment in April 1897 to celebrate Mrs. Forbush's birthday, she did a recitation of "Dolly and Her Mamma."

Harriet Cohen was an Oaklawn School inmate in 1896. During the school's Thanksgiving entertainment of 1896, she publicly recited "The Buttons" and "Columbus."

Lena Deplacito was born in Rhode Island in 1906. Her parents were natives of Italy. She was an Oaklawn School inmate in 1920.

Joanna Degrue was born in Rhode Island in 1906. An Oaklawn School inmate in 1930, she did cleaning within the facility.

Mary Daley/Dailey, during the school's Christmas cantata *The Capture of Santa Claus* in 1897, played Santa Claus. During the school's play *Old Times Made New*, in May 1897, she played Mother Bickerdick. She was an Oaklawn School inmate in 1897.

Mary Ellen Donahoe was born in Providence, Rhode Island on December 7, 1884, the daughter of John and Annie Donahoe. She was an Oaklawn School inmate in 1900.

Eva Gertrude Dawson was born in Rhode Island on March 1, 1889, the daughter of Peter Dawson and Alice (Bailey), natives of England. She had three older siblings and one younger sibling. She was an Oaklawn School inmate in 1900. On August 1, 1908, she married John McLeod in Massachusetts.

Alice M. Dyer was born in Rhode Island in 1909, the daughter of Byron Dyer. In 1915, she was residing on East Greenwich Avenue in West Warwick with her paternal grandmother Cornelia, her father, and her brother Fred (nine). Her father was employed in the dye works. In 1920, she was residing in the same place with her father, grandmother, and brother. She was able to read and write and was attending school. She was an Oaklawn School inmate in 1925.

Johanna J. Dugan was born in Scotland in December 1885. She was an Oaklawn School inmate in 1900.

Josie Dugan, during the school's Thanksgiving entertainment of 1896, publicly recited "Helping." During an entertainment in April 1897 to celebrate Mrs. Forbush's birthday, she performed a solo called "Chinese Song." During the school's Christmas cantata *The Capture of Santa Claus*, in 1897, she played one of the children in the cast. She was an Oaklawn School inmate in 1896 and until at least 1897.

Bertha L. Decker was born in New York in November 1894, the daughter of William Decker and Rosa (Staples). She was an Oaklawn School inmate in 1910.

Dorothy H. Dyer was born in Connecticut in 1909. An Oaklawn School inmate in 1925 and until at least 1930, she did cooking within the facility in 1930.

Irene E. Drury was born in Rhode Island in 1909, the daughter of George Drury and Emma (Holbrook). In 1910, she resided on Greene Street in Woonsocket with her family. In 1915, she resided in Woonsocket with her parents and siblings Esther (fourteen), Marion (nine), and Lillian (four). Her father was employed as a lineman for the electric light company. She was an Oaklawn School inmate in 1925.

Mary Duarte was born in Massachusetts in 1883. Her parents were natives of Portugal. She was committed to Oaklawn School on August 14, 1899, after being charged on two warrants—the theft of $20 from Mary E. Carmon and the theft of $9 from Julia Vera. She pleaded guilty to both charges and was sentenced to remain at the school until 1901.

Mary V. Diaz was born in Massachusetts in July 1892. Her parents were natives of Portugal. She was an Oaklawn School inmate in 1910.

Maude Downey was born in Scotland in 1892. She was an Oaklawn School inmate in 1910.

Norma Pearl Diamond was born in Massachusetts on October 30, 1919, the daughter of William and Frances Diamond. Her father was from Russia and her mother from England. In 1930, she resided on Lawrence Street in Boston with her parents and sister, Zelda (four). Her father was employed as a tailor. She was an Oaklawn School inmate in 1935. In 1940, she was residing in a large boarding house in Washington D.C. and employed as a sales clerk. She died in Warwick on January 15, 1947 at the age of twenty-eight. She is buried in Lincoln Park Cemetery.

Dora Diquattro was born in Rhode Island on January 8, 1919, the daughter of Pasqual and Carmela Diquattro, natives of Italy. She had five older siblings and her father was a street work laborer. In 1930 she was an inmate at the Exeter School for the Feeble-Minded where it is recorded that she had attended school and was able to read and write. She was an Oaklawn School inmate in 1935.

Nellie Dwyer was an Oaklawn School inmate in 1896.

Stella May Douglas was born in Hanson, Massachusetts on November 3, 1904, the daughter of Arthur Douglas and Mina (Robbins). At the time of her birth, her mother was fifteen and her father was eighteen. In 1910, she resided on High Street in Norwell with her parents and siblings Edith (four), Leslie (two), and Florence (one). Her father was employed as a teamer. She was an Oaklawn School inmate in 1920. During that time, her family resided at Franklin Street in Whitman. Her father was employed as a shoe factory laborer.

Mildred Edmonds was born in Rhode Island in 1903. She was an Oaklawn School inmate in 1920.

Charlotte A. Eddy was born in April 1890, the daughter of David and Ada Eddy. In 1900, she resided in Providence, Rhode Island, with her parents and siblings Frank (twenty-one), George (seven), and her mother's oldest son from a previous marriage, Luke Read (twenty-seven). Her father was employed as an engineer. She was an Oaklawn School inmate in 1910.

Forcier Exgefder was born in Rhode Island in July 1882. She was an Oaklawn School inmate in 1900.

Mabel Forget was born in Massachusetts on June 11, 1921. In 1930, she was a lodger in the home of James McCabe and his wife on North Main Street in Pawtucket, Rhode Island. In 1935, she resided on Exchange Street in Pawtucket and attended Jenks Junior High Public School. She was an Oaklawn School inmate in 1940.

Minnie J. Ford was born in Rhode Island in January 1884. She was an Oaklawn School inmate in 1900.

Alice Foster was believed to have been born in 1876 or 1877. She was committed to Oaklawn School on December 9, 1889, after being charged with being a vagrant and disorderly person. She pleaded guilty and was sentenced to five years at the school.

Nellie Fry, during the school's play *Old Times Made New*, in May 1897, played the pharaoh's daughter. She was an Oaklawn School inmate in 1897.

Laura G. Foeri was born on July 10, 1880, in East Providence, Rhode Island, the daughter of Augustus Foeri and Phebe (Brownell). By 1885, Phebe had died, and Augustus was boarding in Providence and employed as a leather worker. During an entertainment in April 1897 to celebrate Mrs. Forbush's birthday, she did a recitation of "The Modest Wit." During the school's play *Old Times Made New*, in May 1897, she played Cornella. She died on April 6, 1916, in Providence, of a heart ailment, at the age of thirty-six. She was an Oaklawn School inmate in 1897.

Gertrude Farrell was born in Massachusetts in June 1883. She was an Oaklawn School inmate in 1900.

Florence (surname unknown) was sentenced to Oaklawn School on July 2, 1893, for five years, charged with "being disobedient and annoying to her parents in many ways." She had been residing in Arctic Center, Rhode Island, at the time.

Minnie Finnegan was born in Rhode Island in December 1885. Her parents were natives of Ireland. During the school's Christmas cantata *The Capture of Santa Claus*, in 1897, she played a frost fairy. She was an Oaklawn School inmate in 1896 and 1897. During the school's 1896 Thanksgiving entertainment, she publicly recited "Dolly." She was paroled to "a good home" on August 20, 1898, becoming an inmate again in 1900. While there, in November 1896, she wrote to the superintendent, "You said that you like us to write you a few lines so I thought that I would. I thank you very much for your kindness to me and I am going to show you that I am thankful by doing my very best and keep all the rules and be a good girl. I must close now. Good bye! From one of the little girls."

Laudia B. Fontaine was born in Lowell, Massachusetts, in 1909. She was an Oaklawn School inmate in 1925.

Helen Alberson F. (surname unknown) was an Oaklawn School inmate in 1896. While there, in November 1896, she wrote to the superintendent, "I thought I would write you a few lines. I have finally made up my mind to be a good girl and to help my teachers all I can and be kind and loving to my schoolmates. I will try to improve each day I am in the school. I am glad I am here. I want to do right because it is right. Good bye!"

Ruth Amy Fenner was born in Rhode Island on May 9, 1907, the daughter of Howard Fenner and Cora (Harris). In 1910, she resided on Mercy Street in Providence with her parents and her siblings Howard (five) and Dorothy (newborn). Her father was employed as a shoe store salesman. Her sister, Dorothy, died in 1912. In 1915, she remained at the same residence with her parents and her brother, Howard. Her father was employed as an ice company driver. Her mother died in 1918 at the age of thirty-one. In 1920, she resided in Providence with her father, her paternal uncle Henry Fenner, and her brother Howard. She was an Oaklawn School inmate in 1925.

Annie E. Fuller was an Oaklawn School inmate in 1896. During the school's Thanksgiving entertainment of 1896, she publicly recited "The Reason" and "Into Her Chamber." By April 1897, she had been paroled to the home of Mrs. Albert G. (surname unknown).

Delia Flaherty was an Oaklawn School inmate in 1887. She was born in 1871, the daughter of Bridget Flaherty and an unknown father. She died on March 10, 1887, of pulmonary consumption/tuberculosis and was buried in the school's cemetery.

Helen Faluett was born in Massachusetts in 1905. Her parents were natives of Italy. She was an Oaklawn School inmate in 1920.

Catherine E. Field was born in Rhode Island on March 16, 1919, the daughter of Warren and Carrie Field. In 1920, she resided on Metacomet Avenue in Warren with her forty-year-old mother, seventy-seven-year-old father, and siblings Carrie (fifteen), Ruth (thirteen), Evelyn (six), Hattie (five), and George (two). Her father was not employed. In 1925, she resided on Meadow Street in Warren with her parents and siblings Carrie, Ruth, Hattie, George, and Evelyn. In 1930, the family was residing at the same location; however, Ruth was not living there, and she had two additional siblings—Daniel (six) and Caroline (three). Her sister,

Evelyn, lived with them and now had the married surname Desmarais. She was an Oaklawn School inmate in 1935.

Pearl Fletcher was born in Rhode Island in 1912, the daughter of Arnold Fletcher and Rosaline (Fournier). In 1920 until at least 1925, she resided on Houston Avenue in Newport with her grandparents Arthur and Mary Fournier, their two young children, and her sister Edna (six). Her grandfather was employed as a carpenter. An Oaklawn School inmate in 1930, she did farm work within the facility.

Elizabeth Graviera was born in Rhode Island in 1905. Her father was from Ireland and her mother from England. She was an Oaklawn School inmate in 1920, at which time she was married.

Bessie F. Garfinkle was born in Rhode Island on June 6, 1917, the daughter of Hyman and Gertrude Garfinkle. In 1930, she resided on Ambrose Street in Providence with her parents and siblings Zelda (sixteen), Joseph (fifteen), and Harry (eight). Her father was from Russia and her mother from Massachusetts. Her parents were both employed as poultry clippers in a poultry shop. She was an Oaklawn School inmate in 1935.

Anna Gardner was born in Rhode Island in 1906. She was an Oaklawn School inmate in 1920.

Rose Gallagher was born in Rhode Island in June 1891. In 1900, she was an inmate of Rhode Island Catholic Orphan Asylum. She was an Oaklawn School inmate in 1910.

Catherine Gonska was born in Rhode Island in 1908, the daughter of John and Theophelia Gonska, natives of Poland. In 1920, she resided on Camden Street in Providence with her parents and siblings Florence (twenty), Helen (sixteen), Adam (fifteen), John (ten), Felis (eight), and Josephine (seven). Her father was employed as a machine shop laborer and her mother was employed as a silk mill machine operator. She was an Oaklawn School inmate in 1925.

Ethel Gibbs was born in 1895. She was an Oaklawn School inmate in 1910.

Mabel Gibbs was an Oaklawn School inmate in 1897. During the school's Christmas cantata *The Capture of Santa Claus*, in 1897, she played Jack Frost.

Evelyn Green was born in Massachusetts in 1915. An Oaklawn School inmate in 1930, she did cleaning within the facility.

Hannah May Gardner was born in Rhode Island on June 28, 1891. In 1900, she was an inmate at the Providence State Home and School. She was an Oaklawn School inmate in 1910.

Cora Godin was born in Rhode Island in 1894, the daughter of Joseph Godin and an unknown mother. Her father was French-Canadian. She was an Oaklawn School inmate in 1910. At the time she was an inmate, her widowed father resided on Arnold Street in Woonsocket with her siblings Picena (eighteen) and Joseph (fifteen), as well as a boarder, Joseph League (twenty-nine). Her father was employed as a teamster and Picena was employed as a spinner in a worsted mill.

Marion Gorton was born in Rhode Island in 1894. She was an Oaklawn School inmate in 1910.

Blanche Gage was born in Rhode Island in 1905. Her parents were natives of France. She was an Oaklawn School inmate in 1920.

Stella Gardner was received at Oaklawn School on May 7, 1895, and was an inmate until at least 1896. It was recorded that she was working as a tailor and that her parents were dead.

Irene M. Goodreau was born in Rhode Island in 1905, the daughter of Frank Goodreau and Catharine (Walsh). Her father was a bricklayer and, following her birth, she resided in Pawtucket with her parents and siblings Francis (five), William (four), George (three), and Charles (three). In 1910, she resided on Lonsdale Avenue in Pawtucket with her parents and siblings Francis, William, George, Harry (three), and Elisie (two). She was an Oaklawn School inmate in 1920.

Aurore T. Gaumond was born on February 10, 1924, the daughter of Ernest Gaumond and Antonia (Bernard). In 1925, she resided on Hadley Avenue in Central Falls, Rhode Island, with her parents and siblings. In 1930, she resided on Garfield Street in Central Falls with her mother, her siblings—Omer (twenty-four), Alfred (seventeen), Jeanette (fifteen), Marie (thirteen), Rita (ten), Raymond (eight), Flore (four), and Yvone (one)—as well as her mother's nieces and nephews—Alexander (twenty-nine), Vepalian (twenty-five), and Yvone (twenty-seven). In 1935, she resided on Pine Street in Central Falls and attended West Side Public Grammar School. She was an Oaklawn School inmate in 1940.

Dorothy Germain was born in 1926. In 1935, she resided in Woonsocket. She was an Oaklawn School inmate in 1940.

Irene Greenwood was born in Rhode Island in 1912. An Oaklawn School inmate in 1930, she did cleaning within the facility.

Ina Mae Gardiner was born in Massachusetts on February 21, 1907. Her education did not go past the fourth grade. She was an Oaklawn School inmate in 1925. In 1930, she was an inmate at the Exeter School for the Feeble-Minded. On November 27, 1935, she was pregnant and an inmate at the Rhode Island State Infirmary. She gave birth to a son there on February 22, 1936. In 1940, she was once again an inmate at the Exeter School for the Feeble-Minded.

Mary Gendron was an Oaklawn School inmate in 1897.

Clara Gedden was born in Russia in 1906. She was an Oaklawn School inmate in 1920.

Alesaudri/Alexandria Gladde was born in Canada in 1906. She was an Oaklawn School inmate in 1920.

Agnes H. (surname unknown) was an Oaklawn School inmate in 1896. While there, in November 1896, she wrote to the superintendent, "As you are trying in every way to make us girls happy and to make our school more like home, we should in return do our best in doing what will please you. This I am going to do. There are so many ways in which to show we appreciate your kindness but, first of all I think, is in telling the truth. Our new teachers will always have my respect and our rules I am going to keep. Being kind and helpful to one another is another thing I can improve on. With the help of God and all our instructors, I hope to succeed in becoming a better girl. Meaning to fulfil my promise in this letter, I will now close. From one of your loving girls." By April 1897, she had been paroled to either the Johnson family or Captain and Mrs. Lee.

Georgette Aldea Heuberger was born on May 24, 1924, the daughter of Frederick Heuberger and Aldea (Parent). In 1930, she resided on Metacom Avenue in Warren, Rhode Island, with her parents and brother Lester (six months). Her father was employed as a building carpenter. In 1935, she resided on Oak Street in Warren and attended Main Street Public School. She was an Oaklawn School inmate in 1940.

Ethel E. Hornby was born in Rhode Island in December 1890, the daughter of John Hornby and Sarah (Hauxley). Her father was from Rhode Island and her mother from England. Her siblings included John (born 1892), Thomas (born 1900), Hilda (born 1902), Gladys (born 1902), Helen (born 1904), Bernard (born 1908), and Alice (born and died at the age of six months in 1909). In 1900, Ethel and John were inmates at the Rhode Island State Home and School. Her mother and father, who was employed as a jewelry polisher, lived on Clarendon Avenue in Providence at that time with their son, Thomas. She was an Oaklawn School inmate in 1910. Her father had died on September 27, 1909, at the age of thirty-nine and her mother lived with her brother, her daughter Gladys, and her son Thomas. Bernard was an inmate at St. Mary's Orphanage in East Providence in 1910 and at St. Andrews Industrial School in Bristol in 1920. By 1930, Sarah and Bernard were living with Hilda and her husband.

Rose T. Hamilton was born in July 1885 in Rhode Island. During the school's Thanksgiving entertainment of 1896, she publicly recited "Who Can Answer?" During the school's Christmas cantata "The Capture of Santa Claus in 1897, she played a chimney elf. She was an Oaklawn School inmate in 1896 and at least until 1900. While there in November 1896, she wrote to the superintendent, "I would be delighted to write to you. I will try and be a good girl and help Mrs. Forbush all I can. I will do my work well and have my lessons perfectly. Dear Mr. Eastman, I would like to come and stay with you a week or two days very much. I know Mrs. Forbush will try and help me to do my best. I do really hope, Mr. Eastman, that you will send a letter saying 'yes, come and stay two days or a week.' From your sincere friend."

Emily Howard was an Oaklawn School inmate in 1896. By 1897, she had been paroled back to her home.

Margaret C. Healey was born in Rhode Island in 1903. Her mother was from Scotland and her father from Ireland. She was an Oaklawn School inmate in 1925.

Sarah A. Heagney was born on August 8, 1885 in Rhode Island, the daughter of Francis and Sarah Heagney, natives of Ireland. She was an Oaklawn School inmate in 1900. In 1910, she was an inmate at the Providence County Jail and worked there in the sewing room.

Maggie Heagney was an Oaklawn School inmate in 1897.

Lizzie M. Hamilton was born in Rhode Island in April 1886. She was an Oaklawn School inmate in 1900.

Florence M. Hood was born in 1907. She was an Oaklawn School inmate in 1925.

Eva B. Hitchins was born in Rhode Island in 1911, the daughter of Henry Hitchins and Lora (Bergeron). In 1915, she lived in Pawtucket, Rhode Island, with her parents and her brother Henry (six). Her father was employed as a cotton spinner. Her mother died on October 4, 1918, at the age of thirty-one. She was an Oaklawn School inmate in 1925. In 1930, she was a prisoner at the Rhode Island Reformatory for Women and worked as a cleaner within the facility.

Hattie Handy was born in 1910. An Oaklawn School inmate in 1930, she cooked within the facility.

Elizabeth Hellew was born in Rhode Island on August 2, 1918, the daughter of Charles Hellew and Margaret (Corey). She had a sister, Helen, born in 1916. In 1935, she was recorded as suffering from heart trouble. She was an Oaklawn School inmate in 1935. She died in 1958 at the age of forty and was buried in Saint John the Baptist Cemetery in Warren.

Helena Hargrove was born in New Jersey on April 14, 1924, and was of African-American descent. In 1935, she resided at 16th Street in Providence, Rhode Island and attended Kenyon Street Public School. She was an Oaklawn School inmate in 1940.

Mary Haskell was born in 1884. She was an Oaklawn School inmate in 1897 until 1900. During the school's 1897 production of the Christmas cantata *The Capture of Santa Claus*, she played one of the fruit fairies. She died on November 6, 1900, and was the seventh (and last known) inmate to be buried in the Oaklawn School cemetery. The daughter of Vincent and Kate Haskell, she was sixteen years and eleven months old when she succumbed to pulmonalis and exhaustion.

Margaret Harrington was born in England in 1902. She was an Oaklawn School inmate in 1920.

Irene C. H. Higginson was born in Rhode Island on December 31, 1918, the daughter of Roughsledge Higginson and Angeline (Radloff). In 1920, she resided at Bullock Point Avenue in East Providence with her parents and siblings Etta (nine), Florence (six), and Roughsledge (four). Her father was employed as a jewelry shop jeweler. In 1925, she resided on Silver Spring Avenue in East Providence with her parents and siblings Etta, Florence, Roughsledge, and Louis (two). Her father died on October 12, 1929, at the age of fifty-five. In 1930, she was an inmate at the Deaconess Home in Fall River, Massachusetts, a school for troubled young girls. She was an Oaklawn School inmate in 1935.

Mildred Hopkins was born in Rhode Island on December 12, 1920. She was an Oaklawn School inmate in 1935.

Margaret Healey was born in 1905. An Oaklawn School inmate in 1930, she cooked within the facility.

Mary Hartnett was born in Rhode Island in 1895. Her parents were natives of Ireland. She was an Oaklawn School inmate in 1910.

Hattie Howard was born in 1893. She was an Oaklawn School inmate in 1910.

Ethel Hutton was born in Rhode Island in 1894 and was of African-American descent. She was an Oaklawn School inmate in 1910.

Emma Harrison was born in New York in 1897 and was of African-American descent. She was an Oaklawn School inmate in 1910.

Adeline Josephine Harvey was born on October 1, 1884, in Lincoln, Rhode Island, the daughter of James Brown Harvey and Virginia (Devoto), natives of Scotland. Her siblings included Angelina (born 1863), Jemima (born 1865), Vincent (born 1868), Caroline (born 1870), Alfred (born 1872), Virginia (born 1874), and Agnes (born 1880). In 1885, she was residing in Lincoln with her parents and siblings. She was an Oaklawn School inmate in 1899. In March 1899, she was being detained at the facility pending action by a judge on the charge of attempting to kill her father by poison. She pleaded guilty, showing no remorse or fear of punishment. Her father had entered the complaint on Saturday, March 2, 1899. She had been residing with her father and her stepmother in Central Falls and was considered a smart and industrious girl. Without any known motive, she sprinkled over her father's dinner pail enough creosote to make him deathly ill, if not kill him. He noticed the pungent odor before eating the food and called the police. She was arrested and proved to be puzzling to the court. Despite facing a sentence of up to twenty years in prison, she showed no concern. She told police that they could not send her to the State Prison under the Juvenile Offenders Act. A well-developed and stout girl, she appeared to want to go to the reform school. As she had never shown any degenerate behavior in the past, it was believed she was suffering from a mental affliction.

Aina/Ania Hegglow/Heggsfors was born in Massachusetts in 1894. Her parents were natives of Sweden and Finland. She was an Oaklawn School inmate in 1910.

Lilian Hatch was born in Connecticut in 1892. She was an Oaklawn School inmate in 1910.

Marion Haddow was born in Central Falls, Rhode Island, on December 6, 1903, the daughter of William Haddow and Marion (Conn). Her brother, Joseph, died of convulsions in 1908 at the age of four months. In 1910, she resided on Cherry Street in Norfolk, Massachusetts, with her mother (a native of Scotland) and siblings Margaret (fourteen), William (thirteen), Clinton (ten), Milton (eight), and Anna (three). Her mother was employed as a restaurant manager. In 1915, she resided in Central Falls with her mother and siblings Clinton, Milton, and Anna. Her mother died in 1917 at the age of forty-five. She was an Oaklawn School inmate in 1920, while Clinton was residing with his maternal aunt and Anna was an inmate at the Rhode Island State Home and School.

Annie Hayward was an Oaklawn School inmate in 1897. During the school's Christmas cantata *The Capture of Santa Claus*, in 1897, she played the snowman.

Bertha Hart was born in 1879. She was a resident of Bristol. After having been committed to Oaklawn School in 1894, she ran away in April 1897 with a boy from Sockanosset School for Boys after they both escaped. They were captured three weeks later and returned to their schools.

Margaret E. Inglesby was born in Rhode Island on November 25, 1907, the daughter of Mary and an unknown father. In 1910, she resided on Smith Street in Providence with her mother and siblings Irene (infant), Lillian (five), Frank (seven), and Florence O'Brian (thirteen), her sister from her mother's previous marriage. In 1915, she was an inmate at the Rhode Island Catholic Orphanage. An Oaklawn School inmate in 1925 and at least until 1930, she did cleaning within the facility. In 1935 and at least until 1940, she was an inmate at the Rhode Island State Hospital for Mental Diseases and was recorded as having a mental disability.

Hope Jordan was born on January 26, 1922. In 1930, she resided on Mallett Street in Providence, Rhode Island, as a foster daughter of Native American couple Olive and Minnie Jackson. Olive was employed as a cake delivery truck driver and they also had another foster daughter named Dorothy (thirteen). In 1935, she resided on Mt. Pleasant Avenue in Providence and attended Nelson Public School. She was an Oaklawn School inmate in 1940.

Myrtle Jordan was born in Rhode Island in 1912 and was of African-American descent. An Oaklawn School inmate in 1930, she cooked within the facility.

Catherine Jessop was born in Rhode Island in 1903. She was an Oaklawn School inmate in 1920.

Anna Jones was born in Rhode Island in 1903. She was an Oaklawn School inmate in 1920.

Louise V. Jones was born in Rhode Island in 1907 and was of African-American descent. In 1920, she was a boarder in the home of Henry and Lillian Mitchell on Logan Avenue in Providence who boarded four other young African-American girls. Henry was employed as a bleachery trucker. She was an Oaklawn School inmate in 1925. In 1930 until at least 1940, she was an inmate at the Exeter School for the Feeble-Minded.

Elizabeth Judge was born on December 11, 1881, in Providence, Rhode Island, the daughter of John and Mary Judge, natives of Ireland. By 1897, she was an inmate at Oaklawn School. She was later taken from Oaklawn School to the Rhode Island State Almshouse where she died on September 5, 1900. At that time her father resided in Providence. A Catholic, she was buried in the State Farm Cemetery.

Beatrice Jardin was born in Portugal in 1910. She was an Oaklawn School inmate in 1925.

Stella Jaskiel was born in Rhode Island on May 18, 1917. She was an Oaklawn School inmate in 1935.

Ethel M. Jordan was born in Rhode Island on June 10, 1917. Prior to becoming an inmate, she resided on Main Road in Charlestown, Rhode Island. She was an Oaklawn School inmate in 1935.

Louisa S. Johnson was born in Rhode Island in February 1883 and was of African-American descent. She was an Oaklawn School inmate in 1900.

Luba J. Kolny was born on April 15, 1923, the daughter of Simon Kolny and Adoleia (Rosa), natives of Russia. In 1930, she resided on Victoria Avenue in East Providence with her parents and siblings George (fifteen), John (twelve), Nina (eight), Olga (five), and Margie (one). Her father was employed as a chemical laborer. In 1935, the family was residing at the same location and she had an additional sibling Mary (four). John, a brother, was born and died in 1917. She had only completed the sixth grade. She was an Oaklawn School inmate in 1940.

Clarice Kammer was born in Rhode Island in 1904. She was an Oaklawn School inmate in 1920.

Loraine Kerwin was born in Rhode Island in 1873, the daughter of Henry F. Kerwin and Loraine (Wilbour). Her mother was first married to James Goddard, a carpenter. They had four children—Julia Goddard (born 1857 and died 1858), Susan Goddard (born 1860), William Goddard (born 1863), and Annie Goddard (born 1866). The family lived in Newport. James died in 1865 at the age of thirty-one. His widow remained in Newport, living with his mother and their three children. She was employed as a seamstress. By 1875, she was living on Walnut Street in Newport with her second husband, Henry Kerwin, also a carpenter, and their children Mabel (born 1872), Loraine, and Eliza (born 1875). She was an Oaklawn School inmate during the 1890s. She died in 1893 or 1894 of pulmonary consumption and is buried in the school's cemetery. In 1900, Henry is listed as being married, not widowed; however, he is living in a boarding house in Boston, Massachusetts, without his wife.

Edith L. Kirk was born in New York in November 1879. Her parents were natives of Scotland. During the school's play *Old Times Made New*, in May 1897, she played Cleopatra. She was an Oaklawn School inmate in 1897 until at least 1900.

Louise Knowles was born in Rhode Island on January 25, 1921, the daughter of George and Annie Knowles. Her father was from Rhode Island and her mother was from Canada. In 1925, she resided on Cranston Street in Providence with her parents and siblings Celia (eight), Rita (six), and Dorothy (three). In 1930, the family resided on Page Street in Warwick and George was employed as a street railway driver. She was an Oaklawn School inmate in 1935. During her time as an inmate, her parents and youngest sister resided on Post Road in Warwick and her father was employed as an attendant at a State institution in Cranston.

Agnes Mabel Kirk was born in Versailles, Connecticut on April 18, 1885, the daughter of Thomas and Mary Kirk, natives of England. She was an Oaklawn School inmate in 1900. On February 28, 1902, she married George Fisher in

Massachusetts. He died on January 2, 1905, at the age of thirty. In 1911, she married Arnold Scurrah in Massachusetts. She died in 1972.

Mary Karczmarczyk was born in Massachusetts in 1908, the daughter of Polish natives Stanislas and Rosie Karczmarczyk. In 1925 she resided on Hedley Avenue in Central Falls with her parents. She was an Oaklawn School inmate in 1925.

Marion Kilroy was born in Rhode Island in 1911, the daughter of William and Minnie Kilroy. Her mother was a native of Portugal. In 1915, she resided on Bay View Avenue in East Providence with her parents and siblings Hannah (seven), John (five), and Lester (three). Her father was employed as a railroad brakeman. In 1925, Marion and William, her brother, resided in the Providence home of her father's sister, Emeline Fales. Emeline's daughter, Betty (eighteen), and mother, Hannah Kilroy (sixty-eight), also lived there, along with two female boarders. An Oaklawn School inmate in 1930, she did farm work within the facility. At that time, her brothers (John and Lester) were living at the St. Andrews Industrial School in Barrington.

Lucy Kimatian was born in Rhode Island in 1907, the daughter of Charles Kimatian and Mary (Tarzian). In 1915, she resided on Douglas Avenue in Providence with her parents and her sister, Rose (nine). Her father was employed by the city street department. In 1920, the family resided on Smith Street in Providence. Her father was employed in coal and wood work. She was an Oaklawn School inmate in 1925.

Lillian G. Knight was born in Massachusetts in 1900. She was an Oaklawn School inmate in 1925.

Bessie Kelley was born in Rhode Island in 1890. She was an Oaklawn School inmate in 1910. Her parents were natives of Ireland.

Lucy Ann Latham was born in Newport, Rhode Island on May 25, 1907, the daughter of Irving Latham and Lavina (Mitchell). In January 1920, she was residing on Bassett Street in Providence with her mother and siblings Lena (eleven), Grace (nine), Anna (seven), and her mother's widowed thirty-seven-year-old brother-in-law, Matthew Caller. Her mother was employed as a private housekeeper. Her father was not in the home. In February 1920, her mother died at the age of thirty-four. She was an Oaklawn School inmate in 1925. Her father died in 1930 at the age of fifty-four.

Juliet R. LaCroix was born on May 14, 1923, the daughter of Henry LaCroix and Yvonne (Tremblay). In 1930 until at least 1935, she resided on Coyle Avenue in Pawtucket, Rhode Island with her parents and siblings Everett, Henry, Eugene, and Richard. Her father was employed as a coal and wood trucker. She attended Broadway Public School. She was an Oaklawn School inmate in 1940.

Ellen Langstaff was an Oaklawn School inmate in 1896 until at least 1897. During the school's Thanksgiving entertainment of 1896, she publicly recited "Deep unto Deep." During the school's Christmas cantata *The Capture of Santa Claus*, in 1897, she played one of the children in the cast.

Rose Virginia Lombard was born in Rhode Island in 1911, the daughter of Joseph Lombard and Sarah (Ammons), and was of African-American descent. Her mother died on October 4, 1914, in Newport at the age of thirty-three. In 1915, she resided on Kingston Avenue in Newport with her father and siblings George (eleven), Doris (ten), Mildred (seven), and Victor (five). Her father, a native of the Cape Verde Islands in Portugal, was employed in digging and grading work. She was an Oaklawn School inmate in 1925. At that time, her siblings were boarded out to other families.

Delia M. Lacroix was born in Rhode Island in May 1893, the daughter of Joseph Lacroix and Julia (Counter), both French natives. In 1900, she resided on Cass Avenue in Woonsocket with her parents and her sister, Mary (four). Her father was employed as a weaver. She and her sister were the only living children out of the six her mother gave birth to. She was an Oaklawn School inmate in 1910. She died suddenly of heart disease on July 13, 1929, at the age of thirty-six.

Blanche Alice Langevin was born in April 1923, the daughter of George Ernest Langevin and Aurelie Victorine (Caouette). In 1925, she resided on Boylston Street in Pawtucket, Rhode Island, with her parents and siblings Dorothy (four) and George (one month). She attended Potter Public School. In 1935, she resided in West Warwick. She was an Oaklawn School inmate in 1940.

Sadie Ann Longbottom was born on July 4, 1881, in Woonsocket, Rhode Island, the daughter of Fred Longbottom and Sarah (Gill), both natives of England. At the time of her birth, they resided on Third Avenue in Woonsocket. Her father was a boss dyer in a woolen mill. She had two older sisters, Pearl (born 1877) and Carrie (born 1879). A brother, Thompson, died in 1872 at the age of seventeen months; she also lost two sisters—Mary died in 1889 at the age of two years, and Martha died in 1874 at the age of seven after being scalded at Enterprise Mill. Her mother died in 1902 at the age of fifty-five. During the school's play *Old Times Made New* in May 1897, she played Hypatia. She was an Oaklawn School inmate in 1897.

Mary Lablanc was born in France in 1903. She was an Oaklawn School inmate in 1920.

Annie Leonard was an Oaklawn School inmate in 1897.

Annie Lennon was an Oaklawn School inmate in 1897.

Katie Lynch was born in 1880. She was sentenced to Oaklawn School on March 3, 1896, for two years, charged with being an idle person.

Mary Lee was an Oaklawn School inmate in 1897. During the school's Christmas cantata *The Capture of Santa Claus*, in 1897, she played one of the children in the cast.

Mary Rose Levesque was born in Massachusetts on February 10, 1921, the daughter of Eugene Levesque and Rosealma (Sylvia). She was an Oaklawn School inmate in 1935.

Papina Marie Maniatakos was born in Providence, Rhode Island on July 17, 1924, the daughter of John Maniatakos and Georgia (Spanos), natives of Greece.

In 1930, she resided on Plain Street in Providence with her parents and siblings Mildred (ten), Theodore (seven), Catherine (two), and Frank (one). Her father was employed as a waiter in a lunch room. She resided in Providence in 1935. She was an Oaklawn School inmate in 1940.

J. Mowry was an Oaklawn School inmate in 1897.

Phebe E. McLean was born in Nova Scotia in 1884. She migrated in 1889. She was an Oaklawn School inmate in 1900.

Mattie Malvose/Maloose was born in Italy in 1876, the daughter of Philip Malvose/Maloose and an unknown mother. She was an Oaklawn School inmate in 1890. She died of pneumonia on May 12, 1890, and was buried in the school's cemetery.

Rita Marie Macomber was born in Connecticut on February 20, 1918, the daughter of James and Rose Macomber, both French-Canadian. In 1920, she resided on Shepard Street in New Haven, Connecticut with her parents. Her father was employed as a rigger in his own shop. In 1930, she resided on Plain Street in Providence, Rhode Island, with her widowed father who was still employed in the same work. She was an Oaklawn School inmate in 1935.

Rose Mary Manzello was born in Rhode Island on June 7, 1916, the daughter of Antonio Manzello and Maria (Defusco), natives of Italy. In 1930, she resided on Republican Street in Rhode Island with her widowed mother and siblings Anna (nineteen), Anthony (eleven), and Lillian (six). Anna was employed at a jewelry manufacturing press. In 1934, her mother was residing on Acorn Street in Providence. She was an Oaklawn School inmate in 1935.

Florence E. Malpas was born in New York in December 1892. Her parents, Charles Malpas and Louisa (Minchin), were natives of England. Her father was employed as a newspaper printer. In 1900, she and her siblings—Nellie (six), Greta (three), and Bertha (one)—were boarders in the home of Minnie Toleman who also had two young children of her own on Romeo Street in Brockton, Massachusetts. She was an Oaklawn School inmate in 1910 along with her sister, Greta. At that time, her mother and siblings—Nellie, Bertha, Harry (eight), Ethel (three), and newborn Eva—resided on Knight Street in Providence while her father resided in a lodging house on Friendship Street in Providence. On March 31, 1913, she married Leo McGale in Rhode Island.

Greta Malpas was born in New York in July 1896. Her parents, Charles Malpas and Louisa (Minchin), were natives of England. Her father was employed as a newspaper printer. In 1900, she and her siblings—Mary (nine), Florence (seven), Nellie (six), and Bertha (one)—were boarders in the home of widow Minnie Toleman, who also had two young children of her own on Romeo Street in Brockton, Massachusetts. She was an Oaklawn School inmate in 1910 along with her sister, Florence. At that time, her mother and siblings—Nellie, Bertha, Harry (eight), Ethel (three), and newborn Eva—resided on Knight Street in Providence while her father resided in a lodging house on Friendship Street in Providence. On

September 26, 1914, she married George Boulais in Massachusetts. In 1920, she was still married but was residing with her parents and siblings—Nellie, Ethel, Eva, and Evelyn (four)—on Washington Street in Providence.

Gladys Irene Mallon was born in Massachusetts on April 2, 1911, the daughter of John Joseph Mallon and Cassie E. (Hastings). Her mother died in 1913 at the age of twenty-two. In 1920, she was a boarder at the Rhode Island Catholic Orphan Asylum. An Oaklawn School inmate in 1930, she did cleaning within the facility.

Isabel "Belle" Mont was an Oaklawn School inmate in 1897. During the school's Christmas cantata *The Capture of Santa Claus*, in 1897, she played a fruit fairy.

Roberta Mathewson was born in Maine in 1897. She was an Oaklawn School inmate in 1910.

Anotonia Mroz was born in Massachusetts on July 22, 1917, the daughter of John and Katherine Mroz. Her father was from Poland and her mother from Russia. In 1925, she resided on Chester Street in Westerly, Rhode Island, with her parents and siblings Walter (six), Edward (four), and Kozmes (one). They were all at the same address in 1930 and her father was employed as a weaver at a fabric mill. An additional brother, John (two), had joined the family. She was an Oaklawn School inmate in 1935.

Elizabeth Marshall was born in Maryland in 1915, the daughter of Lewis and Betty Marshall, and was of African-American descent. In 1920, she resided on Chase Street in Baltimore, Maryland with her parents. Her father was employed as a building laborer. In 1930, she resided on Randall Street in Providence, Rhode Island with her married mother, who was employed as a laundress. Her father was not in the home. It was reported that she was able to read and write but did not attend school. An Oaklawn School inmate in 1930, she did cleaning within the facility.

Filomena Matterese was born in Rhode Island on September 26, 1909, the daughter of Aniello Mattarese and Pia (Limoncetti), natives of Italy. In 1915, she resided on Swiss Street in Providence with her parents and siblings Frank (six), Realina (three), and Lucia (one month). Her father was employed as a cutter in a stocking mill. They were all residing in the same location in 1920. She was attending school and was able to read and write. Her father was employed as a laborer in an iron foundry. She was an Oaklawn School inmate in 1925.

Rose Mickus was born in Basthampton, Massachusetts, in August 1907, the daughter of John Mickus and Rosie (Linzclus), natives of Russia. Her father was employed as a weaver. In 1910, she lived on Emerald Street in Gardner, Massachusetts, with her parents, her younger brother John (one), and two adult male Russian boarders. Her father was employed as a sawyer in a chair shop. In 1925, she resided in Providence with her parents, her brother John, and siblings William (twelve), Minnie (nine), and Nellie (five). She had six additional siblings who died as infants or in early childhood. She was an Oaklawn School inmate in 1925.

Francis Matuka was born in New Jersey in 1908. She was an Oaklawn School inmate in 1925.

Etta Jemima Maynard was born in Providence, Rhode Island, on November 20, 1910, the daughter of Frederick Maynard and Grace (Barrus). In 1915, she resided in Providence with her parents and her sister, Martha (one). Her father was employed as a painter. In 1925, she resided on Water Street in Providence with her parents and siblings Martha, Frederick Jr. (ten), Amos (eight), Grace (six), William (four), Hazel (two), and Mabel (three months). Frederick Jr. died in 1932. An Oaklawn School inmate in 1930, she did cleaning within the facility.

Sabina Gertrude Montey was born in Rhode Island in May 1914, the daughter of James Montey and Alice (Sekator), and was of African-American descent. Her father was from Portugal and her mother from Rhode Island. In 1915, she resided on Beach Street in Narragansett with her parents, her paternal aunt, and her aunt's three children. Her father was employed as an odd job laborer. In 1920, she was residing at the same location with her father, who was divorced from her mother. He was employed as a farmer. An Oaklawn School inmate in 1930, she did farm work within the facility. She died unmarried on January 13, 1943, at the age of twenty-nine, at Mercy Hospital in Philadelphia, Pennsylvania, after acute heart failure that followed a vaginal hysterectomy performed due to uterine fibroids. At the time of her death, she had been residing on Pulaski Avenue in Philadelphia. She was buried in Rhode Island with her father and stepmother.

Alice L. Moore was born in Rhode Island on August 25, 1910, the daughter of William Moore and Matilda (Tremmel). Her father was from Rhode Island and her mother from New Jersey. In 1915, she resided in Providence with parents and siblings, Arthur (six) and Barbara (three). Her father was employed as a stable hostler. In 1920, resided on Talman Street in Providence with her parents and siblings Arthur, Barbara, William (four), George (three), and Richard (one). Her father was employed as a public market stable man. On April 30, 1921, her father died at the age of forty-eight. On April 5, 1929, her mother died at the age of forty-two. An Oaklawn School inmate in 1930, she did laundry work within the facility.

Mary B. Moore was born in Ireland in 1907. She was an Oaklawn School inmate in 1925.

Alberta Mendenhall was born in Pennsylvania in 1905, the daughter of Edward and Arminta Mendenhall. In 1910, she resided on Clifford Street in Providence with her parents, her siblings—John (three) and Lorane (one)—and her mother's siblings (aged nineteen, seventeen, and fifteen) in the home of her maternal grandmother and maternal step-grandfather, Cecelia and John Massey. Her father was employed as a telephone company lineman. In 1915, she resided with her parents on Silver Spring Avenue in East Providence, Rhode Island. Her father was employed as a railroad repairer. She was an Oaklawn School inmate in 1920.

Mary Moore was born in Massachusetts in 1906. Her parents were natives of Ireland. She was an Oaklawn School inmate in 1920.

Mary C. Malone was born in Rhode Island in 1924. She was an Oaklawn School inmate in 1940.

Dorothy Mae Mannix was born in Northampton, Massachusetts, on September 12, 1922, the daughter of William Mannix and Nellie (Paulson). In 1935, she resided on Early Street in Providence, Rhode Island and attended Roger Williams Public Junior High. She was an Oaklawn School inmate in 1940.

Bertha A. Marcoux was born in 1921, the daughter of Alfred Marcoux and Alma (Littlefield). In 1925, she resided on Cross Street in Central Falls, Rhode Island, with her parents and brother Alfred (two), as well as her paternal grandfather, Peter Marcoux. In 1930, she resided on Pine Street in Central Falls with her parents and siblings Alfred, Clifford (four), Richard (three), Roscoe (two), and Pearl (nine months). Her father was employed as a factory laborer. In 1935, she resided in Pawtucket. An additional sibling, Edward, was born in 1939. She was an Oaklawn School inmate in 1940.

Clementine/Salenetinia McMahon/McMahan was born in Massachusetts in 1903 and was of African-American descent. She was an Oaklawn School inmate in 1920.

Alice Mello was born in Portugal in 1905. She was an Oaklawn School inmate in 1920.

Gertrude Martin was born in 1922, the daughter of Alberic Martin and Mary (Collard). In 1925, she resided in Coventry, Rhode Island, with her parents and siblings Gerard (nine), Irene (eight), Florence (five), Lionel (two), and Theresa (eleven months). Her mother died in 1927 at the age of thirty-four. In 1930, her father was employed as a dyer at the print works and the only children residing with him were Florence and Gerard along with a servant, Poisana Boucher. In 1935, she was an inmate at St. Francis Orphanage in Woonsocket along with her siblings, Theresa and Lionel. At that time, her father was living on Harris Street in Coventry and employed as a calendar manufacturer. Theresa and Lionel eventually went back into the home of their father. She was an Oaklawn School inmate in 1940.

Filomene Manera was an Oaklawn School inmate in 1897.

Lizzie Murray, during the school's play *Old Times Made New*, which was performed at the Hospital for the Insane in May 1897, played the wife of Abraham. She was an Oaklawn School inmate in 1897.

Alice Martin was born in Rhode Island in 1906. She was an Oaklawn School inmate in 1920.

Isabel Martin was born on May 16, 1920. She was an Oaklawn School inmate in 1935.

Clara Myles was born in Rhode Island in July 1880. Her mother was from New York and her father from Canada. She was an Oaklawn School inmate from her admittance in January 1897 until at least 1900.

Mary Merchant was an Oaklawn School inmate in 1896. During the school's Thanksgiving entertainment of 1896, she publicly recited "Jemima's Courtship."

Maggie McCoy was an Oaklawn School inmate in 1896. She died on February 12, 1896 and was buried in the school's cemetery.

Edith M. (surname unknown) was an Oaklawn School inmate in 1897. She was paroled that year to a family in North Sterling, Connecticut.

Maria Morena was committed to Oaklawn School on July 22, 1898, for two years, charged with being wayward. She was residing in Bristol, Rhode Island, at the time.

Susie Mathewson was born in 1881. She was originally from River Point, Rhode Island, and was an Oaklawn School inmate in 1897. In August that year, she escaped from the school with inmate Elizabeth Bullock. She weighed about 110 pounds and had light hair, a light complexion, and blue eyes.

Ruth Marie Moore was born in Rhode Island on March 10, 1912, the daughter of Charles Moore and Ella (Sisson), both from Rhode Island. In 1920, she resided in East Greenwich with her parents and siblings Della (ten), Charles (five), Walter (three), and Leander (one). An Oaklawn School inmate in 1930, she did cleaning within the facility.

Sadie N. (surname unknown) was inmate in 1897. That year, she was paroled to the family of forty-year-old farmer Arthur Gilbert Billings of Warwick. She lived with Arthur, his wife Etta (Andrews), their fourteen-year-old son, thirteen-year-old daughter, and ten-year-old son. Etta died four years later, and Arthur died five years later.

Winifred M. Newton was born in Rhode Island in October 1889, the daughter of George Spencer Newton and Harriet (Crandall). Her father was from Connecticut and her mother from Rhode Island. In 1900, she resided in Westerly with her parents and siblings Ernest (fourteen), Harold (five), and Evelyn (one). Her father was a lifelong carriage blacksmith. By 1920, she was an inmate at the Exeter School for the Feeble-Minded. At that time, her parents resided on South Main Street in Westerly with her brother, Ernest. She was an Oaklawn School inmate in 1925 while her parents were residing on Bradford Road in Westerly. By 1930, she was an inmate at the Rhode Island Hospital for the Insane. She did chamber work within the facility. At that time, her parents resided on Church Street in Westerly. Her father was Deacon of the Niantic Seventh Day Baptist Church. She remained an inmate of the psychiatric hospital until at least 1940, where she is recorded as having a mental disability.

Dorothy E. Nelson was born in Rhode Island in 1911. She was an Oaklawn School inmate in 1925.

Florence Nixon was born in November 1885, the daughter of James and Rose Nixon. Her father was from England and her mother from Ireland. In 1900, she resided on Fountain Street in Pawtucket with her parents and siblings James (nine), John (eight), Thomas (six), and William (two). Her father was employed as a dye house dyer. In 1910, her family resided in the same location; however, her father was now widowed, and she had an additional sibling, Elizabeth (ten). She was an Oaklawn School inmate in 1910.

Eliza Nesbit was born in July 1894 and was of African-American descent. In 1900, she was inmate at the Providence Shelter for Colored Children. She was an Oaklawn School inmate in 1910.

Fanny Nesbit was born in 1877, the daughter of George and Mary Nesbit. She is recorded as being "a mulatto." Her parents were employed as servants. She was an Oaklawn School inmate in 1888.

Agatha H. Northup was born in March 1878, the daughter of Daniel Northup and Rozeltha (Sprague). She was an Oaklawn School inmate in 1896 until at least 1897. In 1900, she resided on Pleasant Street in North Kingstown, Rhode Island, with her parents and younger siblings Stukley (twenty-one), Benjamin (twenty-five), Frank (seventeen), Delia (fifteen), Harrie (fourteen), John (twelve), Thomas (seven), and Hope (five). Her father was employed as a fisherman. She was employed as a housekeeper. Her mother had given birth to twenty children, only twelve of whom were alive in 1900. In 1910, she was employed as a servant in the home of attorney Harold Hart, on Murray Street in Broome, New York.

Catherine V. Neary was born on September 9, 1919, the daughter of David and Catherine Neary. In 1920, she resided on Friendship Street in Providence, Rhode Island, with her parents. Her father was employed as a bleachery laborer. In 1925, she resided in Providence with her parents and her siblings, Mary (three) and Ella (one). Her sister, Nellie, died in 1923. Her sister, Mary, died in 1928. In 1930, she resided on Livingston Street in Providence with her parents and her sister, Ella. In 1935, she resided in Providence. She was an Oaklawn School inmate in 1940.

Mary E. O'Rourke was born in Ireland in 1890. She was an Oaklawn School inmate in 1910.

Rosemary D. Oliver was born on August 9, 1926, in Rhode Island, the daughter of Joseph Oliver and Roselyn (Williamson), and was of African-American descent. Her father was from Massachusetts and her mother from Rhode Island. In 1930, she resided on Roger Williams Avenue in East Providence, Rhode Island, with her parents and siblings Joseph (sixteen), Irma (fourteen), Helen (thirteen), Alfred (eleven), Frederick (nine), Florence (eight), Leevon (six), Calvin (five), Jesse (two), and twins Ronald and Roland (ten months). No one in the home was employed but her father had formerly worked as a mechanic in an auto-repair shop. That year, her twin brothers were both placed at the Exeter School for the Feeble-Minded. In 1935, her mother was an inmate at the Rhode Island Hospital for Mental Diseases. Her brothers, Ronald and Roland, had become inmates at the Rhode Island State Home and School. Ronald was noted to have the "disability" of "bad blood." Roland was noted to be deaf. Her brothers, Frederick and Calvin, resided on Mt. Pleasant Avenue in Providence, attended public schools, and were not listed as having any type of disability. Also residing at that address were her sister Florence, who attended Nelson Public School and was listed as having an undisclosed disability; her brother Leevon, who attended Nelson Public School and was determined to have an undisclosed disability; and her brother Jesse who was determined to have the disability of "bad blood." Rosemary also resided at that address and attended Nelson Public School. She was noted as having an undisclosed disability. Her mother remained in the mental hospital in 1940 and died in 1941 at the age of fifty. She was an Oaklawn School inmate in 1940.

Elizabeth "Betty" Olsen was born in Massachusetts in 1923, the daughter of Olan and Bessie Olsen. In 1925, she resided in Providence, Rhode Island, with her parents and her brother, Raymond (one). In 1930, she was a boarder at St. Mary's Home for Children in Providence. She was an Oaklawn School inmate in 1940 until at least 1941. In June 1941, she was an inmate at the Women's Reformatory in Cranston and one of three women who used a painter's ladder to scale a wall and escape. The other women were Mrs. Josephine Worrall (twenty-six), a resident of Cranston incarcerated for robbery, and Emma Roskofski (twenty-two), who was incarcerated for vagrancy. Elizabeth had only recently been transferred from Oaklawn School when the escape occurred, prompting a search throughout New England.

Katie O'Malley was an Oaklawn School inmate in 1897. During an entertainment in April 1897 to celebrate Mrs. Forbush's birthday, she performed a solo of "I'm Going to Write to Papa."

Jeanie Proulx was born in Pennsylvania in 1905. She was an Oaklawn School inmate in 1920.

Dorothy Parker was born in 1923. In 1935, she resided in Woonsocket. She was an Oaklawn School inmate in 1940.

Minnie Pherson was an Oaklawn School inmate in 1888. She died of hereditary phthisis and was buried in the school's cemetery.

Maizie G. Paine was born in Rhode Island in 1910, the daughter of Elijah and Sarah Paine. In 1915, she resided on Danielson Pike in Scituate with her parents, her brother Lester (two), and her paternal uncle, George Paine. Elijah was employed as a farm laborer. In 1920, she resided on Hartford Avenue in Providence with her uncle George and brother Lester at the home of her paternal uncle, Thomas Paine. Thomas and George were both employed as iron foundry laborers. An Oaklawn School inmate in 1925 until at least 1930, she cooked within the facility.

Celia H. Perry was born in Rhode Island on January 29, 1914, the daughter of Marianno and Minnie Perry. Her siblings included Mary (born 1900), Louise (born 1904), and Ethel (born 1908). In 1925, she was an orphan residing in Cottage "C" at the Rhode Island State Home and School. An Oaklawn School inmate in 1930, she cooked within the facility.

Emily E. Porstray/Poutray was born in Connecticut in September 1881. Her parents were natives of Canada. She was an Oaklawn School inmate in 1900.

Dorothy Pires was born on September 20, 1924, in Rhode Island, the daughter of Manuel and Mary Pires, natives of Azores, Portugal. Her father arrived in America aboard the *Don Maria* in 1902. In 1935, she lived with her parents and siblings Alice (twenty-two), Manuel (seventeen), and Joseph (fourteen) on Sharon Street in East Providence. She attended Hoyt School. Her father was employed as a food produce clerk. She was an Oaklawn School inmate in 1940.

Mary Grace Pannone was born in Rhode Island on October 14, 1917, the daughter of Umberto/Albert Pannone and Amelia/Teresa (Pasquale), natives of Italy. In 1920, she resided on Moorefield Road in Providence with her parents and infant sister, Josephine. Her father was employed as a cotton mill laborer. In 1930, she resided with her parents and her siblings, John (eight) and Anthony (six). Her father was employed as an odd job laborer. She was an Oaklawn School inmate in 1935. At that time, her parents were residing on Barbara Street in Providence with her siblings Anthony, John, Josephine, and Anna (one).

Hazel L. Pierce was born in Rhode Island on April 28, 1909, the daughter of John Pierce and Clara (Smith). In 1910, she resided on Caston Avenue in Providence with her parents and siblings Sarah (eighteen), George (fifteen), John (thirteen), and William (four). Her father was employed as an iron foundry laborer. In 1915 and 1920, she resided on Camden Avenue in Providence with her parents and siblings George, John, and William. In 1930, she was residing at the same location with her widowed mother, John, and William. John was employed as a steamfitter, William was employed as a fireman, and she was employed as a private housekeeper. An Oaklawn School inmate in 1930, she did cleaning within the facility.

Veronica Pearce was born in Rhode Island on March 14, 1908, the daughter of Asa Pearce and Agnes (O'Brien). In 1910, she was an inmate at St. Mary's Orphanage in East Providence. In 1920, she resided on Atwells Avenue in Providence with her mother, her brother Daniel (fourteen), and boarder William Kane (thirty-six). Her mother was employed as a press hand in a jewelry shop and her brother was employed as a print shop errand boy. She was an Oaklawn School inmate in 1925, then an inmate at Sophia Little Home for Unwed Mothers in Providence in 1930. From at least 1935 until at least 1940, she was employed as a maid for the family of Herbert Allard, a machinery company owner, on Arnold Avenue in Cranston.

Grace Lillian Place was born in Rhode Island on April 18, 1891, the daughter of Albert Place and Cora (Mowry). In 1900, she resided on Iroquois Street in Providence with her parents and siblings George (nineteen) and Mabel (seventeen). Her father was employed as a teamster. From at least 1910 until his death in 1923, her father lived with his mother in Scituate on the expense of the town. In 1910, she resided on Friendship Street in Providence with her mother, Mabel, and two female boarders. She was an Oaklawn School inmate in 1910.

Sarah Pierce was born in 1893. She was an Oaklawn School inmate in 1910.

Ora Pierce was born in Rhode Island on February 23, 1911, the daughter of William Pierce and Mabel (Thomas), and was of African-American descent. In 1920, she resided on Potter Avenue in Providence with her parents and siblings Joel (eight), Ruth (six), Mary (four), and William (ten months). Her father was employed as an automobile repairman. In 1925, she resided at the same location with her parents and siblings, along with three additional siblings—Rebecca (four) and twins Alberta and Mabel (one). A brother, David, was born in 1929. She completed the eighth grade. An Oaklawn School inmate in 1930, she did laundry work within the facility. In 1940, she was residing back at the same residence with her parents and siblings and was employed as a private housekeeper.

Ruth Ellen Patton was born in Warren, Rhode Island on January 22, 1894, the daughter of William Patton and Sarah (Reynolds). In 1900, she resided in Warren with her parents and siblings William (sixteen), Marion (ten), James (fourteen), and Sarah (nine). Her father was employed as a bakery clerk. She was an Oaklawn School inmate in 1910.

Marion Price was born in New Hampshire in 1910 and was of African-American descent. An Oaklawn School inmate in 1930, she worked as a gate tender within the facility.

Mildred Elizabeth Perkins was born on November 29, 1921, in South Kingstown, Rhode Island, the daughter of David Perkins and Iva (Sheldon). In 1930, she resided on Glen Rock Road in South Kingstown with her maternal grandparents, Edmund and Ada Sheldon, and their other granddaughter, Gladys Cahoone (seventeen). Edmund was employed as a farmer. She completed the seventh grade. She was an Oaklawn School inmate in 1935 until at least 1940.

Anna Press was born in Rhode Island in 1904. She was an Oaklawn School inmate in 1920.

Catherine Pierce was born in Ireland in 1904. She was an Oaklawn School inmate in 1920.

Molly Person was born in Rhode Island in 1900. She was an Oaklawn School inmate in 1910.

Ethel Maud Potter, during the school's play *Old Times Made New*, in May 1897, played Priscilla. She was an Oaklawn School inmate in 1896 until at least 1897. While there, in November 1896, she wrote to the superintendent, "I thought I would write you a few lines to let you know that I am going to be a good girl and help all the teachers all I can. I am going to help the girls to do right and when I go home, I will be a good girl. I pray to God to give me a new heart every night and morning. I am glad I came. I will not be a bad girl again. I would like to go home to my mother, for I have broken her heart, but if God lets me live, I will be good to her. I am the only child she has, and I think I am going to make her happy."

Sadie Person was born in Rhode Island in 1898. She was an Oaklawn School inmate in 1910.

Emma Lena Peckham, during the school's play *Old Times Made New,* in May 1897, played Agnesi of Bologna. She was an Oaklawn School inmate in 1896 and until at least 1897. While there in November 1896, she wrote to the superintendent, "We girls have gathered in the schoolroom to write you a few lines containing some good resolution for the year to come. I am going to do the best I can and to be obedient to all my teachers and to be kind and true to all my schoolmates. I have learned a great deal since I have been here and am going to try and learn more and more each day. I want to grow up to be a good and noble woman and to help others all I can. We girls had a very pleasant time at your house and at the Asylum services this morning."

Gertrude E. Parker was born in Rhode Island on October 6, 1890, the daughter of George Parker and Fannie (Spinney). In 1900, she resided on Newton Street in Providence with her parents and siblings Fannie (fourteen), Gertrude (nine), George (seven), Isabelle (five), James (two), and Bertha (five months). Her father was employed as a machinist. She was an Oaklawn School inmate in 1910.

Mary Ramsbottom was born on October 27, 1923, the daughter of William Ramsbottom and Annie (Smith). In 1925, she resided in Providence, Rhode Island with her parents and her sister, Agnes (four). In 1930, she resided on Pontiac Avenue in Warwick with her parents and her siblings, Agnes and William (newborn). Her father was employed as a dyer in a photograph printing factory. Her mother died on December 29, 1930, of liver abscesses at the age of forty-two. Her father died on December 14, 1934, at the age of forty-seven. She attended William Winsor Public School. In 1935, she was an inmate at the Rhode Island State Home and School, then an Oaklawn School inmate in 1940.

Lucy Rodi was born in Italy in 1904. She was married. She was an Oaklawn School inmate in 1920.

Elizabeth C. Rose was born in Rhode Island in 1910. She was an Oaklawn School inmate in 1925.

Ingoronata Riccio was born in Italy in 1902. She was an Oaklawn School inmate in 1920.

Sarah A. Rankin was born in Rhode Island in April 1885. She was an Oaklawn School inmate in 1900.

Frances Raymond was born in Rhode Island in 1904, the daughter of Jennie (Doris) Raymond. Her father was deceased by 1920. While she was an inmate at the school, her mother lived on Nichols Street in Providence with her mother's sister Mary, Mary's husband William Harrison, and her mother Agatha Doris. Jennie was employed as a baker in a bakery shop. She was an Oaklawn School inmate in 1920.

Abbie M. Read was born in Rhode Island on March 23, 1892, the daughter of William Read and Sabina (McMamman). In 1900, she resided on Crary Street in Providence with her parents and siblings William (twenty), Mary (eighteen), George (sixteen), Sarah (eleven), Sabina (nine), and James (six). Her mother died later in 1900 at the age of forty-two. She was an Oaklawn School inmate in 1910.

Mildred Rudolph was born in Rhode Island in 1894. Her parents were natives of Poland. She was an Oaklawn School inmate in 1910.

Philomena A. Rusico was born in New York in 1907. She was an Oaklawn School inmate in 1925.

Ann Rominyk was born in Rhode Island on December 25, 1919, the daughter of Dimitrou Rominyk and Anna (Tochupski), natives of Galicia. In 1920, she resided in Woonsocket with her parents and siblings Anastasia (six), Katerzyna (two), Mack (eleven months), and two adult male Galician boarders. Her father owned a barber shop. She was an Oaklawn School inmate in 1935. In 1940, she was residing on Sampson Street in Woonsocket and was employed as a waitress at a cafeteria. She was unmarried and living with her six-year-old daughter, Mary Rominyk.

Rosa Raymond was born in Woonsocket, Rhode Island in March 1917, the daughter of Gennessey Raymond and Arzelia (Dumont), both French-Canadians. In 1930, she was residing on Social Street in Woonsocket with her parents and her older sister, Rosilda (eighteen). Her father was employed as a building carpenter. She completed three years of high school. She was an Oaklawn School inmate in 1935.

Mary Rourke was born in 1890. She was an Oaklawn School inmate in 1910.

Lucy M. Rocha was born in Rhode Island on August 27, 1883, the daughter of Enos and Clara Rocha, natives of Portugal. Her siblings included Rose (born 1878), Lena (born 1879), William (born 1880), and Arthur (born 1881). Her father was a barber. In 1885, she resided with her family in Providence. She was an Oaklawn School inmate in 1900.

Mary Ella Stockwell was born on December 13, 1924, the daughter of Frank Stockwell and Eva (Lagasses). In 1930, she resided on Putnam Pike in Smithfield, Rhode Island, with her widowed mother, who had married at fifteen, and her siblings Theodore (sixteen), Ernest (fifteen), Charles (thirteen), Elizabeth (eleven), Harry (ten), Julia (nine), William (six), Rita (three), and Albert (two). In 1935, she resided at the same location and attended William Winsor Public School. She was an Oaklawn School inmate in 1940.

Germania Sims was born in Massachusetts in 1904, the daughter of Elizabeth Sims, and was of African-American descent. In 1915, she was residing on Benedict Street in Providence with her mother and siblings, Anna (twenty-eight) and Nora (eighteen). Her mother was employed as a laundress. She was an Oaklawn School inmate in 1920.

Nellie Sullivan, during the school's Christmas cantata *The Capture of Santa Claus*, in 1897, played one of the children in the cast. She was an Oaklawn School inmate in 1897.

Inez May Sands was born on June 14, 1912, in Pascoag, Rhode Island, the daughter of Oscar Sands and Bertha (Hadfield). In 1925, she resided in Gloucester with her parents, her brother Martin (fourteen), and her grandfather George Sands. Her father, who worked in the logging industry, was from Connecticut and her mother from England. On August 24, 1927, her father committed suicide at the age of forty-eight by shooting himself in the head. An Oaklawn School inmate in 1930, she did laundry work within the facility. By 1935, she was living with her brother Martin on Laurel Hill Avenue in Burrillville and working as a doffer at a worsted mill.

Grace Salisbury was born in 1884 in Rhode Island, the daughter of Clement Eugene Salisbury and Julia (Lake). She resided in Bristol with her parents and siblings Frank (born 1882), Samuel (born 1887), William (born 1892), Clement (born 1894), and George (born 1898). In 1900, her father was serving a sentence at the State Farm and her mother was out working every day. The children took this opportunity to roam the streets instead of going to school, and residents had issued several complaints to police about them not being properly fed and about the depredations being committed by them on the streets, such as smashing windows and stealing fruit. Early one morning, in September of that year, police located Grace, William, and Samuel hanging out in the vicinity of School Street and took the trio to the police station. There, they were left in a room alone for a short time and when police returned to the room, they were gone. They were later located hanging out on Washington Street and were taken to stand before the judge. Grace admitted that they had not had any supper the night before. All three were charged with being idle persons and vagrants. Samuel and William were sentenced to spend two years at Sockanosset School for Boys. Grace was sentenced to spend her minority at Oaklawn School. By 1910, Grace had been committed to the Rhode Island State Workhouse. Inside, she worked as a waitress and was recorded as being unmarried with one child. Clement and Julia were living on Bradford Street in Bristol. Clement had no job, but Julia was employed as a washerwoman. William and Samuel were living there as well, both employed in cotton mills. Frank, Clement, and George were also still there, along with a new sibling, Walter (nine). The two-year-old daughter of Grace, Mary Sherman, was also living with them. By 1925, Grace was married to Dennis Sweet and resided with him in Bristol with their nine-month-old baby, Albert, and Grace's daughter, Mary. Julia, George, and Samuel lived with them.

Louise Bennett Stapleton was born in Providence, Rhode Island on July 7, 1912, the daughter of William Stapleton and Sarah (Hannon). In 1915, she resided on Akerman Street in Providence with her parents and siblings Margaret (four) and John (six months). Her father was employed as an ice company teamer. In 1920, she resided on Valley Street in Providence with her parents and siblings Sarah (eleven), Margaret (nine), Frederick (five), and Lillian (two months). Her father was employed as an ashes and coal teamster. In 1925, she resided at the same location. Her father died in 1928. An Oaklawn School inmate in 1930, she worked as a gate tender within the facility.

Jessie E. Smith was born in Rhode Island in March 1887. She was an Oaklawn School inmate in 1900.

Katie Shea, during an entertainment in April 1897 to celebrate Mrs. Forbush's birthday, recited "Coming of Spring." During the school's play *Old Times Made New*, in May 1897, she played Cecelia. She was an Oaklawn School inmate in 1897.

Abby Shepard was of African-American descent and an Oaklawn School inmate in 1886. She died of consumption on March 25, 1886, and was buried in the school's cemetery.

Ada M. Sweet was born in Rhode Island in June 1885 and was an Oaklawn School inmate in 1900.

Rose Simone was born in Rhode Island on August 6, 1907, the daughter of Giuseppe Simone and Maria (Lombardi), natives of Italy. In 1920, she resided on Prudence Avenue in Providence with her parents and siblings Tony (twenty-one), Theresa (nineteen), Robert (thirteen), Fred (six), and Micheline (four). Her father was employed as a jewelry laborer. She was an Oaklawn School inmate in 1925.

Leica/Lisa Spirito was born in Rhode Island on August 26, 1910. She was an Oaklawn School inmate in 1925. By 1935, she was an inmate at the Rhode Island Mental Hospital, diagnosed with a mental disability.

Phebe Searles was born in Rhode Island in 1894, the daughter of Byron Searles. In 1910, she resided on Batchelor Avenue in Cranston with her father, who was employed as an ice company teamster, and siblings Annie (twenty-three) and Charlie (eighteen). A sixty-five-year-old male boarder also lived there. Although her mother was alive, she was not living in the home. In 1925, she resided with her father and siblings. Her father had a wife living there, Sarah (Pierce), who would have been her mother or stepmother. She was an Oaklawn School inmate in 1910.

Isabel Stevens was born in 1884. She was an Oaklawn School inmate in 1900.

Ethel Smith was born in Rhode Island in 1892. She was an Oaklawn School inmate in 1910.

Alice Smith was an Oaklawn School inmate in 1897.

Grace E. Studley was born in Providence, Rhode Island, in January 1897, the daughter of Orrin Studley and Ella (Chase). In 1900, she resided with her parents in the house of her widowed maternal grandfather Alfred Chase on Burgess Avenue in East Providence. Her grandfather was employed as a shipping agent and her father as a house painter. In 1910, she resided with her parents on Freeborn Avenue in East Providence. She was an Oaklawn School inmate in 1911. Her parents died one month apart in 1917.

Mary Silva was born in Portugal in January 1887. She migrated in 1898. She was an Oaklawn School inmate in 1900.

Virgie Sisco was an Oaklawn School inmate in 1897. During the school's Christmas cantata *The Capture of Santa Claus*, in 1897, she played a chimney elf.

Rowena Spence was born in Rhode Island in 1901 and was of African American-descent. She was an Oaklawn School inmate in 1925.

Maud Stott was born in Rhode Island in 1905. In 1910, she was an inmate at Rhode Island State Home and School. She was an Oaklawn School inmate in 1920.

Celia/Cecelia Salley/Sally was born in Rhode Island in 1905. She was an Oaklawn School inmate in 1920.

Lillian Bernice Sundstrom was born on June 21, 1921, in East Providence, Rhode Island, the daughter of George Sundstrom and Frances (Cook). In 1923, she resided with her parents on Silver Spring Avenue in East Providence. Her father was employed as a clerk. Her father died on March 13, 1924, at the age of twenty-four. In 1925, she resided on Bay View Street in East Providence with her maternal grandparents Ausby and Martha Cook, her mother Frances, and her sister Madeline (one). In 1935, she resided on Wampanoag Trail in East Providence with her mother, her stepfather Howard Waldron, her sister Madeline, and her brother Howard Waldron (seven). Her stepfather was suffering from a broken back. She was an Oaklawn School inmate in 1940.

Anna Sutkartis was born in Rhode Island in 1901. Her parents were natives of Russia. She was an Oaklawn School inmate in 1920.

Eliza Sullivan was an Oaklawn School inmate in 1897.

Mary Souza was born in Maine in 1903. She was an Oaklawn School inmate in 1920.

J. Stevens, during the school's play *Old Times Made New*, in May 1897, played Joan of Arc. She was an Oaklawn School inmate in 1897.

Jenny Stowe was committed to Oaklawn School on September 15, 1884, after being charged with being a wanton and lascivious person in speech and behavior. She pleaded guilty and was sentenced to the school for her minority.

Florence Sutton was born in Rhode Island in 1905 and was of African-American descent. She was an Oaklawn School inmate in 1920.

Annie S. (surname unknown) was an Oaklawn School inmate by 1897 as she was out on parole that year in the home of Samuel H. (surname unknown).

Lenore Strange was born on August 7, 1893, the daughter of Frank Strange and Leonora (Gross). In 1900, her father was found guilty of four counts of breaking and entering as well as larceny and imprisoned at the Massachusetts State Prison to serve four to six years. Her father went by the aliases Frank Henderson and Daniel F. Strange. That year, she and her sister Grace were placed at the Rhode Island State Home and School. She was an Oaklawn School inmate in 1910.

Irene Tasker was born in Massachusetts in 1904. She was an Oaklawn School inmate in 1920.

Marian V. Tate was born in Massachusetts in 1903. She was an Oaklawn School inmate in 1925.

Grace Tiffany was an Oaklawn School inmate in 1897. During the school's Christmas cantata *The Capture of Santa Claus*, in 1897, she played a chimney elf.

Alice Maude Tillotson was born in Phenix, Rhode Island, on March 15, 1888, the daughter of Frank Tillotson and Lydia (Battey). Her mother died on

March 14, 1901, at the age of forty-eight and her father remarried later that year. She had one older sibling and three younger siblings. She was an Oaklawn School inmate in 1905. By 1915, she was an inmate at the Exeter School for the Feeble-Minded.

Augusta Thompson was born in Rhode Island in 1905 and was of African-American descent. She was an Oaklawn School inmate in 1925.

Sarah "Sadie" Trainor was born in 1878, the daughter of John and Sarah Trainor. She was an Oaklawn School inmate in 1894 until 1896. She died of consumption on November 23, 1897, at the age of nineteen, while on parole in Voluntown, Connecticut, with the Gardner family.

Mildred Taylor was born in Massachusetts in 1903. She was an Oaklawn School inmate in 1920.

Lillian Taylor was born in England in 1911. An Oaklawn School inmate in 1930, she cooked within the facility.

Anna M. (Tyrrell) Tresler was born in New York on March 27, 1890, the daughter of Jeremiah Tyrrell and Mary (Dolan), natives of Ireland. She was married by 1908. In 1920, she was an inmate at Exeter School for the Feeble-Minded, unable to read or write. She was an Oaklawn School inmate in 1925 until at least 1930. She did farm work within the facility. In 1935, she was widowed and living on Friendship Street in Providence, employed as a cleaning woman at a hotel.

Lena Tassoni was born in New York in 1914. An Oaklawn School inmate in 1930, she did cleaning within the facility.

Olive Trainor was born in Rhode Island in 1895, the daughter of Hannah Trainor. She was an Oaklawn School inmate in 1910. In 1915, she was employed in a cotton mill and was residing in Pawtucket with her mother (forty-eight), sister Mildred (seventeen), and an adult male boarder. Her mother died the following year at the age of forty-nine.

Clara Tattersall, after escaping from a reform school in Fall River, Massachusetts, was captured at a house in Broad Common in Bristol, Rhode Island and committed to Oaklawn School on October 28, 1897.

Lillian Thibeault was born in Connecticut on August 15, 1919, the daughter of Napoleon and Delia Thibeault. In 1920, she resided in Canterbury with her parents and her sister, Rose (one). Her father was employed as a forest laborer. She was an Oaklawn School inmate in 1935. Just before being sent to Oaklawn School in 1935, she had been an inmate at the Rhode Island State Home and School and worked within the facility as a dining room waitress.

Katie Vaughan was committed to Oaklawn School on August 16, 1910, after being arrested and charged with being a wayward girl. She was sentenced to the school for her minority.

Ruth Vick was born in Massachusetts in 1905 and was of African-American descent. In 1910, she resided in Malden, Massachusetts, with her grandmother

Rebecca Vick, her aunt Rebecca Roderguies, and her cousin Ralph Roderguies (one and a half). Her grandmother and her aunt were both employed as laundresses. She was an Oaklawn School inmate in 1920.

Corinna Veritt was born in Canada in September 1882. She was an Oaklawn School inmate in 1900.

Madeline Wilson was born in Rhode Island on July 28, 1901, the daughter of Frederick Wilson and Louise (Smith). In 1910, she lived with her parents on Cranston Street in Providence and her father was employed as an automobile steelworker. She was an Oaklawn School inmate in 1920. In 1930, she was living in Washington D.C. where she was employed as a restaurant waitress.

Emma Walker was born in Pennsylvania on November 12, 1917. She was an Oaklawn School inmate in 1935.

Jennie Ward was an Oaklawn School inmate in 1896 until at least 1897. During the school's play *Old Times Made New*, in May 1897, she played the Inventress. During an entertainment in April 1897 to celebrate Mrs. Forbush's birthday, she read the opening salutation and did a recitation of "The Smack in School."

Grace Estelle Warner was born in West Greenwich, Rhode Island, on December 20, 1920, the daughter of Carl Warner and Patience (Miller). In 1925, she resided in Warwick at the home of her paternal grandmother Rose Straight and her step-grandfather John, with her parents and her siblings Edward (six), Grace (four), and Joseph (ten months). Additional siblings included Myrtle (1928–1931), Walter (1931–1935), Rachel (1932–1944), Rose (1927–1927), and three others. In 1930, she resided on Pierce Street in East Greenwich with her maternal grandparents, David and Maude Miller. It was recorded that she attended school and was able to read and write. She was an Oaklawn School inmate in 1935.

Anna Elisabeth Watson was born in West Virginia on February 9, 1918, the daughter of Robert Watson and Daisy (McDonough). In 1920, she resided on Main Street in Middleway with her parents and siblings, Evelyn (three) and Blanche (three months). Her father was employed as a farm laborer. In 1930, she resided on Main Street in Warwick, Rhode Island, with her parents and siblings—Evelyn, Blanche, Nina (six), Jessie (four), and Marvin (one)—as well as a boarder, Adolph Raymond (nineteen). Her father was employed as a cloth bleacher in a finishing plant. She was an Oaklawn School inmate in 1935.

Julia Williams was born in Rhode Island in 1905 and was of African-American descent. She was an Oaklawn School inmate in 1920.

Mary West was born in Rhode Island in 1903. She was an Oaklawn School inmate in 1920.

Clara B. West was an Oaklawn School inmate in 1896 until at least 1897. During the school's play *Old Times Made New*, in May 1897, she played Queen Elizabeth. During her stay at the school, she submitted what was supposed to be original work to the *The Howard Times*, the newspaper by and about those within the State institutions. In a subsequent issue, the following announcement appeared, "The verses in our last issue ascribed to Clara West of the Oaklawn School, as original, were found to be cut bodily from another paper. Clara has it to learn, with a good many other things, before she comes to be a woman, that this was a despicable, as well as a criminal, act." While there, in November 1896, she wrote to the superintendent, "I had a lovely time this forenoon. I enjoyed going to the Asylum services very much and I think you enjoyed having us. It certainly was delightful. When we were coming over this morning, we met the Primary boys from the Sockanosset School coming through our grounds. They all kept step with one another, and it certainly did look lovely. I will close now."

During the school's Thanksgiving entertainment of 1896, she publicly recited "Home Joy." During an entertainment in April 1897 to celebrate Mrs. Forbush's birthday, she did a recitation of "The Clerical Wit."

Hattie Wood was an Oaklawn School inmate in 1897. During the school's Christmas cantata *The Capture of Santa Claus*, in 1897, she played a frost fairy.

Liddia White was born in Massachusetts in 1905. She was an Oaklawn School inmate in 1920.

Grace L. Whitman was born in Rhode Island on November 8, 1911, the daughter of Robert Whitman and Elizabeth (Greene). In 1920, she resided on Mineral Spring Avenue in Pawtucket with her parents and siblings Dorothy (thirteen), Florence (twelve), Henry (ten), Mildred (six), Helen (four), and Ruth (one). Her father was employed as a driver for a fertilizer plant. In 1925, she was residing on Larch Street with her parents and siblings Robert (sixteen), Mildred, Helen, Ruth, Marion (five), and Ethel (two). Ethel died in 1929. An Oaklawn School inmate in 1930, she did cleaning within the facility. In 1935, she was residing on Beacon Street in Providence and was employed as a nurse in a doctor's office.

Margaret M. Walbrook/Wallwork was born in England in 1883. She was an Oaklawn School inmate in 1900.

Sidney L. Winston was born in Rhode Island in 1907, the daughter of John and Bertha/Alice Winston, natives of Virginia, and was of African-American descent. In 1910, she lived on East George Street in Providence with her parents and siblings Rosa (thirteen), William (eight), Ethel (four), and infant Anderson. John was employed as a teamster. In 1920, she resided on Pitman Street in Providence with her widowed mother. Her father had died on December 31, 1919, at the age of forty-six. Her mother was employed as a laundress. Also in the home were her siblings William, Ethel, Anderson, Mattie (seven), and John (six). Her mother died on April 7, 1922, at the age of forty-one. She was an Oaklawn School inmate in 1925.

Mary B. Waryas was born in Rhode Island on February 14, 1908, the daughter of William Waryas and Agnes (Suertek), natives of Poland. In 1920, she resided on Arnold Street in Woonsocket with her parents and siblings Annie (eight), Walter (five), and Josephine (one). Her father was employed as a rubber works laborer and her mother as a cotton mill operative. A sister, Katherine, was born and died in 1911. A brother, Sigmund, was born in 1920. She was an Oaklawn School inmate in 1925. In 1926, she married William Charette but was not living with him in 1930. That year, she resided on Olo Street in Woonsocket with her parents, her siblings—Anna, Walter, Josephine, and Sigmund—and her son, William Charette Jr. (two). She was employed as a twister in a worsted mill. By 1935, she was married to Frederick Rose and was living on Public Street in Providence.

Eva S. Woitckan was born in Rhode Island in 1908. She was an Oaklawn School inmate in 1925.

Elsie Evelyn Witherell was born in Rhode Island on January 31, 1897, the daughter of Ernest Witherell and Isabella (Brownell). On January 14, 1900, her father died at the age of forty-two. Five months later, she was boarding in the home of junk dealer Henry Hathaway and his wife, Anne, on Dartmouth Avenue in Providence. She was an Oaklawn School inmate in 1915.

Edna R. Williams was born on May 10, 1895, the daughter of George and Bertha Williams, and was of African-American descent. In 1900, she resided in Mansfield, Connecticut with her stepfather Amos Profitt (a sixty-three-year-old stone mason who had been married to her mother for five years), her siblings Edna (five) and Nellie (three), and her stepbrother Clarence Profitt (thirty-one). She was an Oaklawn School inmate in 1910.

Gabrielle Words/Woods was born in Rhode Island in 1912. An Oaklawn School inmate in 1930, she did cleaning within the facility.

Marion/Marian Weaver was born in Rhode Island in 1907. An Oaklawn School inmate in 1925 until at least 1930, she did cleaning within the facility. In 1935 until at least 1940, she was an inmate at the Exeter School for the Feeble-Minded.

Mabel White was born in Rhode Island in 1890. Her parents were natives of Ireland. She was an Oaklawn School inmate in 1910.

Jane C. West was born in 1883, she was committed to Oaklawn School in September of 1899 for six months, charged with being idle and a vagrant. Having been discovered sleeping in outbuildings in Bristol, she told the judge that she had no home.

Grace Belle White was born in Rhode Island in December 1882. Her mother was from Vermont and her father from Connecticut. She was an Oaklawn School inmate in 1900.

Rose A. Whalen was born in England in 1882. She was an Oaklawn School inmate in 1900.

The Cemetery

In 1886, a place for burials was established on the school grounds. The superintendent's report to the state that year commented:

> A small cemetery has been laid out and fenced for the inmates of the Oaklawn School who may die there without friends to take charge of their remains, one such case having occurred last summer. It was deemed best to have the cemetery of the school upon its own grounds rather than at the cemetery of the other institutions because, for one reason, the distant position of the latter, which would preclude visits of the girls to their former comrade's grave. The cemetery was laid out and plotted by an engineer so that the location of any body may be found by plot, should evidence of its location ever become obliterated. The fence enclosing the cemetery was built and the grading and preparing the ground were done by inmates of the Workhouse. The cost of engineering and material was $33.14.

The hand-drawn map of the cemetery was created by Joseph A. Latham, a sought-after thirty-six-year-old surveyor and civil engineer working out of Providence. In March 1887, he would be hired to map out the Rhode Island State Farm Cemetery.

The Oaklawn School's cemetery plot map, dated July 1886, shows that the cemetery was located some distance behind the school, past the windmill and the shed that stood on the property. The burial ground measured 50 feet long by 25 feet wide. Twenty plots were laid out in four rows with a path between the first and second row and the third and fourth row. There were five plots in the first row, five plots abutting five more plots in middle row, and five plots in the last row. Each plot on the map is numbered from one to twenty. The map contains the names of seven inmates upon the plots in which they are buried. The

The Cemetery

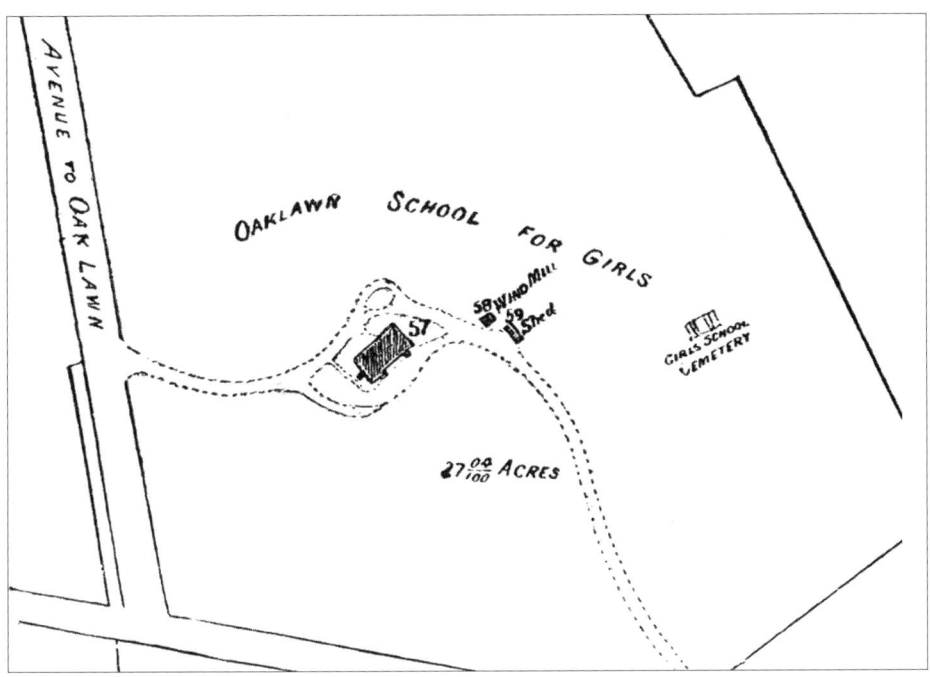

Oaklawn School Cemetery map. (*Rhode Island Historical Society*)

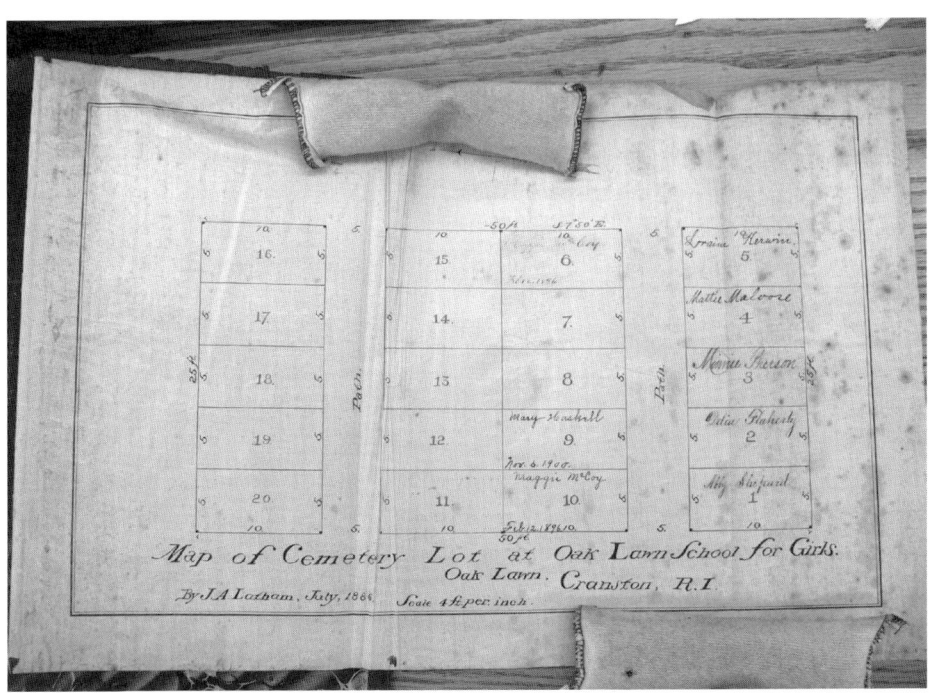

Oaklawn School Cemetery plot map. (*Rhode Island Historical Society*)

first inmate whose name appears on the map, Abby Shepard, died four months before the cemetery was laid out. Her death record contains the notation "Tomb, State Farm." Perhaps her remains were placed in a tomb at another institution's cemetery until a burial place could be prepared at Oaklawn School.

All five plots in the first row were used, the burials being those of Abby Shephard, Delia Flaherty, Minnie Pherson, Mattie Malvose/Maloose, and Loraine Kerwin.

Two plots in the middle row were used for the burials of Maggie McCoy and Mary Haskell. There is no evidence that that any of the other plots had been used. It appears that all of the girls buried there died due to lung issues.

Grave No. 1: Possibly the Abbie Shepard who was born in Rhode Island in 1874 of African-American descent, residing with her forty-eight-year-old cousin Joseph Brown and a sixty-two-year-old woman named Lucinda Brown, on Clayton Street in Providence, in 1880. Her mother was from Rhode Island and her father from Virginia. Joseph Brown was born in Virginia and Lucinda Brown was born in Rhode Island. The inmate interred here died on March 25, 1886, of consumption (lung disease).

Grave No. 2: Delia Flaherty was born in approximately 1871. According to death records, her mother's name was Bridget and her father's name is unknown. She died at the school of tuberculosis/pulmonary consumption on March 10, 1887, and the age of sixteen.

Grave No. 3: Minnie Pherson possibly died in 1888 of hereditary phthisis (a lung condition one is born with which makes them susceptible to tuberculosis.)

Grave No. 4: Mattie Malvose/Maloose was born in Italy in 1876. According to death records, her father's name was Philip and her mother's name is unknown. She died of pneumonia on May 12, 1890, at the age of fourteen.

Grave No. 5: Loraine Kerwin was born in 1873 and was one of the girls who died of pulmonary consumption in 1893 and 1894.

Grave No. 6: Maggie McCoy died on December 12, 1896.

Grave No. 7: Mary Haskell was born in 1884. Her parents were Vincent and Kate Haskell. She died of pulmonalis and exhaustion on November 6, 1900, at the age of sixteen.

The inmates of Oaklawn School always visited the cemetery on Memorial Day, to bring flowers and sing songs. On Memorial Day 1899, the girls marched to the cemetery, each carrying a large bunch of flowers with which they covered the graves. The superintendent spoke briefly before the girls sang their favorite hymns. They then marched to the playground where the rest of the day was spent pleasantly.

On Memorial Day 1900, the girls arose a little later than usual, omitting the regular morning drill. After necessary housework was completed, some of them went to gather flowers to decorate the graves of the six girls who were then buried in the cemetery. At 10.30 a.m., they formed a line and marched to the burial ground. Once there, they sang the hymns "Cover Them Over with Beautiful Flowers" and "Someday We'll Understand" as they marched around the graves and dropped bunches of flowers on each one. They then marched to the playground and indulged in such amusements as swinging, seesawing, croquet, and conversation.

One of the girls described the event in *The Howard Times*:

> As we walked along, we were thinking soberly of the girls who were once like us, members of the Oaklawn School, and hoped they were in that better home above. We sang hymns during which time we marched around the graves and dropped flowers on each, there being six in number. We then marched back to the playground.

Later that year, the number of graves was one more. On November 9, 1900, burial services were held at the Oaklawn School for inmate Mary Haskell, who was one month away from turning seventeen years old. Reverend Nutting was present, and Father Coffey officiated. Relatives and friends of the girl, as well as officers from other institutions, came to pay their respects. The inmates sang and, following the service, her remains were transported to the school cemetery, four inmates acting as bearers. Last rites were performed there, and floral offerings consisted mostly of chrysanthemums, pink and white rose buds and carnations.

On the morning of Memorial Day 1901, each girl was presented with a bunch of beautiful lilacs and lilies of the valley. They marched in double file to the cemetery and decorated the graves. They then sang a selection of songs there before Mr. Eastman made a short speech.

On Memorial Day 1902, memorial services were held in the cemetery, each grave being decked with flowers while the girls again sang "Cover Them Over with Beautiful Flowers" and "Someday We'll Understand."

On Memorial Day 1903, the girls visited the cemetery and decorated the graves with flowers, after which they sang the same two songs they had sung in previous years. They spent the rest of the day on the playground.

On Memorial Day 1905, the girls formed a line at about 10 a.m. According to *The Howard Times*, the girls then "marched to the little cemetery near the building" with the matron and their teachers accompanying them. Each girl was given a bouquet of flowers that they placed on the graves after singing appropriate selections. They then spent the rest of the day on the playground where they took part in various games.

The state eventually sold the property where the school stood to the town of Cranston. Despite the efforts of the designer of the cemetery plot map to ensure that "the location of any body may be found by plot, should evidence of its location ever become obliterated," this cemetery is currently determined to be "lost" as authorities are unable to determine its location. Somewhere within the woods, or beneath a road or parking lot, lie the bodies of at least seven young girls.

Environmental scientist Andy Hall had not spent his life enthralled with history. A native resident of Cranston's Oaklawn Village, he had always lived right down the road from the former girl's reform school and never gave it any thought. It was not until he was digging in his backyard in 2012 and unearthed a rock with initials etched into it that he ever considered reaching into the past.

His research showed that the initials belonged to a man who had lived on his property back in the nineteenth century. Now, somewhat bitten by the history bug, Hall agreed to help a friend of his locate a cemetery she had been looking for. In the course of looking through old documents for some mention of the cemetery, he came across a notation about a cemetery on the property of the old Oaklawn School for Girls. While that was not what he was looking for, he had just unearthed the tip of a new obsession.

Having lived in the area for decades, he had never been aware of any cemetery on the school grounds. Curious, he decided to venture out there and take a walk around, despite the fact that it was the dead of winter and had just snowed. When he did not see anything that looked like a cemetery, he surmised the grave markers were probably just covered over with snow. Emerging from the woods soaked from the ankles down, scratched up by briars and his forehead bleeding, he was determined to go back once the ground was clear.

When later visits still did not produce any hint of a cemetery on the grounds, he assumed the burial markers must have gotten covered over, instead, by time and soil. He delved into research on the deposition rate of leaves within wooded areas to be able to determine how quickly the ground there would have built up over time, and how much it would have risen to cover the stones. He also began to seek out historians and preservationists who might be able to shed some light on the cemetery's location. What he learned was that apparently no one knew the location. Past efforts to ensure that the cemetery could always be located had failed. Over the years, the property has changed hands. There has been demolition, earthmoving, and construction. Where the bodies of seven young girls lie was a mystery that did not sit well with Hall.

To say Hall became obsessed with locating the cemetery is an understatement. He prefers to describe it as "totally obsessed." In his subsequent research, he learned that, most likely, the grave markers would not have been stones with carved names upon them but instead simple wooden crosses that succumbed to the elements over time. "Probably within fifteen to twenty years," he estimates. In addition, it is likely that if the inmates had been buried in caskets, they would have been simple wooden boxes, also prone to deteriorate over time. If caskets were not used, the bodies would have been wrapped in linen along with a brass plate declaring the name of the deceased and the date of death.

The Cemetery

Right: Andy Hall, Cranston resident who became devoted to uncovering the location of the school's cemetery. (*Author's collection*)

Below: Wires deeply embedded in ground may be old pieces of fencing or bed springs. (*Author's collection*)

An old post hole bored into a cement block served a purpose on the grounds at one time. (*Author's collection*)

Using aged hand-drawn maps of the property along with modern aerial views and professional plat maps, Hall compiled overlays and drew out diagrams of triangulations in the hopes that it would help him zero in on one particular spot on this multi-acre piece of property. In trying to locate the area where the cemetery was, his first step was to eliminate all of the areas that it was not.

Hall marked off places where buildings were known to have been, where wetlands existed and where gardens and groves had been laid out. He studied the growth rates of specific types of trees to determine what wooded areas of today would have been absent back in the 1800s. He also used old photographs of the school, measuring the shadows of the structure against the shadows of the trees, to determine how tall the trees were at that time compared to now.

All of this research led to several possible sites for the cemetery, according to Hall, with one resulting in the bodies now laying beneath the parking lot of the Hope Alzheimer's Center that is next door.

To try and better pinpoint a location, Hall appealed to the town of Cranston for permission to bring search dogs onto the property. The town as well as the owners of the Hope Center have been overwhelmingly accommodating in allowing him to pursue the mission of finding this burial ground, Hall said.

The Cemetery

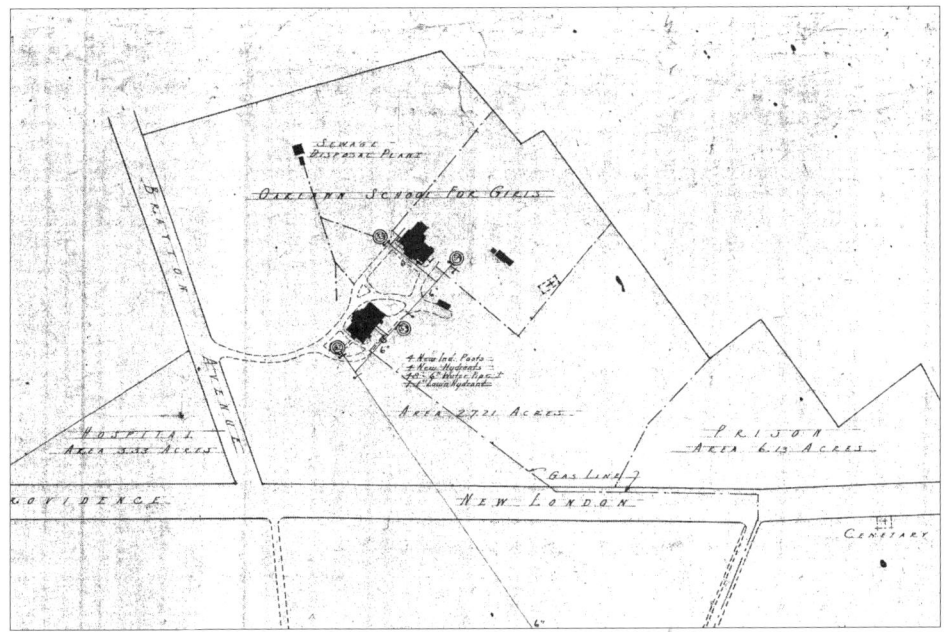

Oaklawn School Cemetery map. (*Rhode Island Historical Society*)

The Hope Alzheimer's Center, now on the grounds that were once Oaklawn School for Girls. (*Author's collection*)

Search dogs seeking out the inmate cemetery on the grounds of Oaklawn School. (*Andy Hall*)

He then approached the owners of Rhode Island Canine Search and Rescue, to obtain their services. This resulted in four dogs, trained in locating human remains, to be brought onto the grounds as part of their regular training exercises. The dogs were first brought to the former Oaklawn School property in November 2012. As the lawns surrounding the Hope Center are regularly fertilized, the detection ability of the dogs was affected by the odor. When the dogs returned, in April 2013, each dog was let to separately search the wooded area across from the ballfield. All four dogs hit on the exact same spot in the woods, beside a large tree.

Hall said his greatest hope is to get someone to come in with ground-scanning equipment, but as of yet, that option has not been offered.

Despite the setbacks, Hall said he will never stop searching for the cemetery, even if that means ambling out there when he is a hundred years old. "It's always bothered me knowing that these are young girls who came from terrible lives and now they're just gone. Forgotten. I've never felt it was hopeless. It's just a matter of time."

Not only does he feel the search is not hopeless, he feels it is destined. "So many crazy things have happened with this," he said. "When I'm there, it feels like home. It feels like where I'm supposed to be."

Andy Hall relaxes on one of the school's old corner stones. (*Author's collection*)

On his first visit to the grounds, he pulled up an aged, dirt-covered mug which he brought home. After washing it off and turning it upside down, he saw the manufacturer's name etched on the bottom: "Hall"—his own last name, which he immediately felt was a sign. Also, there would be more signs that convinced him he was on a mission, including a vivid dream he had about the first girl to be buried in the cemetery, Abby Shepard. He said:

> In the dream, I went into this house and this girl came up to me and I knew it was Abby Shephard. She stood an inch away from me and I knew there some significance about the distance of one inch, but I don't know what. She had on a long blue dress and white socks and her hair pulled back in two ponytails. I then went upstairs, and this man began talking to me and I asked him where the girl was. He told me she had left. I told him that she couldn't leave because I had some questions to ask her. The man said to me, "She's not here for you to find out about her. She's here to find out about you."

While engaged in his searches of the old school property, Hall located the remains of a cobblestone-lined pool, about 8 feet in diameter, which once held 6 inches to 1 foot of water. Hall is not sure what the pool had been built for—whether a tranquil place to sit by or perhaps a place for chickens or other animals to drink.

An old well on the grounds was constructed using cobble stones. (*Author's collection*)

Hall said that after the school closed, the city used the buildings for fire training. The old wells, fire hydrants, and piles of bricks and other building debris are still on the grounds amid thick tree roots and new forest growth.

From walking the grounds with a metal detector to placing flagged markers within grid patterns he has measured out, Hall regularly uses the information he gleans from archeologists and anyone else who comes forward with useful facts, to continue on with the search. He said, "I don't believe that it's only those seven girls who are buried there. I think there are others who were not recorded but I don't have any proof."

If the cemetery is ever located, Hall said that whatever action takes place at that point will depend on whether it is on city or state land. The governing bodies of whatever jurisdiction it falls under can then decide whether to restore and maintain the burial ground, or to move the bodies to another location. Hall believes that even if the burials are not located, the city or state will, at some point, put up a plaque on the property in memory of the girls resting there.

Until that time, he will keep studying the massive amounts of documents in his boxes of map coordinates and crisscrossing the grounds of Oaklawn School with detectors and prods and rakes, though he stresses that the goal in all of this is not that he is personally successful in locating the cemetery but simply that it is located. "I don't care who finds it," he said. "As long as it's found. And when it is, I'll be thrilled. I'll volunteer to maintain it."

The Cemetery

Above: The old well that once served as a water source for the school. (*Andy Hall*)

Right: Oaklawn School Cemetery map. (*Rhode Island Historical Society*)

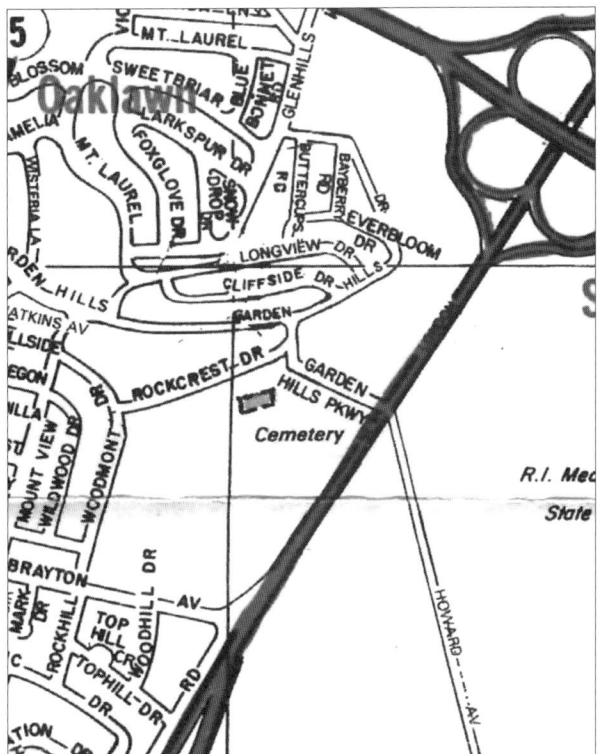

6

THE ONLY HAPPINESS THEY EVER HAD

On February 16, 2019, a psychic medium met with myself (the author), Andy Hall, and two additional searchers (Rene Tougas and Angela Harvey) on the grounds of the old Oaklawn School. When I reached out to secure a medium to perhaps help us locate the lost cemetery, Karen Bruscini immediately volunteered. A holistic practitioner for over twenty years, her *résumé* made her well-equipped for the task at hand. From her Hands of Wisdom and Ancient Wisdom for the New World center on Mechanic Street in Hope Valley, Rhode Island, she is regularly consulted for services in reiki, healing touch, integrated energy therapy, herbalism, and shamanism. In addition, she told me that her interests lie not only in helping the living but those who have passed over as well.

It was a brutally cold day. Rene and I arrived on the grounds at 10 a.m., planning to thoroughly examine the area before the others arrived that afternoon. Packed into three layers of clothing, my head covered with a thick hood, thick boots on my feet, sunglasses protecting my eyes, and a backpack containing a notebook, camera, map, and other necessary items slung over my shoulder, we ventured into the vine-entangled woods.

The low temperature and freezing winds were numbing and my hand so frozen I could barely write. Yet after a while, I settled into the discomfort, fueled by thoughts of what revelations the day might bring.

Andy arrived just after noon and he walked Rene and I through the sections of grounds he has come to know so well, pointing out what stood where during the days when troubled teenaged girls lived, worked and played on that land. Karen arrived just after 2 p.m., followed by Angela, and we all stood upon the pathway near the ballfield to plan out a course of action.

"Where do you want me first?" Karen asked. I told her we would follow her. She nodded in the direction of the Hope Center.

"It's over here. I keep seeing a girl."

She looked across the street toward the ballfield. "There were windows on this side. Where would the windows be?" Andy explained that as the school stood, there would have been windows along the back that looked out over where we were standing.

"There's a little girl with long hair and a gray dress," she went on. Karen began walking toward the parking lot of the Hope Center and we followed. While she had been told that we were seeking the burial ground of the old reform school for girls, the only other information she had been given was a scan of the plot map with seven inmate names on it, and the original map of the school grounds. The only way she would have known details of the inmates, such as causes of death or biographical information, was if she had conducted the same amounts of research that Andy and I had, visiting the State's historical repositories and pouring through old reports.

As we approached the Hope Center parking lot, she asked, "There's only seven girls?" Then she turned to us and smiled. "Not thirteen or fourteen of them?" I had temporarily forgotten about Andy once mentioning that he thought there might be more than seven interments there and that the others had simply not been written on the map.

"Do you think there's more than seven?" I asked.

She nodded with a great degree of certainty. "There's more than seven," she said.

As there were still cars in the parking lot of the Hope Center, Andy stated that we should not go on the property at the moment. The owners had requested in the past that he refrain from conducting any searches on the property until after the center was closed for the day and he wanted to respect that.

We decided to take Karen into the woods, to the area the four search dogs had hit upon. "There is something over here but I don't think it's what you're looking for," she said as we plodded through the trees. "This isn't the little girls' place."

Karen stopped beside a large tree and stood quietly. There was a single grave there she said, but it had nothing to do with the school's cemetery. Although she told us detailed information about the person she said was buried there, she informed me that the person did not want to be written about and I will honor that.

Now able to go upon the Hope Center land, we walked back toward its parking area. "I think the girls are sad," Karen said. "That's why I came out. They want to be remembered." She again described the little girl she had seen earlier and could still see there. "This little girl, she has long brown hair, a gray linen cloth jumper. Her name's not on there (the plot map) and I think her name is Charlotte." Andy commented on the mention of gray linen cloth, explaining to Karen that people who were not buried in coffins, were wrapped in linen shrouds in the olden days.

As we began walking toward the back of the parking area, Karen stopped. "The little girl is with me. She just stopped me right here. She said 'no!' She was walking up the hill with us then she turned off and went down there." Karen motioned toward an area in the center of the parking area. "She giggling and she's dancing around those trees over there. This is where they played. I see two twelve or thirteen-year-olds with her. They were her friends. They have an "M" name, like Mary. I think they watch her when they play together."

Although it is unknown where the school playground was, it was common for the older girls to keep an eye on the younger girls at the school. "They're skipping around the trees," Karen went on. "I think these girls have an attachment here. I think this was the only happiness they ever had in their whole life." She gazed around the parking lot. "You have people right there. Two had typhoid. Did somebody commit suicide here too?" School records and death records have not turned up any mention of a suicide on the property, nor of any deaths due to typhoid fever. However, there is inarguably still much we do not know about the history of the school.

Karen began coughing as she spoke. "That's not me. That's the girl," she said. "Maggie, Margo. I get that she had some sort of infection of her chest." Without having gone and checked the death records or combed through school records, she could not have known that it is believed the seven girls known to be buried in the cemetery all died of lung ailments.

"She's named after her grandmother, Margo," she went on. "Her father was an alcoholic. She says 'my mom doesn't want me' but I don't think her mom didn't want her. I think her mother had mental health issues. The father is incapable of working or anything. He had delirium tremens. The mother just couldn't handle her. She thought she was doing the best thing for her. This place would at least give her a chance for a better life."

Karen continued to cough. She said:

> Her mother had a manic-depressive type thing. I think Margo had a brother too and the brother was older than her. He was like seventeen or eighteen when she was placed here. He went away to get a job in New York. I don't know if he worked on the railroad? But his plan was to come back and get her out but she died before that could happen. All this girl knows is "my mother didn't want me."

Karen then began walking toward the entrance of the Hope Center, where a large area of grass sets within the center of the parking area. "Charlotte is pushing me that way," she told us. She started down the cement pathway that leads through the grassy plot then stopped and stared down at the ground. "I think this is it," she said. "She laid right down there like a little baby."

Karen described how she said Charlotte laid down on the ground in front of her with her hands under her cheek as if going to sleep. She then gazed around the property and said that she felt all of the girls who died at the school had not been buried in the same area. Yet this grassy plot, she said, was the cemetery we had been searching for.

"I'm getting three right here," she said. She asked to see the plot map and I handed it to her. "It doesn't look like this," she said. "They're not that even." As she walked along the area, she said we would go by plot number. Stopping in front of what she said was marked as number thirteen, she stated, "This is Lucy here." The map has number thirteen void of a name or any indication of burial there.

Plots eleven and twelve, Karen said, now lie underneath the cement pathway. She looked at the plot map again. "The lay-out, it doesn't exactly look like this picture," she said.

As she continued to move down the pathway, Karen mentioned that Charlotte was still helping her. She stopped in front of what she said would be plot number six. "This is Margaret," she said. "They called her Magpie. She had curly blonde hair and blue eyes." The map has plot number six void of a name or any indication of burial there.

"Loraine's over here," she went on, walking to what would be plot number five on the map, which contains the name Loraine Kerwin. "I think she's really close to the roots of the tree."

She took a step to the side, next to what would be plot four on the map, which contains the name Mattie Malvose or Maloose. "Mattie's over here. I think these

Psychic medium Karen Bruscini uses a pendulum to communicate with spirits. (*Author's collection*)

two were buried close together. These two were friends. They died close together. Mattie had blackish hair and dark eyes. She only knew her father, I believe."

It is very unlikely that she knew Mattie had been born in Italy and most likely had dark features. It is also very unlikely that she knew Mattie's death record lists only a father's name while the mother is recorded as being unknown. She went on:

> Her father was incarcerated unjustly. She was abandoned by her mother. I think he shot somebody or stabbed somebody in self-defense. He was a good guy and she knew that. She says "I know that. I'm okay."

Going back to the area she believed to be Loraine Kerwin's grave, Karen said the girl called herself "Lori." She said:

> Lori and Mattie were best friends. Lori was very quiet, meek and mild. I think her parents were poor. The mother had schizophrenia or something and the father was trying to make ends meet. Somebody said something and the State stepped in.

Karen then moved on to what she said would be plot number three on the map, containing the name Minnie Pherson. She went on:

> Minnie's over here. She had a bad attitude. I don't think her family could handle her. She was just a child who was high-spirited. She fell a lot, she tells me. She was a rough and tumble tomboy. If she didn't like you, she'd tell you, so a lot of people didn't like her.

Karen gazed around and replied, "I believe that there was some abuse going on here. Physical and emotional. She's telling me that. I'm going to believe this child. There was abuse. Broken bones."

While records overwhelmingly show that the girls loved their superiors as if they were parents, there were allegations of abuse and mention of physical punishments dotted throughout the school's history.

The 1888 report of the Special Committee of the Senate Appointed to Investigate the Management of the State Institutions at Cranston addressed written complaints made by one or more former employees of the school, one being a former teacher, of harsh and cruel treatment committed upon the inmates. The complaints, along with the names of those who made them, were shared with Mrs. Butterworth. The committee investigated the school and questioned the inmates and staff. A hearing was then held and those who had made the complaints failed to attend. The committee reported that "The little ones, while complaining of harsh treatment in the past, agreed that they were well cared for and do not now complain."

One of the written complaints had accused Mrs. Butterworth herself, of abusing eleven-year-old inmate Fanny Nesbit by forcing her to remain in a cold room for so long that her feet froze and toes had to be amputated. The report of Fanny's arrival there, as well as Fanny's own testimony, stated that her feet had been frozen prior to her committal while living at her home in Newport.

The committee found all reports of abuse to be unsubstantiated. It is interesting to note, however, that Minnie was an inmate at the time these written complaints were made. A 1901 report from the school later stated that no inmate had been "punished physically" in more than five years (since before 1896).

A book called *The Dark Days of Social Welfare at the State Institutions at Howard, Rhode Island*, written by Henry A. Jones and published in 1943, describes a former superintendent as a very heavy-set woman who believed in the power of spankings:

> As the years crept on, this woman became so corpulent that her lap was shortened by its rotundity, and her other asthmatic infirmities compelled her to resort to the use of woman's weapon, her tongue, and her burnings on the nether portions of the girls' anatomies were transferred to the higher, if not more impressionable centres, the ears.

The book goes on to say that, prior to 1909, the girls would be led to the front yard of the superintendent's house to perform their exercise and dance routines. Buggies and wagons would then allegedly stop along the side of the road so that the leering men and boys inside could watch. It was reported that the girls loved the attention and applause coming from their passing audience. Apparently, while Mrs. Butterworth and Mr. Eastman saw no harm in this, Clara Forbush did and upon her taking over the role of superintendent in 1909, the public shows were put to an end.

"Delia's over here," Karen said. "She's lonely, out of sorts, out of place." She stood beside what she said was plot number two, containing the name Delia Flaherty. "I think Delia is Delilah," she said. "She keeps telling me 'I was named after a flower'. She was dropped off, definitely. She was unwanted. She had a very stern mother. I think the mother just wanted freedom from her."

Stopping at what she determined to be plot number one on the map, which contains the name Abby Shepard, Karen said she could confirm that she was the first to be buried within the cemetery. "But she's gone from here now," Karen said. She remarked:

> She's moved on. I don't want to offend you, but these girls really don't care about this cemetery. If it ends up being marked and you want to do something nice for them, it might be nice to put a candle on each grave and have a little memorial service for them. I think they would appreciate that. Everyone deserves healing, even

Karen Bruscini standing in the pathway that she believes runs through the location of the cemetery. (*Author's collection*)

those who do not live in our world. The young girls of the school can now be at peace with their journey here on earth. Charlotte, sweet little girl, can now spend her eternity knowing her story is heard and play with her friends Maggie and Mattie around the tall oaks of the pristine land they once called home.

In essence, Karen believes that the inmates buried within the cemetery do not so much care about the burial ground itself being remembered but about the lives of those who lived there not being forgotten.

BIBLIOGRAPHY

All Anderson Herald (IN), 1973
Amarillo Globe Times (TX), 1973
Annual Reports of the RI Board of State Charities and Corrections, 1882; 1883; 1889; 1896; 1901; 1906; 1908; 1909; 1911
Annual Reports of the General Assembly of the State of RI, 1884; 1887; 1899
Annual Report of the RI Public Welfare Commission, 1926
Annual Reports of the RI State Board of Education, 1893; 1894; 1898; 1899; 1901; 1905; 1907; 1917; 1922
Annual Report of the RI State Reform Schools, 1901
Acts and Resolves Passed by The General Assembly of RI, 1887Annual Report of the Penal and Charitable Commission of RI, 1919
Annual Reports of the Women's Board of Visitors to the Penal and Correctional Institutions of the State of RI, 1883; 1903
Annual Reports of the Oaklawn School Superintendent, 1898; 1902; 1904; 1905; 1906; 1913; 1914
Annual Reports of the Oaklawn School Deputy Superintendent, 1904; 1905; 1906
Annual Reports of various Oaklawn School instructors, 1904
Annual Reports of the Oaklawn School Resident Physician, 1909; 1910; 1912; 1915
Annual Report of the Oaklawn School Religious Instructor, 1899
Ancestry.com website
artinruins.com website
Armstrong, M. D., Boston University School of Social Work thesis; Study of Forty-One Mentally Deficient Girls Placed on Probation by The Rhode Island Juvenile Court, from July 1, 1944 to July 1, 1947 (1948)
Billings Gazette (MO), 1973
Bristol Phoenix (RI), 1884; 1889; 1896; 1897; 1898; 1899; 1900; 1908; 1910; 1961
Cranston Directory (RI), 1919; 1922
Cranston News (RI), 1922
Cranston Herald (RI), 1936; 2017
Cranston Today (RI), 1972
Cranston City Times (RI), various years
deckerjourney.com website
Evening News (Washington DC), 1899

Evening Star (Wash. DC), 1911
Evening Bulletin (RI), various dates
East Oregonian (OR), 1911
Evening News (RI), 1912; 1913
Edwards, A. M. and Cheney, H. M., Juvenile Delinquents in Public Institutions, 1933
Findagrave.com website
Howard Times (RI), various years
Herald News (RI), various years
Jones, H. A., Dark Days of Social Welfare at the State Institutions at Howard, Rhode Island, 1943
Letters of various Oaklawn School inmates, 1896–1901
Lincoln Star (NE), 1973
Lima News (OH), 1951
Library of Congress; Chronicling America website
Morning Herald (MD), 1951
Middlesboro Daily News (KY), 1951
Massachusetts Death Records
Massachusetts Birth Records
Moroney, Anna; Boston School of Social Work Thesis; Rhode Island Training School for Girls, 1950
New York Times (NY), 1911
Newcastle News (PA), 1968
Norwich Bulletin (CT), 1912
Newport Mercury (RI), 1924
Newport Mercury Daily News (RI), 1951; 1958; 1960; 1963; 1966
Newport Daily News (RI), 1951; 1953; 1958; 1961; 1962; 1965; 1966; 1969; 1974
Newport Mercury Weekly News (RI)
Newport Directory (RI), 1945; 1946
New Hampshire Marriage Records
Odessa American (TX), 1973
Plain Speaker (PA), 1888
Providence City Directory (RI), 1938
Providence Directory (RI), 1889; 1930
Pawtuxet Valley Directory (RI), 1892; 1894
Pawtuxet Valley Gleaner (RI), 1888; 1891; 1893; 1896
Portsmouth Herald (NH), 1951
Rhode Island City Directories, 1900; 1948
Rhode Island Marriage Records
Rhode Island Death Records
Rhode Island Birth Records
Rhode Island Supreme Court Decisions, 1965
Rhode Island State Censuses
Rhode Island Board of Control and Supply reports; various years
Rhode Island City Directories, 1900; 1948
Records of the Rhode Island Historical Society
Records of the Rhode Island State Archives
Reilly, J., Boston University thesis; Commitments to The State Home and School of RI, 1943
Social Security Death Index
San Antonio Express (TX), 1911
Standard Times (RI), 1970
United States Social Security Applications and Claims index
Westerly Sun (RI), 1925